Bio
Dis   Eliot, Marc.
          Walt Disney :
          Hollywood's dark
          prince

9

WALT DISNEY

WALT DISNEY

Hollywood's Dark Prince

A Biography
by
Marc Eliot

A BIRCH LANE PRESS BOOK
Published by Carol Publishing Group

A Birch Lane Press Book
Published by Carol Publishing Group
Birch Lane Press is a registered trademark of Carol Communications, Inc.
Editorial Offices: 600 Madison Avenue, New York, N.Y. 10022
Sales and Distribution Offices: 120 Enterprise Avenue, Secaucus, N.J. 07094
In Canada: Canadian Manda Group, P.O. Box 920, Station U, Toronto, Ontario M8Z 5P9
Queries regarding rights and permissions should be addressed to Carol Publishing Group,
    600 Madison Avenue, New York, N.Y. 10022

Carol Publishing Group books are available at special discounts for bulk purchases, for sales
promotion, fund-raising, or educational purposes. Special editions can be created to speci-
fications. For details, contact: Special Sales Department, Carol Publishing Group, 120
Enterprise Avenue, Secaucus, N.J. 07094

Manufactured in the United States of America
10 9 8 7 6 5 4 3 2 1

Library of Congress Cataloging-in-Publication Data

Eliot, Marc.
    Walt Disney : Hollywood's dark prince / by Marc Eliot.
        p.   cm.
    "A Birch Lane Press Book."
    ISBN 1-55972-174-X
    1. Disney, Walt, 1901–1966. 2. Animators—United States—
Biography. I. Title.
NC1766.U52D5328   1993
791.43'092—dc20
[B]   92-38788
                                                         CIP

For SARAH

I do not make films primarily for children. Call the child innocence. The worst of us is not without innocence, although buried deeply it might be. In my work, I try to reach and speak to that innocence.

—Walt Disney

There is no theory that is not a fragment, carefully prepared, of some autobiography.

—Paul Valéry

Contents

Acknowledgments

When the subject of a biography is no longer living, the question of authorization becomes somewhat more enigmatic. After all, how does a person authorize a book twenty-five years after his death? In Disney's case, the question of posthumous authorization is further muddled by the politics of the studio that bears his name regarding access to what it calls the "Disney Archives"—its highly guarded repository of information, artifacts, documents, interviews, and photographs about the life of its founder. Only one "authorized" biographer, Bob Thomas, who in 1976 wrote *Walt Disney, An American Original*, has been granted apparently free access to the archives.

In Thomas's case, authorization seems to have come in exchange for studio input on content and presentation. I make this conjecture based on my own experiences. In 1988, I began researching the life of Walt Disney. At that time I did not initially contact the studio. In my view, Thomas's book had already presented what was clearly the studio's approved version of Walt's life, augmented by Leonard Mosley's 1985 "biography," *Disney's World*, which seemed to vary little in approach, attitude, information, or conclusion. In a note at the front of his book, Mosley acknowledged "two other biographies of Walt Disney [in which] I have found nuggets of interesting and valuable information." They are, namely, Walt's dictated autobiography, told to Pete Martin, and later released in 1957 as Diane Disney

Miller's "biography" of her father, and Bob Thomas's "authorized" study. A third Disney book, *The Disney Version* (1985), by Richard Schickel, is less a biography in the strictest sense than an analysis and meditation on the art and commerce of Walt Disney.

These books share many of the same "revelations," details, anecdotes, points of view, mistakes, and omissions. A few examples: No mention is made by Thomas, Mosley, or Miller of Disney's relationship with the FBI. Mosley spends exactly one paragraph discussing the Mojacar connection before dismissing it out of hand. Thomas doesn't mention it at all. Arthur Babbitt, one of Disney's most talented artists, whom Walt came to regard as one of his worst enemies, is never introduced in Miller or Thomas, as Walt Disney insisted Babbitt's name be removed from any studio history. Babbitt is mentioned only briefly by Mosley and Schickel.

The 1941 strike that changed Disney's life and altered the direction of his studio and with it, American animation, is completely omitted in Miller's book, receives a chapter in Schickel, two pages in Thomas, and scant more in Mosley. No mention is made anywhere of Disney's connections to organized crime. The Motion Picture Alliance receives exactly one line in both Thomas and Mosley, and nothing in Schickel or Miller. The fact that Sharon Disney, Walt's second daughter, was adopted is omitted entirely from Miller and Thomas. Lillian Disney, Walt's wife, specifically requested that Thomas not mention it in his book.

When I wrote my proposal for this book, my agent, Mel Berger, to insure confidentiality, sent it by hand to its intended publisher. An offer was quickly made, and a deal was finalized in a matter of days. However, before I had even started to pack my bags in New York, where I was living, for the move to Hollywood to begin researching Disney's life, my editor was contacted by a public relations representative of the Disney studio, Robyn Tynan, who said she already had a copy of my proposal on her desk and was most eager to meet with me to discuss it. Ms. Tynan was put in touch with me directly.

During our initial conversation, she told me, quite candidly, that the studio was not happy that a new biography was being written about its founder, particularly *this* biography. Still, because they were aware there was no legal way to prevent it, the studio had decided to work with me. Upon my arrival in Hollywood, I was to call her, so that I could gain access to the Disney Archives.

I was quite pleased with this development and sent a letter to Tynan to confirm our arrangement. Upon receiving it, she turned it over to the legal department, which amended it to say that the studio had to see the completed manuscript prior to publication and reserved the right to approve its contents.

I refused to comply with this condition. My initial foray to the studio to meet with the head of the archives ended with my being escorted off the grounds by security. This was, I thought, a rather unnecessarily dramatic gesture. When I called Ms. Tynan to find out what had happened, she said she had "forgotten" to inform me my invitation had been canceled.

I then proceded to research Walt Disney's life without benefit of the studio's "authorization," more eager than ever to discover the dark secrets it was so afraid I might learn about "Uncle" Walt, secrets Ms. Tynan continued to insist did not exist. In our final telephone conversation, she told me off the record that I really didn't need the archives at all. Laughing softly into the phone, she explained that no one had ever been given any information by the studio it didn't want them to have, the reason all the other Disney biographies were so alike. If I wanted to see what I would have learned had I been given access to the archives, all I had to do was read Bob Thomas's book. I did. She was right.

Apparently, other recent attempts to gain the studio's cooperation have proved fruitless. As this book goes to press, a book by another author on the history of the Disney studio has been canceled by its publisher because, among other reasons, the author could not gain sufficient cooperation from his intended sources.

While researching this biography, I found that, much to my surprise, it was not difficult to interview those people the studio warned would refuse to speak to me. Perhaps the long reach of Disney's arm is not all that great after all. At any rate, while there were those who would not, in fact, talk to me, and many who would do so only under the cloak of anonymity, which I granted, the list of those who would is extensive.

Before I cite them specifically, I wish to acknowledge up front my editor, Hillel Black. He pursued this book with more energy, enthusiasm, and encouragement, and drove me harder, than any other editor I have ever worked with. I thank him for that. Now to my sources.

I tried to interview Disney animator Arthur Babbitt for a solid year and a half before he finally consented. He had tried in the past to put his participation in the Disney strike and what happened to him as a result of it behind, and knew, once we started, it would bring all the nasty business up again. Mr. Babbitt granted me hours upon hours of interviews and provided me with several key documents. Sadly, he passed away in the spring of 1992. Our interviews became the last he gave in his life, and I regret he cannot read the book he played such a key role in helping me realize.

Animator and author Jack Kinney refused to meet me. He did, however, agree to talk by phone and provided a wealth of information I otherwise would not have acquired. He also granted me complete freedom to quote from his book, *Walt Disney and Assorted Other Characters*, for which I thank him. Mr. Kinney too passed away in the spring of 1992.

Perhaps most crucial to this book were the interviews I conducted with William Cottrell, Walt Disney's then ninety-two-year-old brother-in-law. His contributions are incalculable. In much of what I have written about, he was intimately involved, and age apparently had not clouded his memory. I am extremely grateful to him.

One of the founders of the Cartoonists Guild, Bill Littlejohn, was an excellent and generous source of material regarding the events that led up to the Disney strike and of important documented information regarding Herb Sorrell, Willie Bioff, and the Hollywood Alliance. He arranged for my interviews with Cartoonists Guild attorney George Bodle, who provided additional, essential information about this period.

I was put in touch with Bill Littlejohn by animated filmmaker Faith Hubley, the first person I interviewed for this book. The widow of Disney animator John Hubley, she pointed me in several directions. My connection to Ms. Hubley came via Steve Fleischmann and Dede Allen, two very dear friends of mine.

Disney storyman Joe Grant was extremely generous with his time and his personal archive of documents and materials.

Disney storyman Leo Salkin was equally gracious and informative. Besides several days of interviews, he provided me with several of his own photographs of the strike, many of which have never been published before.

Dave Iwerks, the son of Ub Iwerks, Disney's first partner, sat for several candid interviews and proved quite insightful.

Disney animator and strike leader Dave Hilberman not only agreed to be interviewed but allowed me total access to his incredibly well-kept scrapbooks, which provided a wealth of information.

The following deserve special mention: Marc Davis, Ward Kimball, Cubby O'Brien, Paul Julian, Golda David, Stanley Myers, Roy and June Paterson, Jules Engle, Claire Graham, Bill Hurtz, Sheri Alvaroney, Harry Tytle, John Wilson, Martha Hand (who allowed me to read the unpublished memoirs of her husband Dave), John Reed, Michael Murphy, Lenore Walker, Claire Weeks, Marcielle Ferguson, John Canemaker, Larry Davis, Harry Guardino, Chuck Jones, Miles Kreuger, Ginny Minton, Lee Mishkin, Jack Scagnetti (the source of the photo of Disney and Dolores Del Rio), Charles Shows, Frank Thomas, Shirley Thomas, Ron Miller (for the three brief telephone conversations), and Charles Solomon, with whom I spent an afternoon discussing the nature of Disney's early works, and who helped me acquire several rare, believed-to-be missing photos.

The Valéry and T. S. Eliot quotes are from *T. S. Eliot, A Study in Character and Style* by Ronald Bush.

I wish also to thank Carol-Ann Plamus, a former resident of Mojacar, Spain, who first alerted me to the research regarding Disney's heritage that had been conducted there. During my trip to Mojacar, Tito Del Amo proved a most helpful guide. I also wish to thank the Spanish journalist Paco Flores and Senor Jacinto Alarcon for their time and assistance.

Karen Douglass, one of several professional researchers I worked with, pursued the FBI for more than a year before finally acquiring Walt Disney's FBI file. Her diligence deserves special praise, particularly for her refusal to accept the first version of what the Bureau decided we should be allowed to see. Through her dogged pursuit, we received several additional, revelatory documents from the Bureau.

I wish to cite the extraordinary job Larry L. Piatt performed tracing the Disney family geneology. Gaye Weaver was an excellent reader, researcher, and editorial "eye." Rene Apel was an able assistant in Hollywood. I thank Ace for the time and the tapes.

I also want to thank my agent and friend, Mel Berger.

For personal encouragement and support during the long, often difficult process of writing this book, I thank my best friend, the Chairman of the Board, Dennis Klein, and my favorite uncle, Duane Munde.

Finally, to one and all, identified or anonymous, who assisted in one fashion or another, a final thanks for joining the jamboree.

Author to Reader

FOR MOST of his public life, Walt Disney was known to the world as everyone's favorite "uncle." He was beloved by millions for short cartoons that featured Mickey Mouse, Donald Duck, Goofy, and Pluto, and his full-length features are considered by many to be among the finest representations of that genre. He was hailed as a gentle man, revered as the loving husband and doting father of two adorable children, and honored as one of Hollywood's model citizens. If Walt Disney's life were an open book, one would, presumably, place it alongside the King James Bible.

There was, however, another, darker, more private side to this immensely public figure. Among his many less-celebrated accomplishments, in 1940, at the age of thirty-nine, Walt Disney became a domestic spy for the United States government.

His assignment was to report on the activities of Hollywood actors, writers, producers, directors, technicians, and union activists the Federal Bureau of Investigation suspected of political subversion. Disney perceived his FBI commission not only as his patriotic duty but a high moral obligation. He became as obsessively devoted to spying as he had once been to the making of movies.

Less than a year later, the Disney studio was the target of a massive, debilitating animators' strike. Its most talented artists, frustrated by long hours and low pay, were prevented from organizing for the purpose of collective bargaining. After several failed attempts to establish an independent union, they instigated a job action that began in the early spring and lasted until the end of summer. The leaders of the strike included Arthur Babbitt, considered by many to be the best artist among a staff universally acknowledged as the best in the industry; David Hilberman, another highly respected animator; and Herb Sorrell, an outside union activist. Even before a settlement was reached, each was publicly accused by Disney of being a Communist. For the next several years, the three were subjected to relentless investigation by the FBI and suffered irreparable damage to both their reputations and careers.

Walt Disney believed the strike leaders had committed a profoundly immoral act against the studio. His Midwest Fundamentalist father had brought him up to believe that loyalty to the head of a family was the truest test of one's character. To disobey one's father was an act of immorality that brought disgrace upon the head of the family.

As an adult, "Uncle" Walt considered himself not just an employer of animators but the *paterfamilias* to a group of talented, if immature, "boys," as he often referred to his artists, most of whom he had hired with no prior experience, trained, and given jobs of great opportunity.

When these same artists demanded union representation and struck to force the issue, Disney took their action as an act of familial betrayal, refused to negotiate with them in good faith, and went so far as to align himself with known members of organized crime to reinforce his resistance. Once the strike was settled, Disney determined that those who had led it should pay dearly for their actions.

By the time of the strike, the FBI, under the leadership of J. Edgar Hoover, had established itself as the most effective blunt instrument for the industry's hammering of the activists who sought to organize and unionize the American workingmen and -women who made movies. When the union movement gained its first toehold in Hollywood with the formation in 1931 of the Writers Guild, the FBI took notice. Hollywood, the Bureau knew, had captured the ear of the nation, and when motion pictures talked, the public listened. Fearing that what it considered Hollywood's leftist contingent of writers might use the movies to fuel a nationwide insurgency, the FBI made the film industry the first major target in the Bureau's guerrilla war against subversion via the mass media.

Although Hollywood's conservative element was led by the heads of the "major" studios, when J. Edgar Hoover needed a soldier of unqualified loyalty, he chose Walt Disney, the head of one of the smallest and least powerful independent studios. And with good reason. Early in his career, Hoover, while then a Bureau underling, had become involved with the FBI's 1918 prosecution of World War I draft dodgers. At the same time, a seventeen-year-old Walt Disney first came to the attention of the Bureau, not because he had tried to avoid conscription, but because he had forged his parents' signatures of consent on a letter in a failed attempt to join the army while still a minor.

The Bureau, always on the lookout for potential recruits, made note of the many young men so eager to fight for their country they would lie to get *in* the service. Years later, when the FBI ran a routine preliminary background check on Disney, it discovered that the army, skeptical of his age, had asked Disney to produce his birth certificate after he told the recruiter he was born in Chicago on December 5, 1901. When Walt had requested a copy of the certificate from the Bureau of Records, he had been informed that no such birth certificate existed, anywhere, in any form.

Learning of the missing birth certificate greatly disturbed Disney and deepened the feelings of distance and distrust he already had for his father. As far back as Walt could remember, Elias Disney had been a patriarchal martinet who believed in excessive physical punishment to enforce discipline. A childhood fantasy of Walt Disney, common among abused children, was that his father treated him so badly because he didn't love him, the reason being Elias really wasn't his father.

Now the fantasy took on a deeper and darker dimension. When Disney discovered his birth certificate was missing and perhaps nonexistent, he feared he had inadvertently uncovered a clue to a terrible secret—that his fantasy might not have been a fantasy at all. He might have been, in fact, adopted in infancy, or worse, illegitimate. Thus began his lifelong search to find out who his real parents were. In 1940, Hoover offered Disney the unlimited services of the FBI to help track down his personal past, in return for Walt's assistance in helping to secure the nation's future.

It was an offer Disney couldn't refuse—to at once be able to serve his country, demonstrate his loyalty, confirm his morality to Hoover, the idealized head of this newest of extended families, and unlock the secrets of his own true identity. The temptation was irresistible, with reality and fantasy provocatively interwined. Walt, the wounded patriarch of a stable of "boys" who had destroyed the moral fabric of his studio "family," now had the opportunity to become Hoover's "boy." By doing so, he could not only atone for his attendant shame and mollify the rage he felt for those who had rebelled and therefore betrayed him, but find comfort in the love of a most compelling "foster father."

Disney's first five animated features, *Snow White, Pinocchio, Bambi, Dumbo,* and *Fantasia,* were all completed between 1936 and 1941. This so-called golden period of Disney animation concluded the same year the strike against his studio began. Generally acknowledged as the crown jewels of his animated-film career, each reflects aspects of Disney's single greatest theme: the sanctity of family and the tragic consequences when that sanctity is broken.

In these five films, Disney's heroes all begin with major personality "defects," externalized by lost or missing parental figures. The search for these figures becomes, ultimately, a quest to acquire a spiritual wholeness. The drama is further externalized by a series of objects that threaten the heroic quest: Snow White's poisoned apple; Pinocchio's growing nose; Bambi's forest fire; Dumbo's awkward ears; and in *Fantasia's* climactic sequence, the pervasive darkness of the fearful night itself before the emergence of the reassuring dawn.

Yet Disney rejected any meanings in these cartoons other than the literal ones that rode upon the surface of their plots. Psychological analysis, indeed, any form of introspection, he insisted, meant nothing to him. He had no use for psychiatry in either his work or his life, believing it part of the same Jewish-Marxist conspiracy that had worked to destroy his studio. He also scoffed at the suggestion his relationship with Hoover had its roots in any unresolved emotional conflict with Elias.

Ironically, Disney's real-life emotional blindness proved the source of his great artistic vision. It was precisely this conscious denial that limited his awareness, and therefore his control, of the subtextural power of his movies and freed him from the barriers of cautious self-qualification. Disney's purely instinctive, externalized fantasies were the key to his movies' universal appeal to children of all ages. For youngsters, the fairy-tale plotting of mythic, exotic stories of heroism serve as safe entertainments devoid of any hint of personalization. For adults, their own desired return to the innocence of lost youth adds a thematic, if abstracted, depth to the presentations.

After the 1941 strike, when Disney became disillusioned with animated film, and through his alliance with the FBI, Walt cast himself in the role of his greatest "character" yet, a real-life hero devoted to ridding the nation of the subversive element that threatened the great American family politic. While others pursued individuals within the system, Disney eventually pursued the Hollywood system itself, which he believed had conspired to prevent him from achieving the level of success he thought his work merited. As popular as his films had been, he remained convinced the "Old Boys Club" of mostly immigrant Jews who controlled the three major branches of the system—production, distribution, and exhibition— had worked to limit him to production, where money was spent, while denying him full access to distribution and exhibition, where money was made. Disney, forced to remain outside the industry's mainstream, believed himself to be Hollywood's bastard son.

He externalized the rage this invoked in him by attempting to destroy the structure and therefore the power centers of the industry. Eventually he accomplished his goal as one of the litigants in a landmark Supreme Court case that found the studio system an illegal monopoly. That decision ended the Majors' domination of distribution and exhibition, and further crippled an industry already reeling from governmental investigations into its politics and the new competition from "free" television.

Toward the end of his life, Disney's weekly hosting of the popular television series that bore his name reinforced his public image as everybody's kindly uncle. This image was further enhanced by the monument he built to his own legend, baptized "Disneyland," an amusement park dedicated to the memory of the happy childhood he never had. Disneyland confirmed Disney's place in the iconography of innocent indigenous American childhood, right alongside apple pie, summer vacations, baseball, ice cream, and, of course, Mickey Mouse.

By the time of his death at the age of sixty-five, obituaries mourned the passing of the great American family man who had given the world the pleasure of his films, television programs, and theme parks.

Overlooked in the many tributes were his formation of the Hollywood Alliance and its vigilantelike intimidation of all those it considered subversive; his friendly testimony before the House Un-American Activities Committee (HUAC); his lifelong fear of illegitimacy and his search for the woman he believed might have been his real mother; his twenty-five years of undercover work for the FBI; his virulent antiunion activities; his association with organized crime; and his relentless obsession with putting an end to what he believed was a studio system led by a band of corrupt Jewish European immigrants. In typical Hollywood fashion, death simply made Disney larger than life. His familiar logo signature continued to be universally recognized as a trusted guarantee of quality similar to the Good Housekeeping Seal of Approval.

This is the reason why, in the ensuing years, the preservation and protection of Walt Disney's image has become the single vital priority to those who now control his studio. Walt Disney has become the only name that instantly evokes the universally recognizable image of a man synonymous with family entertainment. As a result, most of the unflattering details of Disney's life have remained among the studio's most closely guarded secrets. Only those papers, letters, and photographs which promote the politically correct image have been released for use in studio-approved and, in many cases, licensed "biographies" which depict Disney's life like a movie star's glossy publicity photo, with all unsightly blemishes simply airbrushed out of existence.

By doing so, those who seek to preserve the commercially viable image of Walt Disney have, in fact, destroyed the artistic integrity of his work. For, in the end, it is only by examining Disney's conflicted inner self that inspired so much of his art—and Disney was an artist of the first rank—that we may begin to appreciate fully its greatness.

Throughout his life, Disney's bright genius emerged through emotional clouds of intense darkness. To put into deep focus Walt Disney's great projections, let us now view them from inside the theater of his troubled soul.

WALT DISNEY

Fathers and Sons

WALT DISNEY descended from a long line of crusaders, expert in the art of self-preservation. In 1066, from the French village of Isigny off the Normandy coast, a small band of peasants joined the army of William the Conqueror to claim the throne of England, among them Jean-Christophe d'Isigny, named for the village of his birth. After the wars, D'Isigny remained in England, anglicized his name, and established two northern villages, Norton Disney and Disney, near Coventry.

The Disneys quietly prospered as farmers until the seventeenth century, when they once more took up arms, this time to support the Duke of Monmouth's attempted overthrow of King James II. When that rebellion failed, the Disneys' land was confiscated, and a price was put on their heads. In desperation, they retreated to Ireland to find shelter within the hermetic safety of the devout Roman Catholic society of County Kilkenny.

High land taxes, poor crops, and a desire to worship as Protestants led to the eventual dispersion of the clan. Several set sail for France, one group ventured further north, and two brothers, Arundel Elias Disney, young, tough, wiry, and gritty, and his brother Robert, darker, warmer, and less prone to temper tantrums, took their families to the New World. They arrived in New York in the fall of 1834. Robert chose to stake his future in the western frontier, while Arundel settled on the Canadian shores of Lake Huron. There he found work in the sawmills and eventually founded his own beside the Maitland River.

His wife Mary gave birth to sixteen children, the eldest among them, Kepple Disney, who, by the time he had married and raised a family of his own, was the heir apparent to the thriving mill. Kepple, however, was something of a dreamer. Much to the disappointment of his aging father, he declined the offer to take over the family business. Kepple hated the bitter Canadian winters and dreamed of one day escaping to a warmer climate. He would listen to stories from the traders who frequented his favorite saloons and whorehouses about the balmy winds that literally blew gold into a visitor's face in the green valleys of Southern California. In the spring of 1878, Kepple set out with his two eldest sons, one also named Elias, who would become Walt's father, and Robert, for America's fabled gold coast.

Failing to make his fortune in prospecting, Kepple decided to remain in America to try his hand at farming. He planted his claim stake for land in Ellis, Kansas, close enough to the route of the Union Pacific to allow for easy profits from the regular shipment of his grains.

Robert worked the land alongside his father, while Elias, lean and tough, preferred the adventure of travel and ran off to join a team laying track, a job that took him from Ellis to Denver, Colorado. Once there, he purchased a fiddle, formed a trio, and played every night on street corners for tips. After several months of this life, Elias decided to return to Ellis, not to farm, a world he did not miss at all, but to see Flora Call, the pretty farmer's daughter who lived on the tract of land next to his father's.

Like the Disneys, the Calls had emigrated to America from England. They arrived in the seventeenth century and settled in New England. In 1849, Charles Call headed west to find his fortune and eventually moved to Ellis, Kansas, as had Kepple. Elias had made up his mind to ask Mr. Call for his daughter's hand in marriage, only to discover, when he returned, Call had sent his brood to Florida. Packing his bag once more, Elias followed them south, caught up with the Calls in Akron, where he asked for and received permission to marry Flora.

The wedding took place in the spring of 1888. Elias took a job as a hotel manager in Daytona Beach, and later that year, their first child,

Herbert Disney, was born. Elias, however, soon became bored with the tedium of enforced domesticity brought about by the presence of a new baby in the house and enlisted to fight in the Spanish-American War.

Seven days of basic training convinced Elias military life wasn't the adventure he had hoped it would be. Managing to secure a medical discharge for a suspect knee injury, he returned to Florida only after Flora's parents promised to buy him his own orange grove in nearby Kissimmee.

Elias settled into a regular dawn-to-dusk routine of citrus cropping until a record frost in the spring of '89 destroyed his harvest. He became convinced he could never make a go of it in Florida. He was also eager to move as far away as possible from Flora's parents, whom he found much too overbearing. As a result, that year Elias brought his family to Chicago.

The city on Lake Michigan, one of the central rail hubs to the Midwest, was in the midst of a major population explosion. From a series of lakeside shacks, Chicago had quickly grown into a thriving cosmopolitan city of more than a million residents. The Disneys soon contributed to that expansion with the birth of their second son Raymond, followed four years later, in 1893, by the arrival of Roy Oliver.

Elias worked as a handyman and carpenter, and after Preacher Walter Parr, of the Christian Fundamentalist St. Paul Church, hired him to build a new wing on the church, Disney became an active member of the congregation. Preacher Parr took a liking to Elias and often found odd jobs to help him out. In return, Disney promised that if he were ever blessed with another son he would be named in honor of the good preacher, a promise kept when, in 1901, a fourth son came to the Disneys, whom they christened Walter Elias Disney, Jr.

In 1903, Flora gave birth to one last child, a girl, Ruth Flora Disney. Within weeks of the baby's christening by Preacher Parr, Elias suddenly proclaimed his outrage at the rapid proliferation of neighborhood saloons, street prostitution, and rising crime. He insisted these offended his Fundamentalist sensibilities and endangered the morals of his children. He uprooted his family and took them to Marceline, a hundred miles northeast of Kansas City, Missouri.

However strong the religious foundation for Elias's protestations, in reality he was more concerned with his own physical well-being in this life rather than his family's spiritual preparation for the next. Elias, like Kepple before him, had a decidedly sacrilegious taste for the good life. He loved smoke-filled saloons, the loose women who worked them, 90-proof whiskey, and dog-eared poker decks that had sustained so many of his nightly flights of fancy. His particular love for a good game of poker had made him an easy mark for professional saloon gamblers. It was his outstanding debt to this congregation that prompted his decision to move from Chicago.

Early in 1903, Elias and his family settled in Marceline, on a fifty-acre fruit-and-stock farm bought by his brother Robert, who had proudly returned to what he claimed had always been his first love, working the land. Like so many disaffected drifters, Elias believed his failure to strike it rich had less to do with his lack of education or professional training than the absence of sufficient investment funds to play the capitalist game. It was this rationale for his own failure that led to his embracing of socialism.

Elias become an active supporter of Eugene V. Debs, leader of the American Social Democratic party. The Disney family's evening dinner now included long diatribes by Elias against the capitalist system and the exploitation of America's working class by the international conspiracy of wealthy Jews in control of the world's investment banks.

Elias's 1906 harvest of lush Wolf River apples provided enough money for him to acquire forty additional acres of land and offer his two eldest sons, Herbert and Raymond, now in their late teens, a portion of the profits from the next season's crop for their commitment to spend another year on the farm.

In spite of the family effort, the third season's only yield was failure, due to a particularly abundant nationwide crop of apples that kept wholesale prices unusually low. Elias took a heavy loss and was unable to pay anything to his two sons. At this point, Herbert, twenty-one, and Raymond, twenty, decided they had had enough of farm life. Their decision outraged Elias, and when they packed their bags and carried out their threat to leave, he vowed never to speak their names again.

Their departure in the fall of 1909 put an even greater burden on sixteen-year-old Roy and eight-year-old Walt, both of whom were required by Elias to spend their days working the farm to earn their keep. He used corporal punishment to enforce maximum productivity and thought nothing of taking a switch to his sons, or the fat part of his leather belt, to administer the "corrective" beatings that became a daily part of the boys' routine. At the slightest provocation, real or imagined, Elias would march Roy and Walt to the woodshed and dispense his brutal punishments.

In the evenings, following a beating, Walt would often lie awake in bed, whimpering. Roy, older and physically stronger, was able to endure the punishments better than his little brother. He would rub Walt's hurts and rock him to sleep with promises that everything would be all right in the morning. Walt would bury his head in the bend of Roy's elbow and ask if the man who beat them was really his father, or just some mean old man who looked like him and wanted only to frighten and hurt him.

On the rare days he wasn't punished, Walt looked forward to that part of the evening when, after he had gone to bed, his mother would read fairy tales to him in her soothing, expressive voice until he slipped gently into sleep.

As reassuring as these visits were, Walt remained confused and frightened by Elias's terrifying violence and couldn't understand why his mother didn't stop the beatings. It was, rather, in his brother's comforting arms that Walt found both the protective warmth he longed for from his mother and the feel of his father's brute strength. Often he would fall asleep huddled close to Roy, then wake up suddenly in the middle of the night and urinate on his brother. Other times, during the day, Walt would sneak into his mother's bedroom and put her clothes on and her makeup. Afterward, he would stand in front of her full-length mirror to admire his reflection. He knew this version of his mother, unlike the real one, would always be there when he needed her.

The boys were not allowed regularly scheduled playtime. In those rare moments they found themselves free of chores, they would play made-up games that inevitably turned to sibling rivalry. They would compete over who could better ride a hog, who could pitch more hay, who could throw the fork farther. When Roy was called upon by Elias to help with some particularly demanding physical chore, Walt, the smaller and weaker of the two boys, found himself mercifully left alone.

During those times, the thing he most liked to do was draw

pictures. Because paper and pencils were rarely available, Walt improvised, usually with a piece of coal on toilet paper. That was all he needed to pass a free hour sketching the gentle farm animals he considered his only real friends. He especially loved the feeling when they brushed up against him while he lay in the tall grass trying to capture their likenesses.

In the winter of 1909, after yet another unprofitable season, Elias came down with typhoid fever complicated by pneumonia and was forced to sell the farm. Upon his recovery, he moved the family to Kansas City, where he purchased a thousand-customer newspaper-delivery route.

If the nature of the family's business had changed, the practice of his sons' enforced participation hadn't. Flora saw to it both boys were enrolled in the nearby Benton Grammar School. Nevertheless, Elias insisted they still had to deliver two daily editions each of both the *Morning Times* and the *Evening and Sunday Star*, seven days a week. This meant their day began at three-thirty in the morning. Elias required the boys to carefully roll each newspaper and hand-drop it on their customers' stoops, and when it rained to place the newspapers inside screen and storm doors.

As the business grew, Elias found it necessary to hire additional delivery boys. Claiming he couldn't afford the extra expense, and blaming his sons for not being able to handle the job themselves, he discontinued their already meager pay. For Walt, this meant he could no longer afford his paper and crayons. Not that it mattered all that much, for now, despite the increased staff, due to the heavy number of new subscribers, there was even less time for drawing.

Walt's work schedule was so exhausting he often took catnaps in the side alleys of the homes along his route. And when the newspaper business proved less profitable than Elias expected, he took out his frustration on his sons, finding reasons to administer the regular whippings that always left Walt weak and dazed with pain.

On his eighteenth birthday, in 1911, Roy decided the time had come for him to leave home. Knowing Walt, only ten, smaller and frailer than most Kansas City farm boys his age, would be left unprotected, Roy spent his last days trying to teach his little brother how to defend himself against Elias. Not long after Roy's departure, the loss of his free labor drove Elias into one of his worst rages.

Predictably, he found fault with something Walt did and ordered the boy to prepare for a whipping.

The beating never took place. That night, up in the bedroom, Elias raised his hand. Walt then had the opportunity to try out all that Roy had taught him. He reached up, grabbed Elias's wrists, and stared into his eyes until, after several seconds, Walt felt his father's strength weaken and his arms fall. Elias left the room. That was the last time he ever came after his youngest son.

A week later, Walt took a job delivering prescriptions for the local drugstore. He used this money to buy additional newspapers to sell on street corners, without bothering to tell his father. He spent the extra profits on art supplies.

At school, Walt managed average grades but showed special aptitude in reading. He frequented the school library, read all of Twain and Dickens, and devoured the adventure books of his favorite hero, Jimmy Dale, junior secret agent. He also showed his abilities in art class, although Disney's strikingly original sketches weren't always what his teachers expected.

One time he drew a series of flowers with human hands and faces. The sketches puzzled his instructors, who had asked the class to draw the real flowers set up as models. Another time, for homework, Walt traced several left-wing political cartoons from one of the socialist magazines his father kept around the house. His teachers sent them directly to the principal, who wrote an angry letter to Elias criticizing him for having such magazines in his home.

Walt also enjoyed playacting in school and in 1912, at the age of eleven, made his first new friend since the departure of his brother. Walter Pfeiffer, like Walt, had an interest in dramatics. They met at rehearsals, and every day after classes, Walt and Pfeiffer played "Jimmy Dale," acting out the adventures of Walt's favorite junior secret agent. The two quickly became inseparable, and Walt began spending afternoons and, over Elias's objections, occasional evenings at his friend's home. In contrast to Walt's, Pfeiffer's father was a warm, chubby, generous man, who encouraged the boys' friendship and helped them playact comedy routines he accompanied on the piano. He liked to take them to the movies on the weekends, which was how Walt first experienced the magic of motion pictures and the art of Charlie Chaplin.

Walt fell in love with the Little Tramp and soon dropped his impression of the Jimmy Dale character in favor of doing "Charlie." He became so good at it he entered an amateur show where he caught the eye of a theatrical touring scout interested in signing him up as a "Juvenile" with a local vaudeville company. Walt tried to work up the nerve to ask his parents to let him perform. But he never actually approached them because he suffered a serious accident one afternoon while making his newspaper deliveries.

As he crossed a street, he happened to see a chunk of ice and lazily tried to kick it. He didn't notice the large nail imbedded in the center of the ice until it was too late. He fell over in pain, with the nail stuck halfway up his foot. He was rushed to the hospital where the wound was treated and he was given a tetanus shot. The doctors told Flora to keep him off his feet for two full weeks.

Those were the first days he ever had the luxury of spending entirely in bed. To pass the afternoons, he eagerly read the many books his mother brought him from the library, drew pictures, and devoured the day's newspapers. He started following the daily comic strips and the editorial cartoons. By the time his foot was sufficiently healed for him to return to school, all thoughts of a career in vaudeville were gone. What he really wanted to do now was to draw cartoons like those that appeared in the newspapers.

In the fall of 1917, Elias sold the newspaper route for $16,000. He believed enough time had passed for him to safely return to Chicago, where he used the money to buy a partnership in the O-Zell Jelly factory. Flora begged Elias to allow Walt to remain behind and finish the school year at Benton Grammar. When Elias first announced his intention to return to Chicago, Flora wrote Herbert, then thirty, whom she had kept up a correspondence with during his travels, and told him what was going on and got him to agree to return home and care for his sixteen-year-old brother.

The separation from his parents invoked in Walt both a deep sadness and an exhilarating sense of freedom. Shortly after they departed, he experienced his first nips of puppy love, developing a crush on one of his classmates. Too shy to approach her directly, he left anonymous drawings filled with hearts and arrows on her desk. The girl never found out who her secret admirer was.

That spring, when school let out, Walt readied himself to make the move to Chicago. Just before his scheduled departure, he received a letter from Roy, saying he was was planning to return to Kansas City, where he had secured a job as a bank teller. Over the objections of Herbert, who was not particularly happy having to baby-sit his kid brother, Walt decided to postpone his move until the fall.

His first week back, Roy filled Walt's head with tales of the adventure and romance he had experienced as a "news butcher," hawking newspapers, candy, cigars, cigarettes, matches, soft drinks, on the Kansas-to-Missouri rail route. Always wanting to be like his brother, Walt lied about his age, saying he was seventeen instead of sixteen, and got a summer job as a news butcher with the Van Noyes Interstate News Company, which serviced several Midwestern cities.

In spite of his enthusiasm, Walt showed little aptitude for the job. By the end of the summer, he wound up owing the company money for unsold inventory. Nevertheless, he considered the experience a great success. The ride back and forth on his designated route, from Missouri to Colorado, had opened up a world to him he had never dreamed existed. Between trips he had eaten in restaurants, walked the streets of big cities, and slept in hotel beds. He didn't mind at all having to pay the company whatever they wanted. To him, no price was too dear to pay for all he had been able to see and do.

When fall arrived, Walt reluctantly joined his family in Chicago, where he was enrolled for his junior year at McKinley High School. He submitted some of his sketches to the school newspaper and was invited to contribute editorial cartoons. By the end of his second semester, he had become the paper's junior art editor. Thus encouraged, Walt signed up for evening classes at the Chicago Academy of Fine Arts, where he came under the tutelage of Carl Wertz and his staff of part-time instructors from the *Chicago Record*. Among them was Walt's newest favorite cartoonist, pen-and-ink caricaturist Leroy Gossett.

To pay for his classes, Walt worked several additional hours a week, in his father's jelly factory, and took part-time jobs at the post office and as a station clerk on the Chicago El.

He also attended the southside burlesque shows to copy the jokes he heard for his cartoons. He would occasionally try them out on Elias, who almost never found them funny. He had no use for comedy, or drawing, for that matter, and urged Walt to spend less time on those frivolous pastimes and more on learning how to run a factory. There, at least, Elias told Walt, if he worked hard enough, he might one day be able to earn a decent wage.

In 1917, America entered the World War I, and Roy, twenty-four, immediately enlisted in the army, eager to join the fighting overseas. That July he was sent for training to the Great Lakes Naval Station just outside Chicago's city limits. As soon as he finished his senior year in high school, Walt packed his bag and visited his brother. Ever the romantic, Roy fueled Walt's curiosity with tales of overseas war stories picked up secondhand from returning vets.

The day he returned to Chicago, Walt made up his mind that he too would enlist. When the local recruiter, skeptical of Walt's age, asked to see his birth certificate, Walt wrote to Chicago's Cook County Hall of Records requesting a copy. A week later, by return mail, he received an official-looking document stating that the Hall of Records had no birth certificate for any Walt Disney born on or around December 5, 1901.

Walt wrote to Preacher Parr, asking if there were any documents in the church that could verify his birth. The preacher wrote back that, to the best of his recollection, Walt had been born at home. Therefore no hospital or church records would exist of his birth. Walt then wrote to the Department of Vital Statistics, whose response only added to the growing mystery; there was an official record of birth for a "Walter Disney," to one Elis [sic] and Flora Disney. However, that birth was recorded for *January 8, 1891*. If that were true, Walt would be *twenty-six years old*, which was, of course, impossible.

Walt finally told his parents he intended to enlist and that he needed a copy of his birth certificate. When they couldn't produce it, he showed them the information from the Department of Vital Statistics. Elias insisted it was all some terrible mistake, that of course a birth certificate existed and he would see about getting a copy of it.

All of this greatly disturbed Walt, whose childhood fantasies that his father couldn't have been his father now reverberated with a deeper, more ominous, resonance. Why wasn't there an accurate record of his birth? What secrets, if any, were his parents hiding from him? Would they ever tell him? Could he ever be sure what they said was the truth? The only thing he was certain of was that he wasn't certain of anything, except that he no longer felt he could trust his parents and wouldn't again from that time on. This infection of doubt would eat at Walt the rest of his days, infusing his future films with a feverish passion that would deepen their dramatic themes.

Walt's first reaction was to run. He asked his parents for a written letter of consent that would allow him to enlist. Flora pleaded with him not to go through with it. Raymond had also enlisted, and she couldn't bear the thought of a third son going off to war. Elias didn't want him going either. He had no use for a war instigated, in his opinion, by the worldwide Jewish capitalist conspiracy.

Unable to convince either of his parents to change their minds, Walt forged their signatures and got himself accepted as a volunteer in the International Red Cross. His first assignment was to go to work for the Chicago Yellow Cab Company. He was ordered to learn how to drive, so he could operate an ambulance. However, during his first week on the job, he became a victim of the 1918 flu epidemic and was delivered back to his parents on a stretcher, courtesy of a Red Cross van.

After he recovered, he was reassigned to South Beach, Connecticut, where, one day after his arrival, the armistice was announced. Along with fifty men from his unit, Walt was assigned for immediate duty in France to care for sick and wounded American soldiers.

Walt spent his eighteenth birthday in Saint Cyr, in a château temporarily converted to a military hospital. That night, the boys in his unit threw a surprise party for him, during which he drank liquor and smoked for the first time, the start of two habits he would keep for the rest of his life. He also spent his first evening with a woman, courtesy of the boys in his company who made it their business to initiate Walt into the brotherhood of man. The next day he had photographs of himself taken in his volunteer's uniform, the arrogant cock of his head, proud thrust of his chest, and tilt of his hat validation that he had finally come of age.

Despite all his dreams of glory, there was, in fact, little for him to do in the weeks that followed. He served as a chauffeur for officers, drove military officials all over France and through the Rhine country of occupied Germany, delivered beans and sugar to military hospitals, and occasionally drove an ambulance.

His days as a driver quickly lapsed into boring routine, smothered by an atmosphere thick with weariness, illness, and misery. To pass the long hours between transports, Walt painted the sides of Red Cross Jeeps with caricatures of his fellow volunteers. He also continued to draw his cartoons and send them to magazines in the United States, all of which were rejected.

This artwork, such as it was, caught the eye of one flannel-mouthed soldier known to the rest of the unit as Cracker. Cracker was always on the lookout to make a quick buck. The two became friends and together hatched a scheme wherein Cracker would buy surplus German helmets, shoot them full of holes, and turn them over to Walt, who for ten francs apiece would decorate them with various German insignia and/or camouflage to suggest they were genuine enemy combat gear. Cracker would then sell them to the other soldiers as authentic war souvenirs. By the time of his discharge, Walt had made nearly $300 from this scam, or as he preferred to see it, from his talent as an artist. It was more money than he had ever seen before in his life.

His service completed, Walt returned on a steamship to New York, checked into a midtown hotel, enjoyed his first hot shower in weeks, changed into civvies, took in the latest Chaplin, ate in the fanciest restaurant he could find, and spent the rest of that night getting drunk and sampling the jazz in several smoky basement nightclubs beneath the streets of Greenwich Village.

The next morning he left for Chicago, where he wired ahead for Elias and Flora to meet him at the train station. His parents were shocked by their first glimpse of the strapping, handsome six-footer who only barely resembled the boy that had run away from home a year before.

That evening, after dinner, Elias sat down with Walt in front of the fire to share a pipe and a pipe dream. The time had come for his son to join the family jelly business. In return for his commitment to the factory, Elias promised Walt an eventual partnership. To Elias's surprise, Walt politely but firmly declined. He had plans of his own. He intended to return to Kansas City and pursue a career as a commercial artist.

At dawn the next morning, he left his parents' home for the last time and caught a train headed for the land of his lost childhood, where he hoped to find his future.

T W O

Kansas City *Ad Infinitum*

AMONG THE FIRST THINGS Walt did after moving into the old family house with Roy and Herbert was to apply for a job as a cartoonist at the *Kansas City Star*. He had delivered this newspaper as a boy, one reason why he was so disappointed when they turned him down without looking at his drawings. The rejection sent Walt into a depression that lasted several days, until Roy pulled him out of it by mentioning an opening for artists he had heard about from one of the owners of the Pressman-Rubin Studios. Pressman-Rubin was the new advertising agency in town whose account Roy handled at the bank.

The next day Walt brought his drawings and sketches to the firm's partners. He was both surprised and delighted when they hired him on the spot, although for years Roy claimed Pressman-Rubin had done so as a personal favor to him.

Walt's first assignment was an easy one for him, drawing farm equipment, egg-laying pulleys, tractors, and silo lifts for Christmas catalogues and illustrations for local "theater programmes." Unfortunately, he lasted only a month before being laid off due to the company's assessment of what it claimed was his "singular lack of drawing ability."

Unable to find any other work as an artist, Walt took a temporary Christmas job at the post office. After work every night he would walk home through the snowy cold, skip dinner, and lock himself in his room until morning.

One evening, a week before 1920's arrival would herald the start of the new decade, a tall, polite young man appeared at the front door, asking if this was where his friend Walt Disney lived. Roy, unaware his brother had made any new friends, invited the fellow in, offered him a cup of coffee, and quickly fetched Walt.

Certain at first there had to be some mistake, Walt appeared surprised when he found it was Ub Iwerks at the door. Iwerks had been hired by Pressman-Rubin the same day as Walt, and as the two worked alongside one another, they quickly discovered they had much in common. Each had grown up on a farm not far from the other. Both wanted a career in commercial art and had been laid off after only a month.

Ub, short for Ubbe, whose parents were Dutch immigrants, and Walt commiserated over their shared fate while having coffee and cakes Roy brought to the parlor. They talked past midnight, when Iwerks suggested that if nobody else were going to hire them, they ought to hire themselves. Disney grabbed a pencil and started making notes. By dawn they were partners in Iwerks-Disney Commercial Artists (as opposed to Disney-Iwerks, which Walt felt made them sound too much like an optical firm). They sealed their partnership with a handshake, both men insisting it was the only contract they would ever need.

Iwerks's visit revitalized Walt, and, just as years ago with Walt Pfeiffer, this new friendship became the prime focus of his life. Iwerks was willing to gamble his future on their shared abilities, and that meant everything to Walt. Time and again during those first days, he pledged to Ub a partnership for life, no matter what, the ardent promise of fidelity made with the kind of intensity more characteristic, perhaps, of young lovers than business partners.

When morning broke, Walt, fueled with fresh enthusiasm, called everyone he knew for leads. Ironically, the new company's first assignment came from Disney's old pal Walt Pfeiffer, who was now a member of the leatherworker's union. Pfeiffer, happy to hear from his boyhood friend, told him his father was about to start a union newsletter. Walt and Iwerks applied for the job to design it, and Mr. Pfeiffer was happy to hire them. Flush with their first success, they next went to see Al Carder, a veteran trade-newsletter editor who had been one of Walt's first newspaper-delivery customers. Carder too had fond memories of Walt. He offered him work space in the rear section of the office in exchange for free consultations.

Although Walt and Ub showed up at dawn every day and worked late into the night, seven days a week, in less than a month they exhausted all their contacts, earning a total of $135 from their one assignment, and Iwerks-Disney's business ground to a halt. Then, on January 29, 1920, Iwerks saw an ad in the paper for a cartoonist. Knowing of Walt's desire to work in that field, he urged him to apply for it. After viewing his samples, the Kansas City Film Ad Company offered Disney $40 a week to start. In spite of his recent declarations of eternal loyalty, Walt immediately accepted a job that effectively ended his "lifelong" partnership with Iwerks.

Disney's first assignment was drawing stick figures for newly popular theatrical "cartoon" ads. Kansas City Ad used an inexpensive and crude form of animation—figure cutouts with arms and legs pinned to wooden dowels that were moved back and forth to create the illusion of motion.

Animated films had been little more than a motion picture footnote until 1919, when "cartoons" enjoyed a sudden burst of popularity due to the unprecedented success of Pat Sullivan's and Otto Messmer's "Felix the Cat" series. Felix's brand of wise-guy humor was an amalgam of the physical comedy stylistics of the silent screen's two most popular comedians, the ethereal Charlie Chaplin and the physically wondrous Buster Keaton. Felix the Cat quickly became the most popular cartoon character of the day. The demand for cartoons became so great, advertising agencies began animating their prefeature ads.

While in no way comparable to the quality of New York animation by such early giants as the Fleischer brothers (Max and Dave), Pat Sullivan, Otto Messmer, Winsor McCay ("Little Nemo,") or John Randolph Bray ("Bobby Bumps"), Kansas City Ad's shorts proved extremely popular with audiences simply because they were animated, and with clients because they were so inexpensive to make.

Kansas City Ad soon found it had more work than it could handle and asked its employees if they knew anyone who wanted to join the company. Walt called Iwerks and told him about the opening, and a week later Ub was hired.

By working on the shorts, Disney learned the basic techniques of moving pictures and animation. He befriended the company's main cameraman, Jimmy Lowerre, who showed Walt the technique of stop-action: Shooting one frame of film and slightly rearranging the stick figures could create the illusion of movement. The more Walt learned, the more he became fascinated with the idea that movement alone could not only project physical performance but also describe emotion.

Thus intrigued, Walt visited the Kansas City library and found two books on animation, a basic handbook by Carl Lutz and the classic work of Eadweard Muybridge on human and animal emotion. He photostatted both and studied them his every free moment. And when he came across an old camera the company no longer used, he asked his boss if he could borrow it. Having received permission to do so, each night after work, Walt locked himself in the garage and spent hours figuring out how to operate the mahogany hand-crank camera. When he was sure he understood all the working parts, he began to shoot footage of his own drawings, moving the camera back and forth, up and down, forward and back, trying to see if he could create the illusion that his pictures actually "moved."

Always an experimenter, Walt became obsessed with the camera's potential. He made up "tricks," loading film tail-first so that the last footage shot came first, then running it from the beginning, head-first, to see the effect. He quickly mastered the technique of stop-action filming, and found that by varying the speed of the shutter crank he was able to simulate fast and slow motion.

Although to Walt it seemed as if he were in the process of reinventing the cinema, there was really nothing particularly original, nor revelatory, in his experiments. All were quite basic and had already been rendered obsolete by the introduction in 1916 of the Fleischer brothers' rotoscope, an invention that allowed artists to duplicate movement by tracing live-action-filmed footage frame by frame. Still, for all their primitiveness, Disney's experiments were, in their way, quite remarkable, considering they were being conducted by someone quite literally shooting in the dark.

Within weeks of mastering the camera, Disney began making original animated films in the family garage after work conceptually and technically superior in every way to the ones he worked on during the day. At least part of the reason was Ub Iwerks's contribution. He could draw better than Walt, particularly human figures. Iwerks often took Walt's original sketches and developed them into fully realized pictures that made his films look better. As Disney's reliance on Iwerks grew, so did the complexity of their relationship. In many ways, Iwerks became an idealized stand-in for Roy.

Walt required a "new" Roy because the old one had begun spending more and more time with his childhood sweetheart, Edna Frances. Roy's "absence" may have been interpreted by Walt as abandonment, causing him to act out his hostility on the closest substitute available. Walt loved to play practical jokes, and the camera he carried around with him everywhere proved an excellent prop. Walt used Iwerks's intense shyness around women as the basis for a series of humiliating gags. Ub was attracted to one of the girls in the office, Margaret Metzinger. Disney made a date with her for dinner and also one with Iwerks, knowing the two would then meet. Walt filmed the whole thing and ran it the next day in front of the entire staff. Ub walked out in embarrassment, and Metzinger threw a bottle of ink at Walt, who couldn't understand why the two didn't enjoy the stunt as much as he did.

Eventually, Walt became convinced he was good enough to compete with Kansas City Ad. Using the name "Laugh-O-Grams," he approached Frank Newman, the owner and operator of a chain of Kansas City movie theaters, which happened to be Kansas City Ad's best clients. Newman was also a key figure in national film distribution. He ran one of the largest and most powerful Midwest film exchanges, where theaters returned their old movies for the new ones that arrived daily from the East and West coasts.

Disney impressed Newman enough for him to set up a meeting with Milton Feld, his general manager, who screened Disney's test reel of shots of local Kansas City residents and familiar buildings interspersed with slides of jokes, news headlines, and public-service curtain raisers. Feld liked what he saw and offered to buy one minute of original "Laugh-O-Grams" a week, at thirty cents a foot. Walt, unaware that "professional" animation cost on the average $25 *per foot* to produce, accepted the deal. On May 23, 1922, a twenty-one-year-old Walt, with Ub's approval, took the remaining assets of Iwerks-Disney Commercial Artists and officially merged them with Laugh-O-Grams, bankrolled by $15,000 he raised from local investors.

To "sell" his concept, Walt knew he somehow needed to personalize it. He created an animated character he called Professor Whosis, who came on-screen between hand-lettered messages with jokes for the audience. Professor Whosis proved such a hit with local audiences, Feld asked for two weekly "Laugh-O-Grams" and raised Walt's fee to $60 a week.

Disney now felt confident enough to resign from Kansas City Ad.

He bought a used model of the same camera he had borrowed from them| and set out to sign up his own roster of advertisers.

While Walt experienced his first taste of cinematic success, Elias underwent his latest failure with the bankruptcy of the jelly factory. The senior Disney, with few options and no money, was forced to leave Chicago, once again under a cloud. He moved back to Kansas City and the old house where Roy, Walt, and Herbert and his family were now living. Walt was delighted by the reunion, which brought the family back together except for Raymond, who had become a traveling insurance salesman and was permanently on the road. Elias, upon his return, agreed to let Walt continue to use the garage as a studio for a rental fee of $5 a month.

The reunion lasted a short time. Within weeks, Roy developed a severe case of tuberculosis that forced him to move to a New Mexico sanitarium for what his doctors predicted would be a long and difficult recuperation. Not long after, Herbert, who now worked for the post office full-time, was transferred to Oregon. Elias, nearing sixty-five and no longer able to work full-time, gratefully and humbly accepted Herbert's offer to bring Flora and their youngest daughter along on the move. As quickly as the big family home had come to life, the house now seemed to Walt eerily empty.

The sudden departure plunged Disney into a new depression. He decided he no longer wanted to live in the family house, especially after Roy's fiancée, Edna, kept coming by to see that he ate regularly. Walt felt her help was intrusive and a poor substitute for his absent brother.

He found an affordable room in downtown Kansas City a few blocks away and rented a nearby storefront to use as a studio. When relocation did not relieve his sadness, he decided to contact the one person he felt closest to outside the family, Ub Iwerks.

Disney easily convinced Ub to leave his job at Kansas City Ad for one with Laugh-O-Grams. He also placed ads in the local newspapers offering free animation lessons to anyone who might be interested in learning "the cartoon business." Disney soon had enough students to start production on his first "real" animated cartoon. It hadn't taken him long to realize that as popular as his "Laugh-O-Grams" were, they were too local to gain him a wider audience. What he wanted to do now was to create a cartoon good enough to appeal to a national distributor.

Walt decided to make a cartoon out of a fairy tale. Not just any fairy tale, but one his mother used to read to him when he was a little boy. Having written a simple adaptation of "Little Red Riding Hood," he shot it entirely with his single hand-cranked camera. In spite of its many technical limitations, the film was good enough so that movie-theater owner Frank Newman could invite local investors to a screening and convince them to buy $15,000 worth of shares in what were now called "Newman Laugh-O-Grams."

With this new influx of cash, Walt started production on a second short, an animated version of "Puss in Boots," another of his favorite bedtime stories. This children's tale possessed one extra attraction, a character who happened to be quite similar to the enormously popular Felix. While Walt worked on the film, Milton Feld, Newman's general manager, as a favor to Walt, sent prints of *Little Red Riding Hood* to New York to help him find a national distributor.

The film was rejected by every major distributor, but Walt did receive an offer from one small, nontheatrical company, Pictorial Clubs—$100 in advance against $11,000 for the delivery of six completed cartoons. Walt immediately put five new films into production.

The office buzzed with activity seven days a week. Walt did some drawing, washed his old celluloids for reuse, and swept up at the end of each day. On weekends, Walt took his Universal camera around town, mounted on the rear seat of his car, shooting raw footage, with a sign hung on his car doors saying the film could be seen the following night at the Isis theater. The management paid for his services with a percentage of the box-office take on the nights his "street scenes" ran. He also shot footage on assignment for the Selznick, Pathé, and Universal newsreels. The relatively high pay, about $1 a foot, always took precedence over animation deadlines.

Unfortunately, shortly after sending Walt the first hundred dollars, Pictorial Clubs went out of business. Disney was saved by the last-minute intervention of Carl Stalling, an organ accompanist for the Newman Theaters and a Newman Laugh-O-Grams investor, who bought an additional $2,500 worth of stock in the company. However, that money was soon exhausted, and Walt had to let his staff go, including Iwerks, who, in the fall of 1922, reluctantly returned to his job at the Kansas City Ad Company.

Before he could decide what to do next, Disney was approached by another local investor, a dentist looking to have a short produced that would promote oral hygiene treatments. The $500 he made from *Tommy Tucker's Tooth* allowed Walt to once again rehire Iwerks and begin work on a new project, a combination live-action–animated film based on Lewis Carroll's *Alice's Adventures in Wonderland*. To save money, Walt came up with a clever variation on the then-popular but expensive technique of Max Fleischer's "Out of the Inkwell" series, which featured superimposed animated characters on "real" backgrounds. Disney simply planned to shoot a "live" Alice against "animated" backgrounds, which were, in reality, nothing more than large drawings.

For his Alice, Disney hired a local actress by the name of Virginia Davis, a child model he had met while both were employed by Kansas City Ad. To keep costs as low as possible, Walt and Ub used themselves as extras to fill out the backgrounds.

In May 1923, even before the first "Alice" was completed, Disney figured he had enough footage to look for a New York distributor. On Milton Feld's recommendation, Walt wrote to Margaret J. Winkler, the New York–based independent distributor for the "Out of the Inkwell" and "Felix the Cat" series.

In his letter to her, Disney boasted of what he considered to be his rather incredible accomplishment: ". . . [I've] just discovered something new and clever in animated cartoons! . . . a new idea that will appeal to all classes and is bound to be a winner . . . a clever combination of live characters and cartoons. . . ."

Walt's brash enthusiasm amused Winkler, who wrote back asking to see his film. Thus encouraged, Walt and Iwerks worked around the clock to finish "Alice" before their $500 was spent. Hard as they tried, they couldn't make it. Rent, food, and payroll killed them, and when Walt's newly hired staff of five local animators quit for lack of pay, Newman Laugh-O-Grams collapsed into insolvency.

Disney was left with little to show for his efforts beyond the bitterness he felt having produced a half-finished film and thousands of dollars in unpaid bills. When he had felt most successful making cartoons, his inspiration had come indirectly from his mother's nighttime fairy tales. Now his feelings of failure led him to borrow a page out of Elias's manual of real life, and he decided to skip town. The only question left was in which direction to flee.

Walt quickly narrowed his choices to two cities: New York, where the best animation houses were located and where he might find a job as an apprentice, or Los Angeles, where Roy's condition had improved enough for him to convalesce in the sunny, dry climate of Southern California. Walt had no problem choosing the security of being with his brother over professional ambition and made plans to join Roy on the Coast.

With his last $40, from the sale of his movie camera, Disney bought himself a first-class train ticket for the West Coast. Ragtag and tired, Walt spent long hours sitting alone and hungry, staring at the panoramic flatlands through the club-car's picture window, marveling at their slow dissolve into the jagged terrain of the Rockies. He was so taken with the passing scenery he failed to notice an elderly well-dressed gentleman approach from across the club car. Curious as to what someone so unkempt might be doing in first class, the man inquired as to Disney's destination.

Walt recalled years later, "I looked up at him and said, with all the assurance of my twenty-two years, that I was going to Hollywood.

" 'Well now,' he said. 'And what's your name, son?'

" 'Walt Disney, sir,' I replied.

" 'And what's your business in Hollywood, Mr. Disney?' he said with a smile.

"I looked up at him with a bigger smile and said, 'I'm going to direct motion pictures.'

" 'Is that so?' the man said, obviously surprised at my response.

" 'Oh, yes,' I said. 'I'm going to direct great Hollywood motion pictures.' "

THREE

Of Men and Mice

IT WAS A BRIGHT Sunday morning in July of 1923 when Elias's brother Robert, now living in Los Angeles, heard the knock on his front door. He opened it to find a young man who introduced himself as his nephew, who, with suitcase in hand, was looking for a place to stay. Although Uncle Robert had never seen Walt before, he welcomed him warmly and offered a room for as long as he liked—at five dollars a week, paid, of course, in advance.

One day after settling into his uncle's house, Walt took a bus to the Sawtelle Veterans Hospital in West Los Angeles, where Roy continued to recuperate from tuberculosis. Upon his arrival, Walt was relieved to find his brother well enough to move freely about the ward. He described to Roy all that had taken place since they had last seen each other, how he now felt he had gotten into the animation business too late, that series like Paul Terry's "Aesop's Fables" and Pat Sullivan's "Felix the Cat" dominated the field. What he really wanted to do was find a job with one of the major Hollywood studios, directing live-action motion pictures. Roy wished him well and offered to help in any way he could.

In Hollywood, Walt had business cards printed announcing him as the Kansas City representative of Universal and Selznick Studios and used one to get him past the front gate of Universal Studios. Once inside, he spent the day roaming the back lots, trying to stay out of the way of the dozens of people constantly moving about. Actors and actresses ran past him in period costumes, men carried scenery the size of walls, extras clustered on corners, trucks moved lights and cables. Standing unnoticed among the traffic, Disney realized this was where he wanted to be, making movies.

He found the employment office and applied for a job as a director and was quickly and impolitely turned away. By the end of the week he had been rejected by every major studio. Down to his last $5 and feeling more like ninety-two than twenty-two, Walt returned to the hospital, found Roy in his room, and broke down in front of him and wept.

After calming his brother, Roy suggested Walt reconsider his decision to give up animation and offered new seed money to get him started. He pledged a monthly stipend of $85 from his military pension if Walt would resume making cartoons. Thus encouraged, Walt mapped out a new plan of attack. He would approach the owners of those independent movie theaters not part of a chain or obligated to the Majors for product and try to sell them his animated curtain raisers.

After being turned down by several, one independent owner-operator, Alexander Pantages, finally offered to view a sample of Walt's work. With additional money borrowed from his brother, Walt rented editing equipment and built a crude studio in his uncle's garage. He worked through the night and put together a reel of stick-figure animation, the best he could manage with no budget and no staff. The next afternoon he delivered the film to Pantages's Hollywood office. A few days later it came back without so much as the courtesy of a rejection slip. Desperate, Walt turned to the East and the one contact he had established during his Kansas City days.

He sent the following letter to Margaret Winkler in New York, along with whatever incomplete "Alice" footage he had:

This is to inform you that I am no longer connected with the Laugh-O-Gram Films, Inc., of Kansas City, Mo., and that I am establishing a studio in Los Angeles for the purpose of producing the new and novel series of cartoons I have previously written you about.

The making of these new cartoons necessitates being located in a production center, that I may engage trained talent for my casts, and be within reach of the right facilities for producing. I am taking with me a select number of my former staff and will in a very short time be producing at regular intervals. It is my intention of securing working space with one of the studios that I may better study technical detail and comedy situations and combine these with my cartoons. . . .

Several days later Disney received this telegram from Winkler:

BELIEVE SERIES CAN BE PUT OVER BUT PHOTOGRAPHY OF ALICE SHOULD SHOW MORE DETAIL AND BE STEADIER THIS BEING NEW PRODUCT MUST SPEND LARGE AMOUNT ON EXPLOITATION AND ADVERTISING THEREFORE NEED YOUR COOPERATION WILL PAY FIFTEEN HUNDRED EACH NEGATIVE FOR FIRST SIX AND TO SHOW MY GOOD FAITH WILL PAY FULL AMOUNT ON EACH OF THESE SIX IMMEDIATELY ON DELIVERY NEGATIVE. . . .

On the strength of Winkler's response, Roy gave his brother an additional $200 over the initial $85, money Walt insisted was an investment, and he made his brother an equal partner in the business. Still short of funds, Walt approached Uncle Robert, who agreed to a $500 loan. Walt offered him a share of the company as well, which he refused, preferring to be repaid with interest from the company's first intake of cash.* On October 16, 1923, twenty-two-year-old Walt Disney signed a contract with Margaret Winkler that officially put him back in the business of making cartoons.

By now sufficiently recovered to leave the hospital, Roy took a small apartment with Walt near the site of their new Hollywood "studio," a small, unused storage space in the back of a large suite of real estate offices where, for $10 a month, the "Disney Brothers" officially opened their doors.

Winkler wanted Walt to use the same girl who had played Alice in the original Kansas City reel. Eager to please, Walt wrote to Virginia Davis's parents in Kansas City and offered them a contract of $100 a month to bring their daughter to Los Angeles. The day after Virginia and her family arrived in California, production began on *Alice's Day*

---

*Roy's return on his $200 investment would eventually make him one of the wealthiest men in Hollywood. Uncle Robert's decision, on the other hand, cost him and his heirs nearly a billion dollars in profits and an ongoing share of the Disney empire.

at Sea. One-third animation, two-thirds live action, *Alice* was shot on a strip of beach between Venice and Santa Monica, with a $200 secondhand model of the same hand-crank Universal camera Walt had used in Kansas City, for a total cost of $750. When it was finished, Walt shipped the film to New York. A few days later Winkler sent the following telegram:

"DAY AT SEA" RECEIVED TODAY. SATISFACTORY. MAILING TODAY DRAFT ON LOS ANGELES BANK WITH DETAILED LETTER.

Two days later Walt received a check for $1,500 and a letter from Winkler advising Walt she still considered his animation inferior, especially the background drawings which Disney himself had created. While she didn't feel this first completed film quite good enough to sell, she agreed to continue to invest in the series.

With the money, Disney began production on a second new short, *Alice Hunting in Africa.* The film placed the little girl on a jungle safari. Some of it was shot on a vacant lot near Hollywood Boulevard and some in Griffith Park, right next to where footage was being shot by Cecil B. DeMille. Winkler's response, while more positive, still contained many critical and technical suggestions. The film looked better than the first, she wrote, but it still lacked the essential element of humor. Walt loaded his third attempt with as many sight gags as he could dream up. Winkler found *Alice's Spooky Adventures*, about the heroine's adventures in a haunted house, good enough to attempt to distribute.

In March of 1924, Walt Disney's "Alice" series debuted in a regional theatrical circuit that included southern New Jersey, eastern Pennsylvania, Maryland, and Washington, D.C., movie theaters. The day after his film opened, Walt got in touch with Ub Iwerks in Kansas City and asked him to come to Hollywood to work on the "Alice" series.

Much to Disney's surprise, Iwerks turned down the offer. Iwerks had once again returned to Kansas City Ad and by now had worked his way up to a salary of $50 a week. What bothered Iwerks was Disney's offer of a job, with no mention of their "lifelong" partnership.

Ub finally agreed to join Disney only after Walt doubled his original offer of $20 a week to $40 and included stock in the new company. Not long after, Walt recruited those he considered the best of the original Laugh-O-Gram student animators, including Rudolph Ising, Carman Maxwell and Friz Freleng.

Walt insisted on putting all profits he made from Winkler back into production, a decision which left the fledgling company vulnerable to any financial crisis. The first occurred when Virginia Davis's mother demanded that Walt double her daughter's salary or find himself another Alice. Walt agreed to raise the child's salary.

The second was far more serious. In August, Winkler informed Walt by telegram that, due to the disappointing returns on the first "Alice" films, she was reducing his advances from $1,500 to $900 per film. If that new arrangement proved unacceptable, she would have to cancel their contract.

Disney was far less concerned with the cutback than why his films weren't more successful. He had no way of knowing Winkler's decision had nothing to do with the quality of his films. Disney's films had, in fact, been among the more successful in Winkler's stable and had begun to build a steady following along the eastern seaboard. However, having recently married Charles B. Mintz, a former Warner Bros. booking agent, Winkler turned over total control of her company to him. Mintz immediately reduced all payouts to the company's suppliers, regardless of how much their films earned.

Roy decided to take over negotiations and, to Walt's pleasant surprise, managed to cut what appeared to be an even better deal for the studio than the one Walt had originally negotiated. For an additional eighteen "Alice" shorts, Mintz agreed to advance the studio $1,800 per film, including, for the first time, gross profit participation. After signing their new deal, the Disney Brothers put some money down on a vacant lot on Hyperion Avenue, three miles southeast of Hollywood Boulevard, and broke ground on what was to be their new, larger headquarters.

Walt felt closer than ever to Roy, believing his older brother had saved the studio from certain bankruptcy. He loved working side by side all day, then going home together, sharing a meal in their one-room apartment, and staying up often past midnight to go over the next day's schedule. As far as Walt was concerned, nothing could be better than this.

To Roy, nothing could be worse. He was still weak from his bout with tuberculosis and required long afternoon naps. That left him the de facto household cook, and he always tried to have dinner ready when his brother came home from the studio. Walt hated Roy's cooking and often loudly complained about it. The two were soon fighting constantly over everything from the evening's menu to that day's misplaced newspaper. Finally, when Roy could take no more, he threw his arms up and told Walt if he didn't like it he could leave. That April, Roy proposed to his Kansas City childhood sweetheart, Edna Frances, whom Walt never liked.

When Walt found out, he refused to believe Roy would break up the team, until Edna arrived in Hollywood with her mother. Convinced Roy meant it, Walt took his brother's decision as yet another abandonment and became convinced that nothing would ever again be the same between them. Walt's rage manifested itself in a series of personal criticisms directed at his brother. For the first time, twenty-four-year-old Walt complained of Roy's general sloppiness around the apartment and poor personal hygiene. His lack of cleanliness, Walt told him, was a sure sign of his godlessness.

Roy and Edna were married on April 7, 1925, in Uncle Robert's living room before Elias and Flora, Herbert, Walt, Edna's parents, and one Lillian Bounds, chosen by Roy to stand up for his bride. Ever the problem solver, because Edna knew no one in Hollywood, Roy arranged for one of the studio's new female employees to be his bride's maid of honor.

The choice of twenty-four-year-old Lillian was hardly arbitrary. Roy believed it was time Walt found a woman of his own and thought this dark-haired girl might be the one. She had the strong features and broad shape of the solidly built Midwestern women he and Walt were used to, the kind of look their mother had, rather than the dewy starlets that seemed to abound in Hollywood. Thick lashes, heavily penciled eyebrows, and red cheeks offset Lillian's strong features, and she smiled with the slightest upturn of the corners of her wide mouth. More than once she had told her girlfriends at the studio, within earshot of Roy, that Walt was an excellent prospect for marriage.

Born and raised in Idaho, Lillian had come to Hollywood for the first time on a brief holiday in the summer of 1923 to visit her sister. While there, she met a young girl by the name of Kathleen, the first new female hired by the Disneys' studio. They became friends, and the girl, who had a crush on Walt, made a pass or two at him that he either didn't notice or chose not to respond to. She told Lillian, "I have a job for you, but I'm telling you about it on one condition: Don't marry the boss." The job, in the inking-and-painting depart- ment, required little skill beyond being able to color. Lillian was about to turn down the offer; then she saw Walt and decided the $15 a week might well be worth her time. Disney hired her primarily because her sister lived so close to the studio he would not have to pay her extra for carfare on nights she worked late.

In the days immediately following Roy's wedding, Walt, looking to avoid the sense of loneliness and loss, for a while considered moving in with Iwerks. But Walt dropped this idea when he began spending greater amounts of time at Lillian's workstation, volunteering tips on how to improve her inking. One night while both worked late, Walt leaned over to show her something on her work board and felt the soft brush of her thick hair against his cheek. He breathed her perfume and felt her dress brush lightly across his trousers. Without thinking, he kissed her on the back of her neck. The next day he asked Roy for a $120 advance, $40 to buy the new suit he would need to wear at his wedding and $75 for a ring. Roy was so happy he insisted they save money and purchase the ring from the same illegal fence who had sold him Edna's. The next day Walt proposed, Lillian accepted, and they immediately set a date.

Just three months after he had watched Roy walk down the aisle, Walt, at the age of twenty-four, married Lillian. The ceremony was held on July 25, 1925, in the Lewiston, Idaho, home of Lillian's brother. Her mother was the only other member of either family to attend. Walt did not invite his parents, fearing the trip might be too much for them, or Roy, whom he still resented for marrying Edna. After the ceremony, the newlyweds boarded a train for Los Angeles.

They spent the early part of their first night alone as husband and wife in the honeymoon compartment, until Walt suddenly developed a toothache. Excusing himself, he stepped into the car's narrow aisle and paced nervously back and forth for nearly an hour. Unable to relieve his anxiety, he visited the club car where he had his shoes shined by the bootblack dozens of times, over and over, deep into the night. This bizarre ritual of cleanliness reprised the rage of Walt's complaints about Roy's "sloppiness" just before his wedding.

By contrast, before Roy broke the news of his marriage, Walt thought nothing of lifting the lid off the corner garbage can, bending over, and putting his face into the trash. He had become fascinated by the patterns the crawling maggots made as they swarmed over rotted food. He often drew the designs onto a small pad to use in some future cartoon.

Upon arriving in Los Angeles, the honeymoon couple transferred to a steamer bound for Seattle. It wasn't until they arrived in Washington that Walt relaxed enough to be able to consummate his marriage. The next day he cut short their honeymoon, claiming an emergency at the studio required his immediate return.

Back in Hollywood, Walt and Lillian moved into a $40-a-month one-room "kitchenette" apartment within walking distance of the Hyperion studio. As a welcome-home present, Roy increased Walt's weekly salary to match his monthly rent.

Walt had a present for his brother as well. Still bitter over what he considered Roy's "betrayal," Walt calmly informed him the name of the business was being changed, from the Disney Brothers Studios to the Walt Disney Studio. Although both knew it wasn't the real reason, Walt claimed a single name was more appealing than a title with the word "brothers." Roy shrugged his shoulders, his standard signature of wordless compliance. Unlike Walt, he had no taste for fame. He preferred the background, where he felt he could more efficiently concentrate on the fortune to be made.

By early 1926, construction on the site of the new studio was completed. Walt and Roy posed in front of their new building, surrounded by their staff of mostly transplanted Kansas City natives, all with arms crossed and smiles on their faces. Walt, feeling he looked too boyish to be taken seriously as the head of a film studio, decided to keep a mustache he had grown on a bet with another animator, because he felt it made him look older and more authoritative.

Walt's delight over his new studio, and the many plans he had for new movies, suffered a blow when Charles Mintz, Margaret Winkler's new husband, arrived in person one morning with no advance warning, bearing grim news. He had come to inform the Disneys in person that due to the exhibitors' continuing lack of interest in the "Alice" series, he was forced to cancel their contract.

Mintz's visit depressed Walt. He locked himself into his office and remained there for the next day and night, refusing to talk to anyone and blaming himself for the company's failure. What he didn't know was that Mintz had been commuting regularly between New York and Hollywood to negotiate a deal with Carl Laemmle, the founder of Universal Pictures, for a cartoon rabbit to compete with the highly successful Felix the Cat series. When that deal was finalized, Mintz figured out a way that would not only have the Disneys create the new character but, if everything went according to plan, the "bumpkins," as Mintz referred to the Disneys behind their back, would wind up begging him to take over their studio to cement the deal.

After letting a few days pass, Mintz paid another visit to Hyperion, this time with "good news." He might be able to save their deal, he told the brothers, if they could come up with an original cartoon character, something on the order of, say, a rabbit.

Laemmle wasn't excited about working with the Disneys. He had little use for what he considered their primitive style of animation, having described it once as nothing more than "out-of-date crap." Nevertheless, Mintz convinced Laemmle to give the Disneys a chance. Laemmle reluctantly agreed, insisting all the while they were wasting their time.

Still unaware of Laemmle's involvement, Walt and Iwerks and the rest of the animators worked through the night and came up with a sketch of a black rabbit that bore a not-so-coincidental resemblance to Felix the Cat. Mintz suggested they name him "Oswald." He then brought the sketches to Laemmle. Genuinely surprised at both the quick delivery and relatively high quality of the drawing, Laemmle authorized Mintz to commission a trial cartoon.

Walt worked on a story while Ub improved the initial sketches of Oswald until he had a fully drawn character. In a single day Walt ground out an outline for a cartoon short he called *Poor Papa*, which was nothing more than a series of unrelated pratfalls. The studio filmed it in a week, and upon its completion Walt personally delivered it to Mintz, who in turn took it to Laemmle. Who hated it. Laemmle railed at its lack of plot, the unsteady camera, and most vehemently, at the way Oswald was drawn, too fat and unappealing.

When Mintz reacted in kind to Walt, Walt destroyed the film's negative and reworked the story and visual character with Iwerks. The entire staff was put to work to make sure the drawings of the backgrounds and characters were the best the studio could produce. Ub also jerry-rigged a motor to steady the camera's vibrations. When they gave Mintz the revised version of the cartoon, renamed *Trolley Troubles*, starring Oswald as the conductor of a cartoonland trolley, he took it to Laemmle, who reluctantly approved it. Mintz then returned to the Disneys with the good news that he had been able to make a deal for Oswald with Universal that put them all back in business. Walt considered Mintz a hero for having remained loyal to the studio.

Early in 1927, Universal Pictures released the first of a projected series of "Oswald the Lucky Rabbit" cartoons, *Trolley Troubles*. Laemmle, notorious for his inattention to detail, mistakenly identified his new "star" in the initial trade announcements as "Oscar the Rabbit." The cartoons were released under the distribution of Charles Mintz's newly created Snappy Comedies, also the name of the corporate subdivision he had created, whose sole purpose was to deliver "Oswalds" to Universal. Mintz, operating as "Winkler," signed exclusive contracts with both Disney and Snappy, thereby creating two corporate stops between Walt and Laemmle.

Trolley Troubles received rave reviews. The public loved Oswald, an affection that translated into sizable profits for Universal and Winkler. The established New York animation houses took notice for the first time of the little West Coast operation that had produced a hit comparable in quality and appeal to anything coming out of the East.

Laemmle was delighted and gave Mintz an order for one new "Oswald" every other week, which Mintz passed on to Disney at their newly agreed advance of $2,250 per cartoon against a percentage of the box-office gross.

Mintz had Disney's checks personally hand-delivered to the Hyperion studio by his brother-in-law George Winkler, who would pick up a finished cartoon in exchange for advance payment on the next. George and his checks were always a welcome sight at the Disney studio. He was given free rein to roam the hallways and chat up the employees.

Although pleased with the success of the series, Walt became upset when he learned, quite by accident, that without his knowledge, consent, or financial participation, Universal and Winkler had merchandised the Oswald character. On his way to the studio one morning, Walt stopped at a local drugstore to buy cigarettes and spotted a counter display for Oswald candy bars, complete with the added line below the product's name advising the purchaser to "Watch for Oswald in Universal Pictures!"

When he returned to Hyperion, Walt told Roy about it, who advised him to do nothing. He assured his brother the publicity would sell tickets to their cartoons, which was what they were in business for, not candy bars. And business was very good. Hadn't they been able to build identical white-shingle ranch houses on nearby Lyric Avenue, for the then-hefty price tag of $7,000 apiece, paid for in cash? The time to bring up merchandise participation, Roy explained, was when their contract expired the following February. Until then they should enjoy their newfound prosperity.

In February 1928, Walt decided to take Lillian with him to New York for preliminary contract-renewal meetings with Mintz. He felt she had earned the trip by her quiet loyalty and willingness to leave the house, where she preferred to be, to come to the studio during the Oswald crisis and help ink and paint, often deep into the night. Their trip, Walt told Lillian, would be a working vacation. A little work, a lot of vacation.

They checked into the Astor Hotel and met Mintz and his wife for lunch the next day. The hotel was one of the favorite haunts of New York's film community, and Mintz took great pleasure introducing Walt to various producers and directors who now came by to meet Hollywood's hot young animator. Afterward, Disney suggested Lillian do some window-shopping along Fifth Avenue while he and Mintz went to the office to do business.

There Mintz ushered Walt in and told him to take a seat. Then, wasting no time, in a quiet, intense manner markedly different from the one he had displayed at lunch, Mintz conveyed what he said would be his one and only offer. Effective immediately, Disney's advance per cartoon was to be cut from $2,250 back to $1,800. If that was unacceptable, the only alternative would be for Snappy to take over all further production of Oswald cartoons. And, Mintz warned Walt, *he would use Disney's own staff to do it!*

Walt, who had come to the meeting looking to increase his advances and even get a piece of the merchandising, was shocked by what he heard. Too upset to speak, he silently stood, nodded his good-bye, and left the office. Back at the hotel, he immediately called Roy, who had stayed behind in Los Angeles to run the studio.

According to their contract, Roy said, the name Oswald and the tag "The World's Luckiest Rabbit" did indeed belong to Mintz's distribution company, Snappy. Worse, Roy told Walt, in his absence, animators Rudolph Ising, Hugh Harman, Friz Freleng, and Carman Maxwell had all had handed in their resignations to accept positions with Snappy.

Left behind by Mintz were Kansas City loyalists Les Clark, Johnny Cannon, Hamilton Luske, and Ub Iwerks, the latter made a stockholder by Walt as well as the highest-paid employee at a salary of $120 a week, nearly five times the amount earned by anybody else, including Walt and Roy. The rest went with Mintz, convinced Disney couldn't possibly survive the takeover.

Besides, there was little love lost between Disney and many of his staff. In their defense, Friz Freleng later explained the animators' decision as having been determined at least partly by Walt's treatment of them. According to Freleng, Disney, in spite of his insistence that everybody on the staff was one big, happy, loyal family, was in reality a "harsh taskmaster, severe and not always reasonable in his criticism. The many early defections were the results of his high-strung temperament and his inability to work harmoniously with his men."

Mintz, believing Walt had no alternative, expected him to accept his offer at the next day's meeting. Out of a sense of "compassion," he would give Disney the option of signing a production contract with the newly formed "Mintz Agency," which would pay production costs and salaries for all subsequent Oswald cartoons, in return for 50 percent ownership of the Walt Disney Studio. Walt asked for time to think it over. Mintz gave him a month.

Walt decided to appeal directly to Laemmle, with whom he tried and failed on several occasions to meet. Laemmle refused to talk to anyone about Oswald except the series distributor, Charles Mintz. Desperate, Walt turned to Margaret Winkler for help. While openly sympathetic, Winkler, who had surrendered all control of the company to her husband, told Walt his situation was hopeless and urged him to take her husband's offer to save the studio.

That evening, Disney lay in his hotel bed, unable to sleep as the darkness deepened around him. Just before three o'clock in the morning, the phone rang. It was Roy. He had figured it out. The thing to do, he told Walt, was simply to give Mintz exactly what he

wanted and to hell with his compassion. Walt said he didn't understand. "Trust me," Roy said. "Do it and come up with another
character and we'll save the studio."

The next morning, Walt walked into Mintz's office and, as his
brother had instructed, calmly relinquished all claims to the Oswald
character and his former employees. Having done so, Walt then
returned to Lillian at the hotel and took a cab to Grand Central
Station where, with great sadness, they boarded a train for the long
ride home.

The story is told that on the train back to Hollywood Walt hit upon
the notion of creating a new cartoon character inspired by a real
mouse that used to live in his old Kansas City office during the
Newman Laugh-O-Gram days. As Walt himself liked to tell it, "Mice
gathered in my wastebasket when I worked late at night. I lifted them
out and kept them in little cages on my desk. One of them was my
particular friend."

Having decided to create a new character based on that mouse, he
told Lillian he had decided to call him Mortimer. Lillian suggested
Mickey instead, insisting Mortimer sounded "too sissy." By the end
of the train ride, Walt had created the image of Mickey on a piece of
paper and worked out the plot for the first "Mickey Mouse" cartoon.

That version, Dave Iwerks, Ub's son, insists, isn't quite the way
Mickey happened. "It's pretty clear now that Mickey was Ub's character. Even the [Disney archives] concedes that Ub created Mickey,
although their version has it that Walt stood over Ub's shoulder when
he did it. The whole scenario of the train story the studio used to be
so fond of is just not right at all."

Actually, according to Dave Iwerks, when Walt arrived back in
Hollywood, he had only the vaguest idea of a new character. He and
Ub put down all their ideas on "character sheets." Walt then brought
in his own proposed sketch of a mouse, which Iwerks rejected
because it looked too much like Walt. Disney confessed he had used
the reflection of his own face as a model.

Taking one of his own sketches of Oswald, Iwerks, with a few
swipes of a pen, changed the ears and rounded the eyes, and in doing
so turned him into Mickey. Walt grinned when he realized just how
easy it was going to be simply to steal Oswald back. Which, having
learned firsthand the way the movie business operated, was exactly
what he did.

FOUR

The Sound of Fame

IN MARCH 1928, work began on the first Mickey Mouse cartoon, its creation shrouded in secrecy behind the closed doors of Ub Iwerks's tiny office. A wall of distrust now stood between the soon-to-depart animators and those who had chosen to stay. With a month left on their contracts, Walt had no intention of letting even a single defector, as he now referred to them, leave so much as one day early to join the competition. Besides, Mintz insisted on delivery of three final "Oswalds," leaving plenty of work that still needed to be done.

Among those who remained loyal, Disney trusted only Iwerks. With ever greater frequency, Ub was assigned to bring to animated life the characters Walt had in mind, a job that ultimately became the expression of what was, really, the character *of* Walt's mind. Thus freed from the confines of physical animation, Disney concentrated on developing stories and supervising his staff.

This shift in his approach resulted in Walt becoming the target of rumors that lasted for decades, mostly by former employees, that he was such a mediocre artist he couldn't so much as draw a straight line.

The rumors dogged Walt and angered him. Finally, twenty years after they began, he admitted publicly for the first time he never actually "drew" Mickey, although he still refused to give proper credit to Iwerks for his role in the cartoon character's creation.

"I started in as an artist in 1919," Walt recalled, "and at that time I drew everything, painted every background, and I carried along as an animator until about the time of Mickey Mouse.

"Now when Mickey came along, he made quite a splash, and it was necessary then for me to give up the drawing in order to organize and run the organization. Mickey Mouse was, to me, a symbol of independence, a means to an end. He spelled production liberation.

"My role [after Mickey]? Well, I was stumped one day when a little boy asked me, 'Do you draw Mickey Mouse?' And I had to admit I didn't draw anymore. 'Well, then you think up all the jokes and ideas.' 'No,' I said, 'I don't do that.' Finally he looked at me and said, 'Mr. Disney, just what do you do?' 'Well,' I said, 'sometimes I think of myself as a little bee. I go from one area to another, and gather pollen, and sort of stimulate everybody.' "

Inevitably, it was Iwerks who over the years would most feel the sting of the self-described king bee's intense desire to take all creative credit. More than once during the development of Mickey Mouse, Roy took his brother aside and urged him to give proper credit to Iwerks for his many contributions. By way of a reply, Walt would angrily remind Roy his only job was to watch the books. He told him in no uncertain terms to keep his nose out of the creative end. Aware of the animator's growing dissatisfaction, Roy tried his best to do what he felt Walt should have done, to acknowledge Iwerks's unique talents. And for a while, Ub remained content to do his job and say nothing to anybody about his frustrations.

WITH PAYMENT received for the final "Oswalds," the Disney studio had a bank of $30,000, enough to produce three $10,000 Mickey Mouse shorts. Walt decided to base the first on America's newest sensation, Charles Lindbergh. Walt recognized in Lindbergh's transatlantic solo flight a metaphor for his own singular flight of animated fancy he believed one day could lift him too into the rarefied air of America's greatest visionaries.

Walt hit upon the name of *Plane Crazy* for his cartoon, a clever double entendre uniting the plot of the film, a solo air flight by Mickey Mouse, with what he saw as the essence of the character. Having settled on a story, Walt turned it over to Iwerks with the warning that they were rapidly running out of money, which meant they were running out of time. Iwerks then produced an astonishing

700 individual Mickey Mouse drawings *a day*. Considering that an average ten-minute cartoon required about 14,000 drawings, a single movement 16, the quantity as well as the quality of Iwerks's singlehanded output was, by any measure, an extraordinary achievement.

It quickly became clear to Disney he would need larger production facilities for *Plane Crazy*. To solve the problem he built a temporary studio onto the side of his Lyric Avenue home, so that Lillian and Edna, both of whom no longer worked at the studio, could assist with the inking and painting. While Edna happily accepted her new assignment, Lillian was less eager to pitch in. She believed that being married to the head of a studio meant she should no longer have to work for it. Warning Disney this was the last time she would do so, she reluctantly agreed to help.

When *Plane Crazy* was finished, Walt arranged for a sneak preview before a live audience at one of the grand movie palaces along Hollywood Boulevard. Sneaks were a common practice then, more casual than today's media-driven affairs. In those days, for a few dollars, a projectionist could be counted on to slip in an extra short before the feature. Most of the time the manager of the theater either knew nothing about it or, not wanting to be bothered, just looked the other way.

Plane Crazy wasn't especially well received that night, and afterward, Roy suggested it might need more work. Walt insisted it was fine the way it was and set up a distributor screening for MGM, who passed on it, as did every other major studio-distributor. At this point, Walt shelved *Plane Crazy* and began working on a second Mickey short.

Gallopin' Gaucho was the initial project for the studio's newly hired team of animators that replaced those who had finally left to join Mintz. Walt began the first day of production the way he did for every new project, seating his staff in a semicircle and standing before them while he acted out the story, playing every character's part as he went along, showing exactly what he wanted them to capture on film.

However, *Gallopin' Gaucho* (Mickey riding a horse instead of flying a plane), like *Plane Crazy* before it, failed to impress either the Hollywood sneak-preview audience who saw it or any of the Majors. With enough money left for only one more try, Disney settled on a third story line for Mickey, borrowed liberally from a popular Buster Keaton film, *The Navigator* (1924), and made Mickey a sailor on a steamboat at war with the captain and in love with the girl.

During production of *Steamboat Willie*, Walt received an invitation to attend the premiere of Warner Bros.' *Jazz Singer*, the studio's much ballyhooed introduction of sound to film. Everyone who saw it that first night, Disney included, heard the voice of Al Jolson come from the singer's mouth and left the theater convinced they had witnessed the end of silent films.

The enthusiasm for talkies turned feverish among those who recognized its commercial possibilities. However, a few in Hollywood believed that while talkies had probably arrived forever, it wasn't necessarily for the better.

To achieve the dimension of sound, it was necessary to freeze the luxurious sweep of the silent film lens, as the new cameras had necessarily to be enclosed in stationary glass cages to muffle their mechanics. What had been an essentially visual medium, able to silently communicate the essence of everything from the Bible to Oscar Wilde to William Shakespeare onto the silver screen, had suddenly become verbose. Actors were now required to stand stiff and still on cue marks so their words could be clearly recorded by overhanging "boom" mikes while their images remained framed by the paralyzed camera.

This marriage of motion picture art and sound technology had produced a breech baby, whose jolting birth cry—"You ain't heard nothin' yet"—shattered the sublimely universal silence of the silver screen. Overnight, nearly every studio in town shelved its upcoming silent production schedules in favor of making movies that talked. Including Disney. The very next morning Walt halted production on *Steamboat Willie* to search for a way to add sound to his already completed footage. After some improvisation with live sound effects and musical instruments, he arranged a test screening for a small group of friends and relatives.

Disney later recalled:

We had a showing with sound. A couple of my boys could read music and one of them could play mouth organ. We put them in a room where they could not see the screen and arranged to pipe their sound into the room where our wives and friends were going to see the picture. . . . The effect on our little audience was nothing less than electric. They responded almost instinctively to this union of sound and motion. . . . It was terrible, but it was wonderful! And it was something new!

The experiment confirmed for Disney his belief that animation's potential for sound was far less limited than features', as the problems of camera noise and placement simply didn't apply in a medium with no live action.

Shortly after the in-house screening, Disney and Lillian boarded a train to New York. RCA had developed a "sound-for-film" system to compete with Warners' and wanted to sell it to independent studios. Disney was interested. Along the way Walt insisted they stop in Kansas City to visit original Laugh-O-Grams investor, Carl Stalling. As it turned out, the visit wasn't a strictly social one. In spite of the mass defection of his original team of Kansas City animators, Disney's sense of loyalty was still heavily influenced by sentimentality. He wanted to hire Stalling, a silent-film theater accompanist, to write original music for *Steamboat Willie*.

Walt and Lillian arrived in New York in time for him to attend an advance screening of the first "sound" cartoon to use the RCA system, Paul Terry's "Terrytoon" talkie, *Dinner Time*. Besides Disney, Terry wasn't the only animation studio interested in sound. Walt had been well aware for a long time that the Fleischers had for the past several years experimented with something they called "Song Car-Tunes," and knew their latest and first commercially viable one was set for release at the prestigious Mark Strand later that year. When Walt read in the trades that Charles Mintz intended to add a voice to Oswald, any doubts he might have had about the future of cartoons was gone. The race was on, and he intended to win.

Filled with anticipation before the screening, Disney was disappointed in the overall quality of *Dinner Time*'s sound, particularly the constant static and the loud rattle and clack of the film's dishes and diners. The next day he telegraphed Roy and Ub his opinion of RCA's system: "MY GOD—TERRIBLE," and described the soundtrack as "A LOT OF RACKET AND NOTHING ELSE."

Disney remained in New York to continue searching for a usable sound system. After rejecting several more, he believed he had finally found the right one after meeting with Patrick Powers and witnessing a demonstration of his sound system, which was clearly superior to anyone else's.

Powers was a veteran distributor of the animated works of many of the industry's pioneers, most notably Pat Sullivan and Otto Messmer's "Felix the Cat," whose success had first prompted Laemmle to develop Oswald the Rabbit. In 1925, Laemmle had signed Powers to a distribution deal similar to the one Universal had with Charles Mintz.

One day early in 1927, after becoming suspicious of Powers's financial reportings, Laemmle paid him a surprise visit for a spontaneous audit of the books. Powers indignantly refused. Tipped off before the impending visit, Powers, in front of Laemmle's disbelieving eyes, defiantly tossed all the financial records out the window. What Laemmle didn't know was that Powers had an accomplice waiting in the alley who piled the records into a truck and drove them across the river to the safety of a New Jersey vault. Powers was summarily fired.

In search of new prospects, he became interested in sound cartoons, and after making an unsuccessful attempt to gain control of one of the many competing sound-on-film companies, Powers developed his own system using technology remarkably similar to the DeForest Phonofilm. Disney, who came from the West Coast, knew nothing about Powers or his previous relations with Laemmle. All Walt cared about was Powers's sound system. He wanted it and made a deal for it on the spot, which, at Powers's insistence, included hiring him as the studio's permanent sound consultant.

During the first months of 1928, Disney and Powers worked on the sound version of *Steamboat Willie* in Powers's New York studio. They coordinated Stalling's recently completed orchestral score, which incorporated an old vaudeville tune "Steamboat Will" and the familiar folk tune "Turkey in the Straw," with the characters' movements and added various sound-track effects and, finally, the high-pitched squeaking voice of Mickey, which Walt supplied himself and would continue to do for the next seven years. As the conversion of the film neared its completion, Powers arranged for several screenings for all the major New York distributors.

While Walt fine-tuned his picture, back in Hollywood the studio, still without any income, faced its most serious crisis to date. Money had become so tight, to meet payroll Roy was forced to sell Walt's prized Moon cabriolet automobile. Unfazed, Walt enthusiastically wired his approval, emphasizing the need to keep the studio afloat at any cost until *Steamboat Willie* was finished.

"A youngster named Jackson had just come to work for me," Walt recalled years later. "I knew he played the mouth organ so I asked him if he knew anything about music and he said a little. Jackson brought a metronome to the studio, and we began to work it out. I brought a blank pad of bar-music sheets. I'd ask Jackson to play a tune on his harmonica, and we'd play out our frames so we had the right ratio of frames to each bar of music.*

"Next I visited a lot of five-and-dime stores and bought a bunch of gadgets—night-club noisemakers, cowbells and tin pans. We had washboards on which we could make scrubbing noises. I bought a couple of 'plumber's friends' and some slide whistles and ocarinas. We played around with those things for a while to work out sound effects; then we began to lay out the score for our sound synchronization. When I say 'we,' I mean my top artist, Ub Iwerks, young Jackson, and myself."

The costs were considerable. A ten-minute silent cartoon cost an average of $10,000 to make. *Steamboat Willie*, because of the increased speed required by sound, needed nearly 20,000 frames, and that pushed the film's budget to over $15,000. None of this seemed to bother Walt, who insisted music and sound play continuously. Each effect seemed to boost the film's costs, and Walt insisted everything Mickey came into contact with had to have an accompanying sound. At one point Mickey picked up an old sow and squeezed it to the synchronized music from an accordion. At another he tickled Minnie's ribs, and the sound track plunked banjo music.

"Why should we let a few dollars jeopardize our chances," Disney wrote to Roy. "I think this is Old Man Opportunity rapping at our door. Let's don't let the jingle of a few pennies drown out his knock."

However, in spite of his conviction and Powers's confidence, screenings of the completed *Steamboat Willie* yielded no takers. At best it was met with yawning indifference, until Harry Reichenbach, an independent promoter for the Colony movie theater in New York

---

*Silent film passed through the projector at eighteen frames per second. Sound, Walt quickly discovered, required twenty-four for proper visual synchronization.

City, saw one of the screenings. Reichenbach told Walt afterward how much he had enjoyed his talking cartoon and asked if it would be possible to screen it as a sneak preview at the Colony.

Walt appeared hesitant to show the film to the public without a firm deal, fearing a negative reaction might kill any chance he had of finding a distributor. However, when Reichenbach offered Disney $500 a week, with a two-week guarantee, paid in advance, Walt, desperate for cash, eagerly accepted the offer and wired the money back to Roy.

On November 18, 1928, *Steamboat Willie* opened at the Colony theater as the curtain raiser for the feature talkie *Gang War*, which starred Olive Borden and Jack Pickford, whose careers would prove as short-lived and forgettable as their film. From its first scene featuring a whistling Mickey Mouse, it was obvious *Steamboat Willie* was what the audience had come to see. Thrilled and enchanted by the little mouse with the funny voice, they enthusiastically cheered his "performance."

The next day *Variety* gave *Steamboat Willie* a rave review, as did the *Exhibitor's Herald*, and the *New York Times*, who called it "ingenious" and "a good deal of fun." It was impressive, amazing even, that this small, independent, single-theater-release film that had received no advance promotion nor advertising happened to be covered by such important and influential publications. Impressive and amazing, yes, but no accident.

Reichenbach, a former press agent with a lot of friends in the newspaper business, insured the profitability of his investment by spending the afternoon of the film's opening tipping the press something special was going to take place at his theater that night. He told them they should make it their business to be there. By the time of the screening, a buzz was in the air about the film and its creator.

The surprising success of *Steamboat Willie* turned into a spectacular coup for Disney. By being the first animator to release a commercially viable sound cartoon, Disney overnight became the hot new talent in Bigtime Town. This was a stunning achievement for the twenty-seven-year-old independent animator with no major studio affiliation or distributor.

And, as it would always seem with Disney, his timing proved exquisite. For if ever an industry needed a new hero, the movies did now. With Hollywood plagued by accusations of immorality accompanied by growing threats of censorship, and about to be plunged along with the rest of the nation into severe economic decline, both *Steamboat Willie* and its maker arrived, as film heroes always seemed to, "just in the nick of time." Even as Mickey Mouse was becoming every kid's newest favorite cartoon character, his "creator," the all-American hayseed from Kansas City with a fondness for farm animals who acted like humans, was about to become the least-likely savior of an industry filled with people—most of whom, in Walt's opinion, behaved like animals.

FIVE

Heroes and Villains in the Real World of Make-Believe

THE PHENOMENAL overnight success of *Steamboat Willie* turned Walt Disney into Hollywood's newest "boy wonder." Overlooked amid all the adulation heaped upon Disney was one glaring omission that could only be described as an act of calculated revenge by him. In spite of the combined effort of everyone at the studio to produce *Steamboat Willie*, in the dozens of interviews he gave to newspapers, he never once mentioned Iwerks's role in the development of Mickey Mouse, an omission which said more, perhaps, about Disney's origins than that of his animated star.

For, early on, Walt had begun referring to Mickey as his "child" and often delighted in going into detail about his impish behavior and the trouble it always got him into, as if he were an independent, living creature. Mickey's character, as Walt saw him—the barnyard innocent, the performer, the adventurer, Minnie's shy admirer— reverberated with scenes that could have been describing Disney's own Midwest childhood. Walt too was a barnyard innocent and, as a child, had loved to perform. He saw himself as much of an adventurer as any twentieth-century entrepreneur, and his shyness around women had marked his teen years with a certain type of loneliness most youngsters usually cure with their first taste of courtship.

By denying Iwerks credit for his role in "giving birth" to Mickey, Walt may have been expressing more than just the symptoms of an excessive ego. He may have been, in fact, trying to avoid any doubt about the "parental" heritage of Mickey, an echo of the lingering childhood fear and uncertainty Disney carried concerning *his* heritage. The denial also externalized the inner rage Walt may have had toward Elias for his suspected role in creating that uncertainty (and toward himself for his conflicted role as Mickey's "father"). That rage easily extended to Carl Laemmle for having stolen, or "illegally adopted," Oswald. With *Steamboat Willie*, Walt discovered how to make cartoons talk, its success sounding the powerful weapon of revenge that had until now lurked silently within his artistic arsenal.

THE FILM'S POPULARITY now prompted the same distributors who had rejected the cartoon to fall over one another in the rush to bid for the rights to the little mouse that had so captivated the public and critics. Not that anyone in Hollywood thought the movie was any great work of art, any more than they did *The Jazz Singer*. There were certainly more entertaining and sophisticated animated shorts around than *Steamboat Willie*, yet, simply put, Disney had shown he could produce cartoons that not only talked but made lots of money, and *that's* what made his cartoons the best.

As it happened, the timing of *Steamboat Willie* gave the animated cartoon an added value no one could have predicted. The film premiered just months before the economic collapse of the late twenties that signaled the onset of the Great Depression. Wall Street's tumble produced a resurgence of dozens of civic-minded organizations, supported by many in the federal government who believed the country's financial decline was the inevitable result of its moral one. And they insisted a good part of the blame had to be placed at the fancily shod feet of those who walked the boulevards of America's Sin City, Hollywood.

To defend itself against the renewed groundswell, the leaders of the film industry, the studio heads, searched for a role model of unassailable moral fiber whose wholesome movies could only be seen as fun for the whole family. In the midst of growing accusations of immorality, which they feared were at least in part a thinly veiled revival of the same anti-Semitism that had first driven them out west, the heads of the studios pushed the man they considered their best hope to the front of the pack, that good Fundamentalist family man and filmmaker, Walt Disney.

TWO OF THE ENDURINGLY POPULAR myths of the history of American film are that Hollywood gave birth to the movies and that the industry's pioneers were Jews who had immigrated from Europe. In truth, the American motion picture industry began on the East Coast as the exclusive dominion of the urban American turn-of-the-century entrepreneurial elite. Christian names such as Dickson, Casler, Marvin, Koopman, Long, Smith, Scull, Kleine, Marion, Berst, and Méliès headed such early studios as the American Mutoscope Company, Kalem, and Vitagraph. Among these companies, the most powerful was the Wizard of Menlo Park, Thomas Alva Edison, the head of the studio that bore his name.

For more than a decade Edison had been the unchallenged premier maker and distributor of mostly esoteric, nonnarrative, silent motion picture "studies." Edison was greatly disturbed by the sudden, sweeping popularity of the new century's first novelty, street-corner nickelodeons, amusement parlors that first appeared on New York's Lower East Side. He felt they cheapened the sophisticated art of film by offering "peep show" films and other lurid diversions meant to satisfy the carnal pleasure of the workingman.

In 1910, Edison formed the first motion picture alliance, which came to be known as the "Trust." Its purpose was to protect the public (and his own financial interests) from the kind of immoral trash produced by what he termed the "Jewish profiteers," who not only ran the nickelodeons but made their own movies to show in them.

The Trust was publicly dedicated to the preservation of the industry's moral integrity and privately devoted to protecting Edison's profitable monopoly. Not only were nickelodeon operators and filmmakers denied membership in the Trust, but they were prevented from buying raw film stock and projection equipment, all of which Edison held patents on and absolutely controlled.

In response, an independent group of mostly immigrant Jewish filmmakers, led by Carl Laemmle, formed their own distribution organization, or exchange, as they called it. They organized an effective, if illegal, underground to import foreign raw film stock and equipment that allowed them to keep making movies.

By 1912, the films of Laemmle and his partners had become more popular than those of the Trust. Edison, frustrated by his inability to wipe out his competition, resorted to hiring goon squads. They smashed the nickelodeon arcades and set block-long fires in the neighborhoods that housed them. All the while Edison justified his actions in the name of preserving the nation's morals.

The mob tactics of the Trust caused the independents to put as much distance between themselves and Edison as possible. One by one they migrated west, until they reached California. There they found cheap real estate, a perfect climate, and the natural protection of a three-thousand-mile buffer zone. California gave them a second chance to make their movies. The films they made redefined the American motion picture and the industry that produced them. Unlike their early East Coast counterparts, the heads of Hollywood's studios were less interested in artistic experimentation than profit. They put on the screen what sold the most. The public was willing to pay to see films filled with sex and violence, and Hollywood was more than happy to make them.

By the early twenties, all that remained of Edison's Trust was the issue it had raised regarding the moral content of motion pictures. The federal government kept a close watch on Hollywood, the new capital of the film industry, to make sure the movies it produced remained "socially acceptable."

However, Hollywood's moguls had no idea of what was meant by "socially acceptable" films. They didn't know if their movies were moral or immoral and couldn't have cared less. To them, films were strictly vehicles of profit, not instruments of expression. The more money a film made, the better it was. As such, they ran their businesses *like businesses* and treated their writers, directors, actors, and scenery movers as clock-punching employees rather than artists. Whenever the industry came under attack for being morally corrupt, none of Hollywood's owners believed the problem had anything really to do with morality.

Which, of course, was precisely the problem. Among those who correctly perceived Hollywood as dominated by Jews, to many in government and the private sector nothing more than heathens, unable to comprehend, let alone project, the essence of Christian morality. They believed Hollywood's Jewish businessmen had corrupted an art form for the sake of making money, and by so doing had contributed to the widening moral corruption of America. They were, in Henry Ford's words, a perfect example of America's growing problem, its turn-of-the-century influx of "the international Jew."

And the behavior of Hollywood's Christian talent pool employed by the Jewish moguls reinforced this canard. From the teens through the early twenties, a series of drug and sex scandals and sensational murders rocked the film capital, culminating in the 1921 alleged rape of party-girl starlet Virginia Rappe by comic actor Roscoe "Fatty" Arbuckle. The sensational Arbuckle case intensified the public's demand for governmental regulation of what it perceived to be the morally corrupt film industry. In 1922, formal legislation was introduced in Congress to create a national board of film censorship.

Fearing government intervention, the heads of the major film studios formed a self-regulating organization, the Motion Picture Producers and Distributors of America (MPPDA). To head it, they appointed Postmaster General Will Hays, former traffic cop, onetime national chairman of the Republican party, and, as it happened, an Elder of the Presbyterian church. The Jewish power faction in Hollywood hoped choosing a Christian to regulate the moral content of their films would improve the overall image of its industry.

Hays's appointment stalled the movement toward federal censorship but didn't end it. There were many in Congress who felt the very formation of the MPPDA was an admission of guilt. They continued to press for federal legislation.

Nor was Hays's presence universally welcomed in Hollywood. By 1924, there were those who were adamantly opposed to any sort of regulation of film. Charlie Chaplin spoke for many that year when he came out against what he termed the MPPDA's brand of "Presbyterian censorship."

Still, for the next several years, as the country prospered, the movie industry and the government coexisted in relative peace, until the financial collapse of Wall Street brought renewed pressure on the government from the most powerful interests in the private sector to regulate the moral content of motion pictures. This latest attack on the moral vacuity of American movies and the men who made them was led once more by those looking for a link between the nation's economic downturn and its moral one. And with each new attack, the nation's Jewish-American studio heads felt the chill of anti-Semitism cool Hollywood's balmy, and quite profitable, climate.

In 1929, needing a "hot" issue to boost his newspapers' sagging circulations, William Randolph Hearst ran a series of editorials demanding the revival of federal censorship to regulate the growing immorality of motion pictures. No friend of either Jews or the film industry, he considered newsreels, shown in effect "free" along with the features, a threat to his newspapers.

Hearst's campaign received much support in Congress, where the definition of movie morality had expanded through the years to include not only sexual provocation but political subversion. In March of 1929, U.S. Senator Smith Brookhart summed up what he considered the deteriorating situation in Hollywood as nothing more than a battle for profit at the cost of sexual and social morality between competing studios, led by "bunches of Jews."

What Hollywood desperately needed was a new hero who not only extolled the right virtues but understood what they were in the first place. What Hollywood got, as if on cue, was Walt Disney's *Steamboat Willie*, the perfect nonsexual, apolitical movie starring a harmless little talking mouse who courted his sweetheart by singing her a song. Overnight, every major studio in Hollywood that had for the better part of a decade turned out the kind of lurid, violent, sexually suggestive fleshpot films guaranteed to put money in their banks, was now eager to align itself with not only the very popular, but now suddenly politically correct, filmmaker.

Walt, however, rejected all offers. After his experience with Laemmle and the loss of Oswald had left him locked out of the distribution mainstream, Disney had come to value his creative independence. "I wanted to retain my individuality," he recalled years later. "I was afraid of being hampered by [major] studio policies. I knew if someone else got in control, I would be restrained, held down to their ideas of low cartoon cost and value."

Disney now wanted a distribution deal, to which none of the Majors would agree. As much as they needed him, they would not permit an unaligned, independent filmmaker to gain a position of influence and power among their Old World brotherhood. The actions of the studio owners had come full circle. In their refusal to deal with an independent, and a Christian one at that, they had ironically echoed the exclusivity that had caused Edison to form his infamous Trust.

Walt did accept a personal invitation from his old nemesis Carl

Laemmle to talk things over. Disney was delighted that the man who had refused to see him during the Oswald crisis had now come courting. Laemmle offered substantial financing, national distribution, and unlimited free use of the same animators he had once stolen from Disney. In return, Laemmle sought the same thing every other studio wanted, the copyright to the Mickey Mouse character. Disney took great satisfaction in turning Laemmle down.

When it became clear he would not accept the terms offered by the Majors, Disney made a deal with Pat Powers giving him rights to distribute Mickey Mouse cartoons on a "states' rights" basis, a less reliable and less profitable system than the unified, presold networks. Powers agreed to pay Disney $2,500 for each new cartoon in return for 10 percent of the gross and a firm commitment by the studio to continue to use the Cinephone sound system. Later on, however, when Roy went over the fine points of the contract, he discovered the studio was obligated to pay Powers $26,000 a year in license fees, for ten years, for exclusive use of Cinephone.

Roy complained about the exorbitant fee to Walt, who insisted the deal with Powers was a good one. Shortly thereafter, the studio began production on four new Mickey Mouse sound shorts. One of the first things he did was to make Carl Stalling the studio's resident musical director. By the end of 1929, Stalling had scored the first two silent "Mickey"s, giving Disney four completed sound cartoons for Powers to sell.

In the next year and a half, the studio produced thirty-one "talking" shorts. Mickey's soaring popularity eclipsed not only his closest animated rivals, Felix the Cat and Oswald, but such human performers as Buster Keaton, Harold Lloyd, Al Jolson, and even the once untouchable Charlie Chaplin and his little tramp.

Disney's cartoons, combined with Hays's introduction of a set of rigid guidelines known as the Production Code, seemed for the moment to halt the government's campaign to impose regulations on the content of Hollywood films. A "grateful" industry, while still unwilling to grant Disney a decent distribution deal, publicly hailed Walt and his cartoons for their high moral quality.

However, as the twenties dissolved into the thirties, federal intervention wasn't the only threat Hollywood faced. Organized labor had begun the movement to unionize Hollywood's workers. Organized crime, attracted to the film industry's high cash flow, wanted a piece of the American dream as well. Ironically, because of Disney's great popularity and presumed wealth, coupled with his independent and therefore vulnerable status, both the unions and the mob placed his studio among their prime targets. Before long, like a couple of big bad wolves, they too would come huffing and puffing, to blow down Disney's door.

BECAUSE OF THE LIMITED box-office potential of cartoons, compared to features, the Walt Disney Studio's popularity far exceeded its profitability. Whatever money was generated, the terms of Walt's distribution and licensing deal gave Powers most of the profits.

To try to improve his cash flow, Walt announced a new series of animated shorts under the umbrella title of "Silly Symphonies." The idea was to make cartoons with musical sound tracks and as little dialogue as possible, to maximize their international appeal.

Roy thought it was a mistake to take time, money, and manpower away from Mickey, the studio's meal ticket. Powers frowned upon the idea as well, as his distribution commitment was specifically limited to Mickey Mouse. Both men were unable to persuade Walt to abandon|the "Silly Symphonies." Disney came up with a story line for the first short about skeletons rising from their graves at night to make merry. It was loosely based on Saint-Saëns's classical *Danse Macabre*. Disney then assigned Stalling the job of scoring *The Skeleton Dance*.

When it was finished, Walt, who had come to trust the opinion of the public far more than his brother's or distributor's, sneak-previewed the short at Hollywood's famous Carthay Circle Theater. William Cottrell, Disney's brother-in-law,* accompanied Walt to the screening. He later recalled:

> It was around eleven o'clock at night, New Year's Eve. As soon as the Disney logo came on, a roar went up from the crowd. Walt was surprised by the level and intensity of the reception. Of course it was a holiday crowd, and it was late, but still, they

---

*In 1927, while working at the studio, Cottrell met and married Lillian's sister, Hazel Bounds, who had taken a secretarial job there. In addition to being Walt's first cameraman, Cottrell became one of the studio's most talented storymen. He was Disney's lifelong friend, traveling companion, and trusted confidant.

just loved the picture, so much so that the manager immediately booked the cartoon for a regular run.

The preview confirmed for Walt that the "Silly Symphonies" could be as successful as Mickey Mouse. Powers, impressed with the results of the Carthay Circle booking, quickly made a deal with Walt to distribute the series.

While the "Silly Symphonies" proved a solid box-office hit, cash flow at the studio remained a problem. When Powers was unable to come up with an explanation for what Roy believed were a series of unusually low payments, he began to suspect his distributor might be keeping two sets of books. Distribution figures started arriving late and didn't match the box-office receipts. Unknown to Powers, Roy had learned about the discrepancy by hiring an independent auditing firm to monitor the film's attendance. He decided to go to New York with his brother and personally confront Powers.

Walt suggested they obtain the services of a lawyer to accompany them and chose a newcomer to Hollywood whose exploits had been written up in the local newspapers. Gunther Lessing had recently arrived in Hollywood seeking to make his fortune as a lawyer to the stars. No sooner had he taken office space than he began to haunt the offices of the city's newspapers, looking for some free publicity by telling the gossip columnists he had just returned from Mexico where he rode with and advised the infamous Pancho Villa.

A self-promoter, Lessing's actual involvement with Villa was limited to handling the settlement of the estate for the assassinated Mexican revolutionary's widow. Unproven rumors persisted for years that Lessing had actually had a hand in Villa's death.

With great interest, Walt had followed the daily newspaper accounts of Lessing's Mexican adventures and decided anyone tough enough to ride with Villa would have no trouble with Powers. Roy was also impressed, particularly with Lessing's intimidating physical appearance. He was a large man with a wild shock of red hair who dressed in heavy three-piece tweeds that caused him to sweat profusely, giving his face a swarthy, menacing cast. It was a look of intimidation Lessing used to his advantage. When he spoke, his loud voice had a natural bray to it like the sound of a wounded wolf.

In January 1930, Walt, Lillian, Roy, Edna, Bill Cottrell and his wife Hazel, and Gunther Lessing journeyed by train to New York.

The evening of their arrival, Walt assembled everyone in his hotel room to announce a change in the game plan. He had decided to make his initial visit to Powers the next day, alone, out of respect for all that he had done in the past for the Disney studio.

At that meeting, Powers angrily denied any fraudulent actions on his part, despite Disney's hard evidence. Walt calmly reminded Powers their contract included a one-year "out" clause that, if invoked, would end their association. Powers retaliated by reaching into his suit and pulling out a telegram from Ub Iwerks stating his intention to leave the Disney studio to start his own. Ub would be backed by Powers, who guaranteed distribution in return for a commitment to use the Cinephone sound system.

Powers suggested that if Walt backed off, he, Powers, would tear up Iwerks's signed contract. At this point Walt ended the meeting. When he arrived back at the hotel, Roy told him that while he was gone, Iwerks had telephoned to announce his resignation.

"Forget about Powers," Walt told his brother. "It's Ub we should be concerned about." Roy placed a call to Iwerks and, after trying for several hours to persuade him to change his mind, reluctantly worked out a deal over the phone for Iwerks to surrender his contract and company stock for a onetime payout of approximately $3,000 in cash.*

Knowing it was only a matter of time before the Disneys realized what was going on, Powers had made it his business to search for a weakness in their camp. Having befriended Iwerks, he believed he had found it. As a "favor" to Ub, Powers let him know the studio was in critical financial trouble. He told Ub in confidence that Disney had seriously overextended himself with the "Silly Symphonies" and probably wouldn't last the year. When tipped by Iwerks the reason for Disney's New York trip, Powers responded by offering Iwerks something he knew he wouldn't turn down: the chance to run his own studio.

According to Ub's son, Dave Iwerks, "Ub and Walt were both very hardheaded, and because of that any differences between them became major. My father felt overlooked and underappreciated at Disney. He'd begun as a partner and was now an employee. When

---

*Had Iwerks kept his shares, they would be worth approximately half a billion dollars in today's market.

Powers gave Ub the chance to start his own studio, he jumped at it. And why shouldn't he have?"

In a single day Disney had lost his best artist, his distributor, and a sorely needed $150,000 in unpaid royalties Powers still owed. Roy and Walt worked out a strategy whereby he and Lillian would remain in New York while the others, including Lessing, returned to Hollywood. Disney was now desperate for a distribution deal and met once again with the heads of the major studios, beginning with the ruthless, demanding Louis B. Mayer at the New York headquarters of MGM.

Although the squat, balding, bespectacled Mayer had been quite vocal in his dislike of Disney's movies, having once dismissed Mickey as being doomed to failure because "every woman is afraid of a mouse," Disney's success changed Mayer's mind, and he offered to back Walt. However, the deal quickly fell apart when Mayer received a warning from Powers that he would sue anyone who interfered with his contract, still in effect, for the exclusive rights to Disney's films.

Powers also informed Walt he intended to challenge the one-year "out" clause. Undeterred, Walt continued his search for a distributor not as easily intimidated as Mayer and found one in Harry Cohn, the New York–based president of Columbia Pictures, whose gutter-tough crudeness made Powers seem, by comparison, a boy scout.

Cohn, often described in the industry press as "the meanest man in Hollywood," was a stubby man with thick features and balding black hair who always kept a cigar clenched between his teeth. He bore a remarkable resemblance to Al Capone, reinforced by a tough-guy manner that made him hated and feared by rival studio heads on both coasts. The Columbia studio hallway that led to his office was known by his employees as "the last mile." Among his more endearing qualities was his admiration of Mussolini, so strong that Cohn had his New York office remodeled into an exact duplicate of the Italian dictator's. Cohn's favorite expression was "I don't get ulcers, I give 'em."

When he first met Disney, he was impressed with what he later referred to as Walt's "spunk." Shortly afterward, Cohn called Frank Capra, his favorite director, for an opinion on Disney's future. Capra, a big fan of Mickey Mouse, advised Cohn to do whatever it took to sign Walt. Cohn then offered to distribute Disney's cartoons. Walt, unconcerned by all he had heard about Cohn, accepted the offer, his first formal association with any major studio.

When Powers heard of the arrangement, he followed through on his threat and sued. Cohn retaliated by acquiring the services of a team of top New York lawyers. He then had countersuit papers hand-delivered by some "personal friends," a couple of imposing, flat-nosed street toughs. Powers quickly backed off and agreed to a onetime buyout from Disney of $50,000 against any and all future claims.

Just as one crisis seemed to ease, another replaced it. Carl Stalling, Disney's resident music director, suddenly announced that he too was resigning to join Iwerks at his new studio. Powers had persuaded Stalling to defect by offering to double his salary to $300 a week. With Iwerks and Stalling hired, Powers then went to Mayer and quickly struck an exclusive distribution deal with MGM. Mayer had no problem dealing with the man who had so recently threatened to sue him over Disney, once it became clear MGM would get the benefit of Disney's stable of talent at a fraction of what it would have cost only a month before.

Cohn, meanwhile, concluded his deal with Walt, agreeing that starting February 7, 1930, he would advance $7,000 a cartoon, nearly three times what Powers had paid, and let all copyrights to Mickey Mouse remain with Disney.

In the face of extraordinary obstacles, Disney once again managed to save his studio from going under. Exhausted, he and his wife could now board a train in Grand Central Station for the journey back to Hollywood. Several hours each day, Walt sat alone in the club car staring through the picture windows at the passing countryside, his fingernails loudly *clackity-clacking* on the sill in time with the rumble of the train's wheels as he thought about Iwerks, the man he once considered his best friend, and why he had betrayed him.

As the time and towns passed, Walt's mood darkened. Unable to sleep at night, he stared silently at the ceiling of his compartment until the early hours of the dawn. He lost his appetite and skipped meals, preferring to sit in the club car with a scotch and soda while Lillian dined alone. By the time they arrived in Los Angeles, Walt was so depressed he stopped talking to his wife and everybody else.

Back in Hollywood, he stayed in his office most days, brooding silently as he stared out his window, unable to focus on anything having to do with making movies. In the evenings he argued with Lillian over the slightest issues, what she made for dinner, if the sheets were changed that day, what she wore around the house, after which he would lock himself in the study and weep, uncontrollably, for hours.

Thirty years later, in his late fifties, Disney offered this explanation for his behavior: "I guess I was working too hard and worrying too much. . . . I had a nervous breakdown. . . . Costs were going up; each new picture we finished cost more to make than we had figured it would earn when we first began to plan it. . . . I cracked up."

At the age of twenty-nine he felt more like fifty-nine. Undoubtedly, he had been left emotionally exhausted by the pressure to save his company during the Powers affair and the personal devastation of Iwerks's defection. However, what had finally pushed him over the edge was the realization, and the fear, that he was about to become a father.

All during the 1930 New York trip, in the midst of the crisis that had threatened to shut the studio down permanently, Lillian insisted they start planning a family. It was a subject she raised often during their first five years of marriage. When pressed, Walt would point out the uncertainty of their finances as the reason they shouldn't have children yet. This time, however, Lillian let Walt know that she felt at her age, twenty-nine, it was time she had a baby, and no excuse was going to change her mind.

It wasn't long after that Walt suffered a relapse of the sexual impotency that had plagued him during their honeymoon. At Lillian's insistence, he submitted to a full medical workup. Recognizing the delicate state of Disney's emotions, the doctor recommended immediate hospitalization, a suggestion Lillian rejected. The only alternative, the doctor told her, was a complete break for her husband from the pressures of the studio, the presumed cause of the anxiety. He advised an extended vacation with lots of rest and relaxation.

Only two weeks after returning from New York, Walt, Lillian, and Bill and Hazel Cottrell embarked on a trip through the Americas, leaving behind a full schedule of cartoons in production.

The group traveled by train to Washington, D.C., New Orleans, New York and down the Atlantic coast. In Key West, Florida, they boarded a cruise ship bound for Cuba, stayed for a week, then continued on to Panama. After traversing the Canal, Walt chartered a private yacht for the return journey along the Pacific coast to California.

By the time they arrived back in Hollywood, two months later, it seemed Walt was once more himself. Apparently, the trip had done him a world of good. Indeed, his mood had begun to noticeably shift during the long days at sea. He told Lillian he agreed with her that they should try to have a baby. At the same time he formulated dozens of new plots for Mickey Mouse and the "Silly Symphonies."

And something else. According to Bill Cottrell, Walt's mood first began to change in New York City, where the first seeds of a new, as yet unformed, idea were planted: "We went backstage at Radio City because Walt wanted to see how they did things with that incredible stage. Then we went to the Statue of Liberty. 'Let's go up to the top,' Walt said. I think we climbed twelve flights, after taking the elevator up as far as it would go. Now Walt was a very patriotic man, without doubt, but I don't believe that was the reason why he wanted to go to the statue that day. He was intensely interested in why millions of people would go out of their way to see it. That's the real reason he went. He just wanted to know what it was about a statue that could attract all those tourists."

SIX

Fairy Tales and Fatherhood

WHILE *Steamboat Willie* brought the Disney studio a great burst of public attention, the heads of the Majors considered it more a triumph of technology than a truly great motion picture. Many privately felt Disney's newfound fame would last about as long as the run of his celebrated cartoon talkie and thought it wise to maximize his value to the image of their industry.

Not surprisingly then, in 1931, the members of the Academy of Motion Picture Arts and Sciences nominated not one but *two* of his cartoons for Oscars in the category they had created especially for the occasion, the Best Short Subject.

The just-turned-thirty Disney found himself among some older, more established, and very strong competition, especially from Laurel and Hardy and Mack Sennett. However, the Laurel and Hardy comedies were peppered with naughty flappers and sexual innuendo and were thus too cynical for the times in their outlook on the institution of marriage. As for Mack Sennett's bungling Keystone Kops, these movies had mocked official authority for too many years. By comparison, Disney's "Silly Symphonies" *Flowers and Trees*— flowers dancing to the music of Mendelssohn and Schubert—had a bucolic air of innocence, and its innovative use of color made it the easy choice for an industry eager to showcase its commitment to wholesome, highly moral family entertainment.

To underscore its intention, the Academy gave Disney's other nominated short, the interestingly titled *Mickey's Orphans*, a special award simply to pay homage to Walt's by-now celebrated mouse. This additional award was only the second time the Academy had bestowed such an honor on a filmmaker, the first having gone to one of the original inspirations for Mickey's "character," Walt's childhood idol, Charlie Chaplin. Walt attended the ceremonies in black tie and was warmed by the accolades from those he now considered his peers. Lillian also attended although, unlike her husband, she had no use for such celebration. She was uncomfortable in the spotlight and decided, from this point on, to refrain from putting herself on display as if she were an ornament in a fancy store window.

To Walt, the two awards represented the mark of great achievement. He saw himself now not among Hollywood's pioneers but a technical wizard who had single-handedly advanced the art of animation.

By 1931, when he first considered making a cartoon in color, his motivation had been far less esoteric. In the two years following the sensational debut of *Steamboat Willie*, the studio's box-office returns had peaked and flattened. What Disney felt he needed was another technical innovation to boost his films' popularity.

His idea to use color had actually begun after the creators of a new and still-experimental film process they called "Technicolor" went in search of animators to sell their system to. When they approached Disney, he immediately recognized their products' potential. Color, like sound, had been around for years in one form or another, long before Disney discovered it for the first time. The prints of many early silent feature films had been tinted or, in some cases, their individual frames painstakingly hand-painted. A color cartoon actually appeared in 1919, eleven years before *Flowers and Trees. The Debut of Thomas Cat* utilized a system known as "Brewster Color," which was abandoned shortly thereafter because of its prohibitive expense.

In the early thirties, the Technicolor laboratory believed it had finally solved the two basic problems that had prevented color from being widely adapted by the film industry: its cost and relatively brief shelf life before prints started to fade or turn purple. However, the industry remained skeptical, and when it was unable to interest any of the Majors in its system, the company turned first to the independents and, as a last resort, to the animation houses.

The only other studios that showed any interest in Technicolor besides Disney's were Pioneer Films, a small, independent live-action house, and Ub Iwerks's new animation studio. To close his deal, Disney insisted on and won the right of animation exclusivity. This was a critical point to Walt, who had learned that Iwerks was planning a series of sound and color cartoons with classical-music sound tracks he intended to use to compete directly with "Silly Symphonies."

In spite of Walt's sense of urgency, Roy believed color was a huge financial gamble the studio simply couldn't afford to take. He reminded his brother that the first twelve "Silly Symphonies," of which *Flowers and Trees* was the sixth, had been presold to and by Columbia at a fixed rate. Furthermore, the studio's average budget for a black-and-white cartoon had escalated to $10,000, from which it could reasonably expect a maximum return of about $45,000. Color cartoons would cost at least twice that much to make, with a maximum potential profit increase of only about $5,000, resulting in a net profit reduction of approximately $5,000 per cartoon. Besides, Walt intended to finance the research necessary to have his own technicians correct the problems Technicolor couldn't.

Over his brother's objections, Walt finalized the deal with Technicolor and ordered all of *Flowers and Trees*'s black-and-white footage scrapped in favor of starting over in color. After it won the Oscar, the studio received what Walt later described as "an avalanche" of new bookings.

Still, the newfound fame did not translate into dollars. The profits from the increased bookings were offset by the rise in production costs and ongoing research to perfect the process of making color cartoons, which wouldn't be completed until 1935, when the first color "Mickey" finally appeared. As a result, the studio continued to suffer cash-flow problems.

At least part of the reason was that from its earliest days Hollywood conducted business as a series of cash transactions in which nobody in a higher position of power paid anyone lower on|time. Conversely, the more power a recipient had, the faster he received his payment. As a result, royalties from the distribution of cartoons, a relatively low priority but the Disney studio's sole source of income, always arrived late, often several weeks, sometimes months.

No one suspected the kind of larceny practiced by Powers. Harry

Cohn's disposition on any given day was the determining factor as to whether he signed checks, and on most days he just didn't feel like paying people. When he did, like everyone else in Hollywood, he paid last those with the least power and influence. While Columbia Pictures was considered the "Poverty Row" of Hollywood's Majors, compared to Disney's little independent cartoon studio on Hyperion, Cohn was huge. As far as Cohn was concerned, Disney should have been happy to be getting paid at all. If he had any complaints, all he had to do was speak up, which, of course, he didn't, fearing an angered Cohn might withhold payment for an even longer period of time.

The week before Christmas 1931, things came to a head when Roy was unable to meet payroll. In a last-ditch effort to bridge the crisis, he came up with the idea of issuing gold tokens and promissory notes in lieu of paychecks to the staff. Most were outraged by what they considered the Disneys' cavalier insensitivity, especially so close to the holidays. As he had with Iwerks, Walt believed the staff's silent acquiescence was a demonstration of their satisfaction, especially since none complained about having to wait for their pay.

THE TWO THINGS Disney shared with the major Hollywood studios were his assumption he could arbitrarily bend the rules of employment, including the temporary suspension of salary payouts, and, not surprisingly, his resolute opposition to unionism, a growing problem of the industry.

The onset of the Depression had revitalized Hollywood labor's interest in formal organization. As early as 1927, Louis B. Mayer had sensed the potential threat of the labor unions. He proceded to organize what he considered a conciliatory forum among the heads of the major studios to listen to the growing complaints of the industry's employees regarding their low rate of pay and generally poor physical working conditions.

While Mayer's Academy of Motion Picture Arts and Sciences assumed a sympathetic posture, it was, in reality, less interested in increasing salaries and improving working conditions than establishing a united management front. So much so that in 1931, after another precipitous drop in box-office revenues, the heads of the major studios imposed an industry-wide 50 percent pay cut on all salaried writers. Similar reductions for actors, directors, technicians, and laborers soon followed, which further divided Hollywood into two opposing, increasingly hostile factions.

At approximately the same time, Chicago's notorious Al Capone tried to establish his own beachhead in Hollywood. Capone had long admired the exploits of his "cousin," Charles "Lucky" Luciano, who along with Benjamin "Bugsy" Siegel and Meyer Lansky had effectively infiltrated every economic strata of working Hollywood. In addition, John Rosselli, a former protégé of the Chicago kingpin, had established a major Los Angeles–based gambling network.

Capone's many mob operations included the formation of a nationwide bootlegging network whose best and most profitable market was Hollywood. Convinced motion pictures were an even better cash cow than illegal whiskey, Capone planned to use his trademark methods of muscle and, if necessary, murder to take over one or more studios. However, before he had a chance to make his move, he was arrested and convicted of income-tax evasion, which effectively ended his grand strategy to dominate Hollywood.

While Capone was in prison, Frank Nitti took over his turf. Nitti, like his predecessor, believed the mob's future lay in Hollywood. However, his plan was far more subtle, built upon a strategy of infiltrating the film industry's unions. To that end he enlisted the special services of his old friend and mob associate, onetime hit man Willie Bioff.

Bioff's most recent specialty was the intimidation of local Chicago theater and nightclub owners who failed to accommodate mob-controlled unions. Along with his partner George Browne, the head of the Chicago local union of the International Alliance of Theatrical Stage Employees (IATSE), Bioff and Browne were "made" as a reward for helping Nitti and the mob gain a stranglehold on every theater and nightclub in Chicago.

Then, as if on cue, the Majors' 1931 imposition of across-the-board salary reductions caused the Hollywood local branch of IATSE to threaten retaliation with a formal industry-wide job action. In response Nitti promptly dispatched Browne and Bioff to Hollywood. It didn't seem to bother anyone that Browne, Bioff, and Nitti, like Capone, Siegel, Luciano, Meyer, and Rosselli before them, not only were known to be members of organized crime but made no secret of their association. The heads of the studios welcomed anyone to their side in the ongoing battle to keep salaries and benefits as low as possible. And Frank Nitti promised Hollywood's leaders Browne and Bioff would do just that.

WHILE THE Majors and the mob together worked to oppose unions and industry laborers, the Disney studio remained, for the moment, out of this particular confrontation. Walt's troubles were far more fundamental than the distribution of profits. Profits were something to which he still aspired. His problem, thanks to Harry Cohn, remained a serious lack of cash flow, which had become so bad that unless a solution was found, and quickly, bankruptcy seemed inevitable.

The solution to Walt's difficulties came from the most unlikely of benefactors. As it happened, a wealthy New York merchandiser by the name of George Borgfeldt had two children who were fans of Mickey Mouse. When Borgfeldt decided he wanted to give them Christmas presents with Mickey and his girlfriend Minnie's faces on them, he simply licensed their image from Disney for use on toys, books, and articles of clothing. From the moment they became available, items with Mickey and Minnie on them flew off the shelves.

Having discovered this new source of revenue, Walt began searching for more merchandising arrangements. He quickly struck a deal with Bibo and Lang, a small New York publishing firm, for *The Mickey Mouse Book*, a sixteen-page volume that included an original story by a precocious eleven-year-old who happened to be Bibo's daughter; a game; pictures of Mickey; and the lyrics to an original song. *The Mickey Mouse Book* sold 97,938 copies its first year in print.

Disney then licensed to the King Features Syndicate the rights for a Mickey Mouse newspaper comic strip, which became an immediate international hit, even more so than the studio's animated shorts. The comic strip was responsible for Mickey Mouse becoming a familiar face in every corner of the world. By 1932, Mickey Mouse Fan Clubs had a combined enrollment of more than a million members in the United States alone, with new clubs opening every day.

At the year's end, more than eighty major U.S. companies, including General Foods, RCA, and National Dairy, were selling millions of dollars of Disney-related merchandise, which resulted in a $300,000 windfall for the studio. Disney received about half, which accounted for one-third of the studio's entire net profits.

Walt then signed William Banks Levy as the studio's European merchandising representative. Disney knew Levy from the days when both had been with Pat Powers, liked him, and, more important, trusted him. Levy proceeded to close deals for everything from toothbrushes to dollhouse-size kitchen sinks, all bearing the trademark Mickey Mouse ears.

Experience soon revealed to Disney the weakness in his arrangement with Borgfeldt, in which royalties to the studio increased with the number of items sold, when, in fact, the bulk of a novelty item's sales life was notoriously brief. As a result, Borgfeldt realized a much larger profit than Disney. Walt soon ended their association and hired Herman "Kay" Kamen to run the studio's newly formed in-house marketing division.

Shortly after he signed on, Kamen's first order of business was the immediate adjustment of all existing contracts. Having accomplished that, he set out to build what eventually became the largest and most successful in-house studio merchandising operation in the world.

His very first deal, for Mickey Mouse ice-cream cones, resulted in the sale of ten million the first month they were made available to the public. He also put together a series of logo deals, all extremely profitable, including one with Lionel trains for the manufacture of a Mickey Mouse handcar, a toy that proved so popular the sales from it alone rescued the struggling toy-train company from imminent bankruptcy. The deal Kamen made with the Ingersoll-Waterbury Company for Mickey Mouse watches resulted in the sale of two-and-a-half-*million* units the first two years.

Ironically, Walt Disney's reputation as the world's most famous animator had resulted less from his abilities as an artist than as a merchandiser. It was Disney's timely addition of sound and color to his films, followed by his propitious commitment to the merchandising of Mickey Mouse, that rescued his studio from impending insolvency.

And no one was more aware of it than Walt, who also understood that merchandising profits depended on the continued success of his cartoons. That was why, in the days immediately following his two Oscars, he moved quickly to fill the creative gap left by the departure of Ub Iwerks.

Finding a replacement did not prove easy, since the best animators in the business were still on the East Coast. Walt figured the best course of action was to apply what he had learned from merchandising to create his own in-house training division. After being turned away by several other local schools, Walt found a receptive ear at Chouinard's Art Institute of Los Angeles. Its founder, Nelbert Chouinard, a woman less concerned with profit than with education, was impressed by Disney's concept and agreed to work with him.

Chouinard's, begun in 1921, benefited financially from the many World War I discharged veterans who attended classes paid for by the government. So much so that in the mid-twenties, Mrs. Chouinard introduced a series of scholarships for talented high school students, one of whom was a young man by the name of Don Graham. To help pay his living expenses, Graham served as the school's night janitor. Mrs. Chouinard agreed to allow Disney to hold animation training classes in the evenings, provided Graham could teach them.

Although he was a talented painter, Graham had no actual experience in animation. Still, his enthusiasm and personable manner impressed Disney, who invited his new instructor to the Hyperion studio lot to help him gain a practical firsthand knowledge of the process of animation.

Disney recalled years later:

> I made a deal with [Graham] to come out and work with me, to sit with me and know my problems. That, in turn, gave [him] the chance to know what we had to work on. [He] sat right in the room with me . . . in what we called our sweatbox [a tiny, poorly ventilated room hardly bigger than a supply closet, where animated sequences were projected for the purpose of demonstration]. Fifty percent of my time was spent in the sweatbox going over every scene with every animator.

Graham's classes proved so popular that Disney soon shifted them to the daytime and leased a small building directly across Hyperion for the students. Many Graham "graduates" became part of the creative nucleus that produced Disney's greatest animated movies. While they were a source of great pride to Walt, it was a pride focused more on self-congratulation for having come up with the notion of the school, rather than on the talent it produced.

Walt treated his animators in the same fashion the heads of most

Hollywood studios treated talent—as employees rather than artists. They remained mostly anonymous, their unique styles and individual contributions most often lumped under the umbrella of "Walt Disney Presents." Even more so than at the live-action studios, where actors and actresses enjoyed the privileges of celebrity, the only "stars" at Disney's studio other than Walt were his cartoon characters. Disney, never a great sharer, preferred to think of his studio as essentially a one-man operation.

All of which added to Walt's reputation as Hollywood's resident animation "genius," a reputation he cannily nurtured by pursuing personal relationships with the most influential syndicated Hollywood columnists, including Hedda Hopper and Louella Parsons, at whose suggestion Walt first grew his pencil mustache to make him look more "debonair." Ed Sullivan and Sidney Skolsky regularly ran stories about Disney in their columns that hailed his work. They took their cue from the mood of the industry, often citing the quality of his films as the best proof of Hollywood's "new" morality.

The Disney studio's growing reputation attracted some of the best talent in the industry, including many established animators who emigrated from New York for a chance to work with Hollywood's new hero. Ben Sharpsteen made the cross-country journey after several years at the East Coast–based Hearst, Terrytoons, and Fleischer studios, as did Dave Hand, the creator of the Fleischer studio's "Andy Gump"; Rudy Zamora, a Fleischer animator; Tom Palmer, a New York director of cartoons for the Van Beuren Studio; Ted Sears, one of Fleischer's best storymen; Burt Gillett from Hearst International; Jack King from the Bray studio; and Webb Smith, a gag-and-joke man from Hearst International. All came west hoping to work for Walt. Those who were hired had to agree to salaries far below what they were used to, in return for the privilege of working for Walt Disney and the promise of creative freedom.

As Disney's studio expanded, even the influx of money from merchandising proved insufficient to offset operating expenses. To meet the rapidly growing payroll and the escalating costs involved with the production of quality animation, it soon became necessary to put the studio through yet another round of belt-tightening. Never wanting to appear the bad guy, Walt charged his resident attorney, Gunther Lessing, with explaining the economic facts of life to the staff.

Jack Kinney, a Disney animator, remembered what took place that morning in the winter of 1931: "We were told to report to the new soundstage, where we gathered promptly at five, all the boys and girls, wondering what was up. 'Gunny' Lessing had just returned from a trip to New York. He came on strong with a terribly sad story of conditions there—people going around with the seats of their pants worn out, and other distressing news of the Great Depression—ending up by passionately asking us to take a 15 percent cut in salary."

Which everyone did. When Lessing asked if anyone had any objections, the fear of losing jobs silenced any expressions of dissatisfaction and resentment.

Nevertheless, patience was wearing thin among the staff. The demand for new color cartoons forced Walt to push them beyond all reasonable expectations. To augment his primary source of cheap talent, Graham's classes, Walt placed dozens of ads in newspapers all over the country advising young people with artistic abilities interested in learning animation to apply for a job at the studio. The standard Disney pitch declared:

WE'RE AFTER ARTISTS

We're hunting men. Walt Disney's staff is expanding so rapidly Walt needs more capable, well-trained artists. We're looking for smart fellows who have something on the ball.

There are opportunities in animation for artists interested in every sort of work—opportunities for both creative work and advancement in salary. The work is not confined to caricature alone. Every phase of fine art is used. For artists of talent and ability, jobs are open. Write for further information.

According to one animator who got his start with Disney from an ad like the one above: "Walt wasn't really interested in hiring so-called professionals at all. For one thing it would have cost too much money. He preferred taking on 'apprentices' who would do the bulk of the work for nothing. He considered their art lessons enough of a payment by themselves. The ten to fifteen dollars a week he started most animators out with was really just carfare, rent, and cigarette money."

Walt finally decided to go to New York and personally meet with

Harry Cohn to discuss the possibility of Columbia doubling the advance for each cartoon from $7,500 to $15,000. Production costs, Walt explained to Cohn, had risen from a profitable $5,400 to a highly unprofitable $13,500.

Cohn's response was an immediate and nonnegotiable no. He reminded Disney there was a depression on, that money was tight everywhere. When Walt suggested it might be better for the both of them if they ended their association, Cohn pulled their contract out of the top drawer of his desk, tore it up, and threw the pieces in Walt's face. The next day Lessing was notified by Cohn's attorneys that Disney was expected to repay in full the still-outstanding "loan" of $50,000 Columbia had advanced to buy out Powers.

When Carl Laemmle heard about Disney's break with Columbia, he immediately offered to repay Walt's outstanding loan and take over distribution at whatever price he wanted. Walt only had to surrender the copyright to Mickey Mouse, something he had always refused in the past.

This time, however, Disney, fearful of being left without a distributor, considered Laemmle's proposition until Joseph Schenck bettered it. Schenck offered to advance Walt $15,000 for every new cartoon he could produce.

A producer with a reputation for making money, Schenck had been brought in by the founders of United Artists to stabilize their financially troubled studio. United Artists had originally been conceived by Charlie Chaplin, Douglas Fairbanks, Mary Pickford, and D. W. Griffith as a place to make original, creative films unencumbered by studio bureacracy. Due to the lack of imposed discipline its creators had wanted to avoid, UA slipped into a collective state of nonproduction. By 1933, it had become, in reality, little more than a fancy distribution house, specializing in ready-made independent movies. When Schenck made his offer to Disney, Chaplin privately warned Walt he should be careful, that everyone in Hollywood was out to steal everything from everybody else. Chaplin told Disney what he already knew from his experience with Carl Laemmle: Above all, no matter what anybody advised, for no amount of money should he ever sell out to a major studio.

Fresh on Chaplin's mind was the experience of Buster Keaton, who in 1928, on Joseph Schenck's advice, had accepted an offer of $3,000 a week to give up his own studio and make movies for MGM, the studio then headed by Schenck's brother, Nicholas. Keaton now considered the move the greatest mistake of his career. So did Chaplin, who never tired of using Keaton's experience as an object lesson for those who felt vulnerable to the lure of the studios.

To get Disney to sign, Schenck offered Walt a descending sliding-scale percentage of the profits to insure more money and an earlier payout. Schenck knew that having Disney under contract made it possible for UA to guarantee filmmakers a Disney cartoon would open their features. Later that year, Schenck left UA to help found Twentieth Century, where he tried several times without success to convince Disney to incorporate his studio as a subdivision. Two years later Schenck merged his studio with Fox, to form Twentieth Century-Fox.

As 1933 DREW TO A CLOSE, Walt returned to Hollywood eager to get back to making movies. Among his first goals was to help perfect the process of Technicolor, and revamp the physical characteristics and behavior of Mickey Mouse. Mickey's original design had consisted of a combination of perfect circles and tubes, what some animators describe as the "rubber hose" style. Walt offered this rationale for his decision to alter what was generally considered the studio franchise:

> The life and adventures of Mickey Mouse have been closely bound up with my own personal and professional life. It is understandable that I should have sentimental attachment for the little personage who played so big a part in the course of Walt Disney Productions and has been so happily accepted as an amusing friend wherever films are shown around the world. He still speaks for me and I still for him.

It was among the most revealing public comments Walt had ever made about his "relationship" with Mickey. Referring to his animated character as if it were a living creature wasn't, in and of itself, all that unusual. Nor was Walt's rather coy admission of the fact, not previously well-known, that he was the voice of Mickey Mouse. Symbiotic creator-character acts had become quite popular, perhaps none more so than Edgar Bergen and his dummy Charlie McCarthy. However, whereas Bergen's live act relied on the joke of Charlie's not being "real," underscored by Bergen's physical presence, Disney's films utterly depended upon the audience's absolute acceptance of the "reality" of Mickey Mouse, controlled by the godlike invisibility of his creator.

In a way, Mickey Mouse was, of course, very real. Indeed, his original wise-guy attitude, taste for adventure, and physical heroics fairly reverberated with the essence of his original inspiration, Charlie Chaplin. At the same time, Mickey's chaste love for Minnie and his overall redemptive innocence had continued to reflect the inner feelings of little Walt toward his favorite storyteller and primal love, his mother.

Disney's decision to replace Mickey with a new one whose features resembled a newborn baby's—large head, round stomach, tiny arms and legs—added a dimension of depth without sacrificing the essential quality of innocence. Mickey's face acquired a wider range of expression, particularly in the eyes, while his physical movements became more sophisticated. Walt also wanted Mickey's personality adjusted, his wise-guy attitude replaced by one more wholesome and childlike, his overall behavior gentler and less aggressive.

Disney would put Mickey through nothing less than a fully textured and multicolored rebirth, to replace the bare bones of his own childhood associations with a fully realized, animated "individual" the whole world could not only laugh at but love. This transformation would take on heroic proportions and be repeated over and over again in Disney's greatest characters and, in doing so, perfectly reflect his own real-life transformation, from his bare-bones life of an anonymous, impoverished, abused child to the fully realized, creative animator the whole world came to love.

There was also, perhaps, a darker aspect to Walt's changing relationship with Mickey. The successful metamorphosis of the character meant, in a sense, that Walt had done his job and was now finished. As with a parent whose child has grown, the time had come to say good-bye. The worldwide institutionalization of Mickey Mouse had given him a life of his own. There was little left for Walt to do than wish his prodigy well.

Or kill him off. For there was a sense of sibling rivalry at work as well, a narcissistic jealousy between Walt and his vastly more popular animated reflection. Walt may have been reassuring himself, as well as his audience, when he insisted that "he still speaks for me and I still for him." Nevertheless, his next major project would bear no character that resembled in any way, shape, or form, a mouse, let alone the celebrated rodent whose creation had come to overshadow its jealous creator.

Perhaps it was no accident, then, that Disney returned to the scene of his childhood, the source of his greatest creation to date, for fresh inspiration. Walt often told anyone who asked that he ate, slept, and breathed cartoons. This statement took on a deeper meaning one night when he awoke sometime after 2:00 A.M., got out of bed, went to the standup desk he kept next to it, and scribbled a note to himself. His dreams had awakened him. On a piece of paper he scribbled "The Three Little Pigs."

As with virtually all his great creative revelations, Walt had once again let his unconscious be his guide. His dream to make a ten-minute film out of "The Three Little Pigs" was, like the inspiration for Mickey Mouse, rooted in his memories of his relationship to his mother and to Charlie Chaplin. The Grimm fairy tale tells the story of three pigs whose characters are illustrated by their approach to the building of their houses. Two use flimsy materials that are easy to work with and take little time, while the third laboriously builds his with brick and mortar. When a wolf comes along, he blows away the first two houses but can't get past the door of the third. This was yet another of the stories Walt's mother had read to him when he was a little boy, and the dream had come to him not long after Walt caught a revival of Chaplin's 1921 silent film *The Kid*, a movie based on the relationship between a tramp and his "adopted" child.

In *The Kid*, Chaplin's Tramp finds a newborn baby abandoned on his doorstep and takes it in as his own. The emotional center of the movie is also its physical middle, the dramatic victory of the Tramp over the officials from the local orphanage who years later have come to take the little boy for placement. In response, Chaplin literally rises to the occasion, racing over the rooftops with angel-like grace to cut off the orphanage's wagon and rescue his child.

Disney made the image of the orphanage officials pounding at the Tramp's door into the prime physical and thematic leitmotiv for his version of "The Three Little Pigs"—the wolf at the door—a lift so blatant that when Louella Parsons asked him about it, Walt replied, "Well, that might not be such a bad imitation."

For the first time, plot became a major factor in a Disney film. Because the story of "The Three Little Pigs" is essentially illustrative rather than pastoral, that ultimately it is the material of one's character, rather than the building blocks one chooses for his house, that determines one's fate, Disney correctly sensed he had to find a way of physically defining morality. Disney did not want three identical characters to *heighten* the sense of drama, but three individuals to *deepen* it. With *The Three Little Pigs*, Disney's animation achieved emotional perspective.

According to Chuck Jones, another of Hollywood's legendary animators:

> For American animation, *The Three Little Pigs* was the turning point. Disney's animation [had at first] defined characters by what they looked like—in films like *Steamboat Willie*, the villain was the big, ugly guy and the hero was the little guy—and everybody moved the same. In *The Three Little Pigs*, the three pigs *looked* more or less the same but each *acted* differently, each had a different personality.

To impress his staff with what he was after, Disney ordered repeated screenings of *The Kid*, pointing out how it was really the Tramp's character that had not only motivated his physical accomplishments but made them cinematically effective. Disney continually pointed to Chaplin's soaring rooftop run as the dramatic equivalent of his transcendent moral conviction. At times Disney would stop the film and act out original scenes for *The Three Little Pigs*. He would literally *become* the Big Bad Wolf, hunched over and menacing as he tried to blow the first pig's house down, then shift suddenly to the character of the pig, shivering with fear as he tried to keep the wolf from his door. Back and forth he would go, from wolf to pig, three times, each time changing his portrayal of the pigs with a shift of an eyebrow or the twist of his body, stooping, stretching, snarling, cowering, laughing, crying, praying, until the last pig heroically conquered the wolf.

Walt stunned his captive audience with the power of his performance, leaving several of the grown men openly weeping at what they had just witnessed. One who saw it recalled it as being "as good as anything Chaplin had ever done."

The key assignment to direct *The Three Little Pigs* went to Burt Gillett, a former Hearst International animator who had joined the studio four years earlier, in 1929, and whose use of detail had always impressed Disney. Fred Moore was rewarded for his work in helping to revise the image of Mickey Mouse by being assigned the job of drawing the three individual pigs. To create the Big Bad Wolf, Disney relied on Norm Ferguson, who had gained Walt's attention by creating the popular character of "Pluto" the dog.

And for the film's musical score, Walt surprised everyone, including Roy, by announcing he had rehired Carl Stalling. In spite of his anger at Stalling for defecting, Disney still admired his considerable talent and felt he simply was the best man for this job. Moreover, Disney considered Stalling a trophy of battle in the ongoing war with Iwerks.

Walt wanted the pigs to sing as they built their house. When Stalling proved not very good at writing lyrics, Disney decided to lease a song from an outside publisher. However, when none would reduce their regular feature-film rates, Walt asked two of his in-house storymen, Frank Churchill and Ted Sears, to make something up. The result was "Who's Afraid of the Big Bad Wolf," a song that went directly from the lips of the three pigs to the top of the song charts as it became the nation's unofficial Depression-era anthem, and also one of Disney's most profitable ventures, as all song publishing remained the sole property of the studio.

While the tune's strong moral message was sung by the "wise" pig in a verse extolling the virtues of hard work, it was the "silly" pigs' refrain—Who's afraid of the Big Bad Wolf?—that everybody identified with.

So pervasive was the message of the refusal to surrender to fear, many believed it was the inspiration for one of Franklin Delano Roosevelt's most memorable Depression-age rallying cries—"The only thing we have to fear is fear itself."

The song's widespread popularity was only one aspect of the ten-minute film's unprecedented success. *The Three Little Pigs* proved popular beyond all expectations, Walt's included. Its uplifting theme of moral courage in the face of overwhelming odds struck a hot nerve with America's Depression audiences.

The public simply couldn't get enough of it and rushed to see it, boosting attendance figures of whatever movies it preceded. So intense was the public's demand, UA had trouble striking enough prints to supply all the movie houses that wanted to book it.

By the end of 1933, its first year in release, *The Three Little Pigs* had grossed more than $125,000, a previously unheard-of amount of money for a cartoon short. By the end of its record-breaking, two-year first run, during which time it played in one or more theaters somewhere in the country every day, including five separate bookings in New York's Radio City Music Hall, its gross exceeded a quarter of a million dollars.

Steamboat Willie and the merchandising campaign that followed had made Mickey Mouse an international star. After the success of *The Three Little Pigs*, it was a quite satisfied Walt Disney upon whom fame now focused its spotlight. Every week, it seemed, another prestigious, and previously unavailable, Hollywood organization threw a banquet in honor of its newest favorite son. Tickets for the dinners became the hottest items in town.

One such dinner, given by Hollywood's exclusive Writers' Club, was highlighted by the nation's favorite sophisticate-as-everyman, Will Rogers, introducing Hollywood's favorite everyman-as-sophisticate, Walt Disney. From the raised dais he shared with another honored guest, his primary artistic inspiration, Charlie Chaplin, Disney gazed down at every studio head who had at one time or another slammed their front gates in his face. Now they were there to honor him. This event would be a night he would remember the rest of his life; his official entrée into the gaudy pantheon of Hollywood's liveliest legends.

Disney's deification was by no means limited to Tinseltown. That December, the prestigious Chicago Art Institute selected several Disney cartoons for inclusion in its permanent collection. To celebrate the occasion, the Art Institute announced a major retrospective of Disney's first hundred animated films.

That same week *Parents* magazine awarded a medal to Walt Disney for distinguished service to children, personally presented by Dr. Rufus B. von Kleinsmid, president of the University of Southern California. At the same time King Features syndicated newspaper columnist J. P. McEvoy published an open letter to Disney that underscored just how important his contributions had been to the overall image of the film industry.

Hollywood, declared McEvoy, was

Mad about you! The only fault I have to find with you at all is that you don't make enough pictures. If I had my way I would turn all the studios over to you and let you make all the pictures from now on. . . . I would suggest the new [Production] code for the movies . . . is a little music and a grand chorus of producers, distributors, and writers singing "Who's Afraid of the NRA?" led by Willie (Mickey) Hays.

Disney's popularity proved so pervasive it crossed the line that separated popular culture from "serious" art. International film journals analyzed Disney's cartoons with the same intensity they did the movies of such internationally celebrated filmmakers as Charlie Chaplin, Buster Keaton, D. W. Griffith, and F. W. Murnau. On December 29, 1933, Disney was awarded entrée into the British *Who's Who*. That same day *Scientific American* published an extended piece exploring the "new" science of film animation, highlighting the techniques developed by Walt Disney and his studio.

Walt's public adulation was mirrored by his acceptance into Hollywood's elite social scene. That Christmas of 1933, Disney received a personal invitation from Victor McLaglen to join the exclusive weekend polo games played in Riverside stadium. Polo had become the sport of choice among Hollywood's Young Turks, with McLaglen's game the most desirable as well as most difficult to be asked to join.

Walt also accepted an invitation from the Riviera Polo Club. At thirty-two, he was among the club's youngest members, whose inner circle included such Hollywood luminaries as Will Rogers, Darryl F. Zanuck, Leslie Howard, and Spencer Tracy.

Recalled Disney's brother-in-law Bill Cottrell:

Walt became very friendly with Spencer Tracy in particular. In fact, Tracy was one of the very few people outside the immediate family ever invited into the Disney home. Lillian didn't, as a rule, like strangers invading her privacy, and Walt, for the most part, went along with it. I do remember, though, seeing Tracy there on several occasions with his wife. I believe he was, for a while, whom Walt considered his best friend.

In addition to admiring Tracy's acting, Disney enjoyed his personable offscreen manner and sharp, understated wit. The two also shared a taste for expensive scotch, red sunsets, and horses. Tracy, an excellent rider, took Disney under his wing and taught him the finer points of polo.

Walt became such a devotee of the game he insisted all his animators learn it. He initiated mandatory riding lessons every Sunday morning in Griffith Park, a directive that didn't sit very well with those employees whose only day off was now being commandeered by their boss.

When Walt was invited to join the Rancheros Visitadores (Visiting Ranchers) riding club, he accepted immediately, along with animator Dave Hand, an excellent horseman in his own right. Walt and Hand took part in the Rancheros's annual rides over the Santa Ynez Range to the mission, where all participants received the blessing of the resident padre.

"It was good to see Walt enjoying the open country, free from the cares of his office," Hand recalled. "However, at times we might just as well have brought along tables and chairs. Walt would talk more and more about his new ideas, always ending with directions for me to see that certain new or different operations were effected or workers transferred or revisions of schedules upon our return to 'civilization.'

"We were sitting around the campfire telling stories one night when Joe, the wrangler who took care of our horses every night, told us about his earlier cowboy days. The story he told was about his being lured away from a rodeo meeting to a nearby ranch supposedly peopled by two lonely women, definitely against his [Disney's] puritanical upbringing. I noticed Walt was staring into the fire with a blank, faraway expression, probably thinking up a new feature or cartoon idea.

"The next night we happened to be alone with Joe. I asked him to tell that story again. This time Walt listened and came alive, enjoying every moment, laughing as if he'd never heard it before. The funny part was, I was sure he hadn't."

Disney purchased a half-dozen polo ponies he intended to house in the stables of the new, larger house he was building for himself, Lillian, the recently hired servants, and one other person as well. Shortly after the release of *The Three Little Pigs*, Lillian announced she was pregnant.

Walt publicly expressed his joy at the prospect of becoming a father, telling friends how much he hoped Lillian would bear a son. In private he was stunned, having long believed he was physically incapable of impregnating a woman.

Throughout their eight years of marriage, Lillian had insisted and Walt had agreed to submit to every treatment available to increase what had been diagnosed as his unusually low sperm count. The doctors' reports made no mention, if the doctors were even aware of his problems with recurring bouts of impotence, that it might have anything to do with his apparent infertility. Among the curative treatments Walt submitted to were the packing of his genitals in ice for hours at a time and injections of liver extract directly into his thyroid gland.

Much to Walt's dismay, something had apparently worked. As Lillian's delivery date neared, Disney increased his already considerable drinking, his chronic cough worsened, and his smoking increased to three packs of cigarettes a day. In addition, his bouts with insomnia extended to weeks at a time, the facial tics and eye twitches from which he periodically suffered returned with renewed intensity, and he obsessively washed his hands several times an hour, every hour.

During this time the one person he felt he could turn to for comfort, understanding, and sympathy was Spencer Tracy. The two spent many nights together closing the Polo Lounge of the Beverly Hills Hotel with the actor steadying Walt as he frantically fibrillated toward fatherhood.

In contrast, Lillian was elated at the thought of approaching motherhood, seeing in it the opportunity to infuse her life with the kind of meaning it had lacked since she had married Walt. Having come from a middle-American working-class background, Lillian had little use for what she considered the cheap glitz that passed for "high society" in Hollywood and no longer attended any of the functions to celebrate the "Disney phenomenon" that Walt never missed. As a result, Walt was seen around Hollywood by himself so often that journalists who didn't know he was married, and a lot of them didn't, often described Disney as one of Hollywood's most eligible bachelors.

Although Lillian occasionally agreed to supply answers to written questions, or allowed the studio's public relations department to do so for her, she almost never granted interviews to journalists. Aside from the very few friends she had besides her sister Hazel and Roy's wife Edna, she simply couldn't stand the idea of even being in the same room with people she didn't know. Disney eventually had to build a private screening room in his house just so they could watch his movies together. She never gave parties of any kind and discouraged Disney from bringing guests into their home.

Shortly after she became pregnant, the Disneys were invited to pose for the famed photographer Clarence Sinclair Bull, an invitation Walt naturally assumed Lillian would decline. However, much to his surprise, she agreed—professing a longtime admiration for the photographer's work—if the session took place in the living room of her home.

The sitting produced a portrait in which Lillian, in a conservative white dress, is reclining on a leather sofa, while Walt, in a suit and tie, stands above and behind her. Neither is looking at the other, nor smiling. The stiff, joyless formality the photograph captured was described by one close friend at the time as having perfectly defined the essential qualities of their eight years of marriage.

On December 19, 1933, Lillian gave birth to an eight-pound, two-ounce baby girl, whom the Disneys christened Diane Marie. When Lillian and her new baby were ready to leave the hospital, Walt surprised her by driving to the front door of the family's new home, overlooking the studio, in the nearby foothills of the Los Feliz district just north of Hollywood.

It was an impressive-looking place, far more extravagant than the one on Lyric Avenue. This ranch-style, picture-windowed home, with a pool dug out of the mountainous rock that surrounded it, seemed a perfect place for Lillian to raise her child. The insides were still bare, except for the few belongings Walt had moved from the old house. Lillian would soon decorate it with fine midwestern-style furniture, lots of wooden-framed chairs and sofas with floral patterns, to make it feel like a real home.

To COMMEMORATE the birth of his daughter, Walt declared that from now on, the first day any new Disney picture opened, orphans everywhere were to be admitted free.

SEVEN

Disney's Folly—The Making of *Snow White*

SHORTLY AFTER *The Three Little Pigs* opened, the leaders of several Jewish organizations met with Disney to express their concerns about a scene in which the Big Bad Wolf disguised himself as a Hebrew peddler to trick one of the pigs into opening his door. Although he agreed to remove the offensive scene—the peddler in robe, beard, and glasses became a nondescript door-to-door brush salesman in future releases—Walt insisted to friends he hadn't intended anything more than a spoof of Carl Laemmle's many unsuccessful attempts to blow down the Disney studio's house.

The Three Little Pigs remained in continuous release for the rest of the decade. Because of the Wolf's enormous popularity, Disney starred him in a series of cartoons that emphasized the humor of his ineffectiveness rather than the menace of his threat.

The following year Walt decided to film an original animated story he called *The Golden Touch*, a "Silly Symphonies" based on the old King Midas fairy tale, wherein everything the king touches turns instantly to gold until, much to his dismay, he discovers he cannot touch anything, especially other people.

Walt insisted on directing the film himself. It was his first directorial attempt and looked it. The continuity was choppy, the storytelling preachy, the dialogue pretentious. Walt, in one last attempt to show the king was really a regular guy, ended the film having him going out for a hamburger.

The film proved an embarrassing failure. Walt withdrew it from distribution, and it has not been seen since by the general public. Although no one at the studio would criticize the film to Walt's face, behind his back the staff was delighted by the folly of his directorial debut. They laughed when one employee suggested the king should have cried out for a turkey and then eaten the film's raw footage. *The Golden Touch* marked the beginning and end of Walt's directing career.

In 1934, THE FIRST significant profits from Kay Kamen's *Three Little Pigs* merchandising campaign finally arrived. Three Little Pig and Big Bad Wolf dolls, sold by Kamen to coincide with the film's release, brought in hundreds of thousands of much-needed dollars. Even more importantly, the windfall proved for the first time the studio's ability to turn a profit. Disney was now able to set a meeting with Joseph Rosenberg, UA's financial advisor and studio liaison at the Bank of America.

Based on the box-office receipts of *The Three Little Pigs* and the sales figures from the related merchandising campaign, Disney was able to secure a million-dollar line of credit for the studio. Rosenberg worked directly under A. P. Giannini, the legendary founder and board chairman of the Bank of America. Giannini also had extensive dealings with Harry Cohn and remembered Disney and the profits Cohn had made from their distribution deal. The bank's chairman personally approved Rosenberg's recommendation to establish Disney's line of credit.

As a result, Walt was able to formally commence the studio's next major undertaking, a project he boasted to the trades had never been attempted before in the entire history of film: a feature-length animated motion picture.

Disney's reasons for wanting to move into features were more pragmatic than artistic. The Depression had produced a significant drop in overall movie attendance, which prompted theater owners to offer free plates, raffles, and double features to lure audiences, all of which either greatly reduced or eliminated entirely the necessity and budgets for cartoon shorts.

To make the move, Disney first had to complete his expansion program. He focused his attentions entirely on that goal, personally interviewing every individual who applied for a job at the studio—and by now there were many. They came from all over the country, eager to work for the man who had given the world Mickey Mouse. Walt made the final decision on every applicant, hiring more by instinct than any other criteria. Many of the men he chose during this drive eventually took their places among the most talented animators, artists, and storymen of their generation.

Among them was one former magazine illustrator and a relative newcomer to animation, Marc Davis. "Early in 1935," Davis remembered, "Disney was looking for people who could draw perhaps a little better than the staff he already had. Animated features would require a different, better caliber of art. The pay, of course, was absolutely minimal. Artists who were hired all started with the same salary, $15 a week."

Ward Kimball was barely twenty when he was hired by Disney in 1934, even though he had little more than inspiration and desire to put on his résumé: "When the cartoon *The Three Little Pigs* was released, I saw it six to ten times. Instead of going to New York and becoming a magazine illustrator, I thought maybe I should try working for Walt Disney and Mickey Mouse. I packed up a portfolio of samples and, with just enough gasoline to make the round-trip [drive, from Stanford University], made my call to the old Hyperion studio.

"The receptionist told me to leave my portfolio and they would contact me later. I explained I didn't have enough gas to make another trip and could they please look at my samples while I waited. They sent my stuff directly to Walt Disney's office. The answer soon came back. I was to start work the following week."

Frank Thomas and Ollie Johnson, both also from Stanford, joined that same year. They worked as a team almost from the time they began at the studio and spent their entire professional lives at Disney. Davis, Kimball, Thomas, and Johnson, those newly hired and those who had been with the studio the longest, including Les Clark, John Lounsbery, Milt Kahl, Wolfgang "Wollie" Reitherman, and Eric Larson—these were the animators who would remain with Disney and prove the most loyal, the "Nine Old Men," as he later called them, after the members of the Supreme Court for whom appointment was not only the privilege of a lifetime but a lifetime privilege.

Other talented artists came aboard during the expansion drive, and for reasons that would have less to do with their artistic abilities than their personalities, politics, sexual proclivities, or, according to at least one former staffer, religious affiliation, were sooner or later eliminated from placement among the first rank of Walt's personal high court. Perhaps foremost among these was Arthur Babbitt, one of the few animators Walt hired who had previously worked for a competing studio.

Babbitt, feeling the pinch of the Depression, left his position at the Paul Terry Animated Studios in New York to enter the more lucrative field of commercial art. One afternoon he happened to catch a screening of the "Silly Symphonies" *Skeleton Dance* in a local theater and was so impressed he went home, packed his bags, relocated to Hollywood, and applied for a job at Disney.

Babbitt was the most intellectual of Disney's animators and probably the most singularly talented, responsible for many of the classic and classiest moments in Disney's features, including the renowned Chinese mushroom dance from *Fantasia*. Babbitt brought along his friend and fellow Terry man, Bill Tytla. Disney hired Tytla as well.

Joe Grant came aboard after his work as a local newspaper caricaturist caught Walt's eye. "I actually got a call from Walt himself, after he saw my caricature of King Kong, asking me to come to the studio and meet with him."

Disney offered Grant a job doing caricatures featured in the 1933 short, *Mickey's Gala Premiere*, to be shown at that year's Academy Awards celebration. When the picture was finished, Disney decided to keep Grant on the payroll.

Walt's hiring of Grim Natwick, Hamilton Luske, and Shamus Culhane signaled the completion of this phase of the studio's expansion. From an original staff of six full-time animators the studio now had more than fifty, plus fifty assistant animators; a resident twenty-four-piece orchestra; dozens of storymen, gag writers, ink-and-painters, cameramen, technicians, secretaries, messengers; even shoe-shine men, one of whom remained with the studio for forty-five years, the only full-time African-American employee during Walt's lifetime.

Walt prided himself on knowing everyone's face, if not their name, and believed the studio functioned as one big happy family. To that end he tried whenever possible to employ friends and female relatives of his animators, who were exclusively male, for low-level artwork, such as ink-and-painting, or clerical positions.

Marcielle Ferguson, animator Les Clark's younger sister, recalled how she got hired: "I'd just graduated from high school and was looking for a job. I'd majored in art, and my brother said he thought he could get me a job at the studio. Les went to Walt and asked if he could find a place for me, and Walt said, sure, bring her in. I had no special artistic skills, but it didn't seem to matter to Walt. I started as a painter, and then I worked as an inker and then a checker, for a total of about seven years. Everybody who worked there, it seemed, had someone else in their family who also worked for Disney."

Michael Murphy, an electrician at the studio in the fifties, recalled: "There was a guard at the front gate at the Burbank studio who'd been with Walt since the Hyperion days. He didn't do anything, really, except show up for work and get a little tipsy now and then, but everyone knew he had a job for life because he'd stuck with Disney during some hard times and Walt would never fire him. There were a lot of characters around the lot whose only qualification was that Walt liked them."

Frank Thomas echoed that opinion: "Walt had this thing about loyalty. He wouldn't fire someone he believed had been loyal to him no matter how mad he got at them over something. He'd say, 'Maybe we got 'em in the wrong place.' He had this fantastic ability to cast a person in the job that was just right for him, very often a job that hadn't existed before."

Perhaps nowhere was Walt's loyalty more in evidence than when he hired his boyhood pal and onetime stage partner, Walt Pfeiffer. Disney targeted Pfeiffer as a potential director, even though he had no experience nor special interest in making movies. The general consensus among the animators, essentially correct, was that Pfeiffer was hired because he'd been a childhood friend and was now down on his luck.

There were many at the studio who didn't appreciate what they thought was the capriciousness of Walt's loyalty. When it came to on-screen credits, in particular, Walt was thought to hog the glory. All his pictures came under the single producer credit, "Walt Disney Presents." The more famous Walt became, the greater the resentment among those who felt slighted for their contributions.

Perhaps in retaliation, from behind Hyperion's gates the old rumors began recirculating throughout Hollywood that Disney couldn't so much as sign his own name—the famous curlicue signature that was the studio's logo was just another of the departed Iwerks's many uncredited creations.

Disney did, in fact, have one of his artists, not Iwerks, create a corporate logo based on his signature, a prettier version of Walt's actual handwriting. He took great pride in it, and when called upon to actually affix his signature, he always made a big production out of inscribing what was, actually, a well-practiced copy of the copy.

According to Les Clark, Walt "lacked the patience ever to master the art of relating drawings to each other. . . . Whatever the reasons, as the techniques of animation progressed, Walt understood less and less of how it all worked. He knew the ingredients a scene should have and what the acting should be and what could be done with a scene that was not quite working, but he could not sit down at a desk and make the drawings that would demonstrate his ideas."

Recalled Arthur Babbitt: "Actually, he had no knowledge of draughtsmanship, no knowledge of music, no knowledge of literature, no knowledge of anything really, except he was a great editor. He oftentimes didn't know what he was going after, but he could spot something that was wrong in a piece of work. Many times he couldn't tell you what was wrong, nor could he ever tell you how to fix it, but he could spot it if it was wrong."

Ward Kimball concurred. "He couldn't draw very well, but he knew what was wrong, if the gag wasn't put over. He was a great gag man and had a great sense of story."

Here, an actual discussion held at a story meeting for a Goofy picture:

> *Walt:* You might want to size up the value of a good screwy chase against this stuff down here . . . second board, bottom row.
> *Jack Finney:* That should be feverish as hell. We won't stay on that long. Just a couple of little gags and the gun goes off.
> *Walt:* Snap it up! He gets the hotfoot—the tail gag—he runs like hell—the tiger grabs him, and the force pulls them both back. The gun goes off . . . then, the devastated forest. They both go up, but when they hit the ground, they're out . . . right from the explosion. . . .

This is funny, on your last board. It might be better to take out some of the stuff that might stall.

From the bunny-hug—go right out and into the last board. That second board is the kind of stuff that is liable to stall . . . last row. You have one stop there—the tiger playing with him like a kitten. I was just thinking, what does he do there—tear off the sole of the Goof's shoe? Does he lick his foot? The tiger could just lick his foot, and the Goof is taking it . . . laughing.

Jack: We could get a close-up of the rough tongue . . . sandpaper effect.

Walt: I thought he could just be having fun tickling him. What is he doing there, eating the shoe? What is the Goof doing where he has him in the pincer-hold? I wonder if the Goof could do something to him.

Jack: The same idea as the cat and the mouse. We won't have to have much narration.

Walt: What do you do—just come down on a bunch of eyes? You could come in and come up close on a pair of eyes. Maybe you come to a close-up—here's these eyes, still in the dark, and a match is struck—then reveal the elephant and the Goof. The Goof is lighting a pipe. Then, from that, let the lights come on. It's like having them against a dark drop . . . yes, and get birdcalls, *caw caw caw*, all kinds of funny sounds. What were you getting on that silent spot? Try twigs breaking now and then, etcetera. Let an echo follow the roar. Then, after that, nothing but silence—a twig could snap here and there. To get silence you need little contrasting things to create suspense, a few little sounds to make it sound silent. . . .

Walt was disturbed by the ongoing rumors of his lack of drawing skills, for reasons having perhaps less to do with his artistic abilities than his emotional makeup, if such a distinction may be made. As the self-proclaimed father figure to a staff he had personally selected, whose members he insisted were more like a family than employees, these rumors inflamed one of Walt's most nagging ongoing fears: That no matter how hard he worked and what degree of success he achieved, rather than proving how different he was from his father, it only seemed to confirm how much like Elias he really was.

And because he reacted emotionally to the rumors, he failed to recognize them for what they actually were: the early rumblings of dissent among a staff angered by Disney's refusal to acknowledge, and therefore fairly compensate, their contributions. In a field where public recognition meant higher pay, Disney's animators felt seriously shortchanged.

Typical of the growing hostility among the staff was the response to a March 19, 1934, letter published in a local Hollywood paper inquiring as to who created Felix the Cat—Pat Sullivan or Walt Disney. The following week this letter appeared in the same paper, from an anonymous Disney animator:

> In answer to "Fightin's" request for information about Felix the Cat:
>
> I am sure Felix the Cat was created by Pat Sullivan. Walt Disney created Mickey Mouse. This character was improved by Ub Iwerks, who created Pluto, Clarabelle Cow, and, I think, Pegleg Pete, all [eventually] used in Disney's productions.
>
> Walt Disney's personal achievements, since the creation of Mickey, have been largely the use of his ability in the fields of production, business, publicity, and direction, rather than his actually doing any of the things to which his name is signed. He does not draw the newspaper strip; neither does he draw any of the movies. The entire operation is done by others under his direction. Although much credit is due Disney, a great deal must be given to the account of those who perform the actual work. After all, they make the pictures.
>
> —An Animator

The unsigned letter was read aloud by one of Disney's animators during lunch hour. He was loudly cheered. This rare demonstration of open camaraderie was in marked contrast to the staff's usual method of venting anger, by seeing how many of Walt's "House Rules" they could break without getting caught.

These rules included no drinking of any kind on studio property, an admonition that didn't apply to Walt, who often drank in the afternoons behind the closed doors of his office. Although Disney suspected some of his animators kept bottles stashed in their workplaces as well, he chose to look the other way.

He did, however, remain adamant when it came to the use of proper language in the presence of women. He expected his animators to behave like gentlemen at all times. When someone did, on occasion, slip in Walt's presence and use a four-letter word in mixed company, the result was always immediate dismissal, no matter what type of professional inconvenience the firing caused.

If Walt acted the martinet to his men, to the studio's female clerks and inkers and painters he remained the epitome of courtliness. The women adored him for that as much as they enjoyed what one described as his dashing, elegant good looks, especially, according to another, his "Errol Flynn pencil mustache."* The women never confused Roy and Walt, although they were brothers. To them, Walt was the handsome one; Roy was more owlish-looking, with a round head, receding hairline, and hollow round eyes. Walt always seemed to smile with his lips more open on one side of his face to show off his great teeth. Roy, on the other hand, almost never smiled and kept his lips clenched tight.

In Walt's opinion, the "girls," as he called them, were always so much more cooperative than the men, eager to work all hours of the day and night, six days a week, seven if necessary, for their "hero."

During times of crisis, usually precipitated by insufficient cash flow, Walt often declared "For Girls Only" one-week vacations, effective immediately and without pay, as a way of making the necessary temporary layoffs as painless as possible. Invariably he would be greeted with thank-you notes, occasionally perfumed, gushing words of appreciation for his kindness and consideration.

Disney, ever on the lookout for the slightest hint of scandal among his staff, at first objected to the presence of nude models regularly hired by Don Graham for his art anatomy classes. However, Walt gave his reluctant approval after Graham insisted they were a vital part of the training program. As Disney had feared, extremely detailed drawings of the models quickly became highly coveted collector's items among the male staff and sometimes provoked the kind of artistic debate not directly related to cartoon animation.

One time after class, a former artist recalled, an argument broke out between two animators about the nature of a particular body-part movement. They resolved the argument when a young, attractive

---

*Although Disney kept his mustache the rest of his life, one of the strictest rules for his employees at Disneyland was that the boys and men have no facial hair of any kind. In 1991, the staff of the amusement park went on strike to protest the rule. The strike leader was fired, and the rule remained in effect.

female inker, known for her enjoyment of a good time, came by to pick up some cels. "It doesn't move like that," the animator said. Reaching into the shirt of the young girl, he pulled out her naked breast, flopped it up and down in his fingers, and said with great authority, *"That's* how it moves!"

On December 5, 1936, Disney's thirty-fifth birthday, at Roy's urging the studio's animators gave a party for Walt. It was held after hours in the studio's soundstage, a large room about three hundred square feet filled with various instruments and noise-effects equipment and a large screen. To protest being forced to pay homage, a couple of the animators got together and made a reel of the studio's world-famous mouse "consummating" his relationship with Minnie, their pointed metaphor for the way they felt they were being treated by Disney expressed in the act Mickey performed on his girlfriend. When the lights came up, Walt stood, applauded, praised the footage, and asked which talented animators were responsible for such fine work. The men responsible quickly raised their hands, and the smile immediately fell off Disney's face. "You're fired," he said to them, and left the party without saying another word.

After that, the staff kept their socializing to a minimum, wary of the tightening grip of what some staffers now referred to as "Waltalitarianism," fearing a single misinterpreted word to anyone could result in immediate termination. Under these conditions, few friendships between animators developed at the studio, and even fewer relationships between men and women.

When word filtered back to Walt that Arthur Babbitt was conducting private art classes for some of the studio's animators in his home, Disney immediately confronted him, demanding to know why.

"The young animators were very much interested in life drawing," recalled Babbitt, who had volunteered to tutor the new recruits on his own time. "So they showed up in my home in droves. I had to seat them on the floor, on top of orange crates. Then Disney heard about these private classes in my home and called me into his office. 'You know,' he said, 'Art, I understand you've been running these classes in your home.'

"I said that was right. 'Well,' he said, 'it wouldn't look very good in the papers if it came out that a bunch of Disney cartoonists were drawing naked women in a private home.'

"So I said, 'Well, what would you suggest?'

" 'You can use the soundstage right here,' he said. 'Set up a class here in the studio; then it would be all right.'

"Which was exactly what I did."

After that, Disney felt he had to watch Babbitt. Admittedly, he was the studio's most talented animator but also, in Walt's opinion, its biggest potential troublemaker.

EARLY IN 1935, Walt completed the story outline and production schedule for his first animated feature, *Snow White and the Seven Dwarfs*. While there was much enthusiasm among the animators for making a feature, Roy had strong reservations about the huge investment of time and money the film required.

Roy was concerned about meeting the additional salaries necessary to making the film. Although the starting base pay for most animators was still under $20, Walt had instituted a complex bonus plan based on the number of total hours per week an employee had put in at the studio. Disney's intention was to insure that during the making of *Snow White*, by rewarding loyalty, he could prevent any of his best animators from defecting. As a result, some of the artists who had been at the studio the longest took home as much as $300 a week (the same salary as Walt and Roy), while others hired during the great expansion earned $20 for doing essentially the same work.

Under this arrangement, Roy warned Walt, the budget for a feature that would undoubtedly require huge amounts of overtime would surely become astronomical. Not to worry, Walt assured Roy, the elimination of just ten shorts from the annual budget would easily make up for any cost overruns. That answer was as disturbing as the original problem to Roy. The shorts were the principle source of profit for the studio. To eliminate them for the sake of a film that would take years to complete just didn't make any sense.

Walt also insisted they now had to increase the physical size of the studio to accommodate the newly expanded staff. Walt claimed expansion indicated success, not failure, and approved the construction of a new Ink and Paint Building.

It was no secret on the lot that the studio's finances fluctuated like a spiking fever. Rumors constantly swept the working halls of an impending shutdown. One moonless February night, Walt called a meeting of the entire staff to be held on the main soundstage and issued 65-cent dinner chits, his favorite way of monitoring attendance. Rumors flew that this time the studio was actually going under.

There was, therefore, a great collective sigh of relief when Walt stood in the center of a circle of his employees like a wagon master awaiting an Indian massacre and announced that he had gathered them all together to proclaim officially the start of production on *Snow White*. After a burst of enthusiastic applause, Walt decided to act out the film's entire scenario for them. He played every character and scene: the young girl, the seven dwarfs she "adopts," the evil queen obsessed with beauty, her seduction of stepdaughter Snow White with the poisoned apple, and the arrival of Prince Charming. Once again Disney amazed his employees with his ability to shift from one portrayal to another.

A mood of hushed awe came over his audience as he slowly completed his performance by turning and seeming to actually recede into the happily ever after. A stunned silence followed, until finally one person began to clap. What followed was a thunderous round of applause, which Walt acknowledged with a smile, a nod, and the holding up of one hand, palm out, fingers spread apart. One witness later recalled the performance as effortless as "a drop of mercury rolling around on a slab of marble."

The next morning, with great fanfare, Disney issued a statement to the press that he intended to make a full-length feature film of the Grimm Brothers' classic *Snow White and the Seven Dwarfs*.

As enthusiastic as Walt appeared about *Snow White*, the nineteenth-century fairy tale hadn't been his first choice for moving into features. He had originally planned an animated version of *Alice's Adventures in Wonderland*. As early as 1931, Disney had begun preproduction on the Lewis Carroll classic that he abruptly halted when Commonwealth Pictures released its full-length, live, "all-talking" version.

Two years later Disney thought about reviving *Alice* in a combination live-action–animation format reminiscent of his early "Alice" series, to star Mary Pickford in the title role against animated backgrounds. Pickford, who happened to be one of the founders of UA, the studio's distributor, was so eager to work for Disney she offered to finance the film's half-million-dollar budget out of her own funds. Disney reluctantly canceled this production when Paramount announced it had begun filming a live-action, all-star *Alice*.

Walt next considered a live-action–animated version of *Rip Van Winkle*, featuring Will Rogers. Once again, Disney found himself doublejumped by Paramount, which held exclusive long-term rights to the Washington Irving story.

Walt then thought of making an animated version of *Babes in Toyland*. That idea had to be shelved as well when Hal Roach, who held the rights to the Victor Herbert operetta he had recently acquired as a vehicle for Laurel and Hardy, refused to let Disney negotiate for them.*

Walt had originally earmarked *Snow White* for a "Silly Symphonies." He had first viewed a silent version of the film in 1915 at a special screening for Kansas City newsboys when he was fourteen years old, one of the first films he had ever seen. The story had remained a sentimental favorite ever since. In 1933, the Fleischer studio released its own short version of the fairy tale starring its popular female character, Betty Boop. After seeing it, Walt believed the Fleischers had compressed too much story into too little time. With the other ideas for films no longer feasible, Disney finally decided to expand his own version of *Snow White* and make it his first feature.

The nation's morning papers all carried the news of Disney's latest project, hailing it as yet another innovation from Hollywood's newest favorite wunderkind. Reaction among the industry's insiders, however, was less enthusiastic, the general consensus among them being that this time Disney may have gone too far. A five- or ten-minute cartoon was one thing. Nobody, they believed, would sit through an animated feature of a gothic fairy tale. *Snow White* quickly became known as Disney's folly throughout the back lots and executive offices of the Majors.

WALT'S FIRST PRODUCTION decision was to choose a director for the feature. That assignment went to his riding partner and perhaps the closest personal friend Walt had made among the staff, Dave Hand. Hand had become privy to many of Disney's most private thoughts and feelings, particularly about Ub Iwerks, for whom Walt continued to harbor bitter feelings. "Walt confided to me that Ub did nothing

---

*Disney eventually made animated versions of both *Alice in Wonderland* and *Rip Van Winkle* (*The Legend of Sleepy Hollow*).

but 'fix' his car all day [and that] mechanics could be had much cheaper than the price of an animator."

The assignment to direct *Snow White* had been considered a plum and was sought by every animator on the lot. At one point Walt had promised the job to his brother-in-law, Bill Cottrell, but at the last minute decided Hand was the better man for it. There were also some who felt that Walt wanted to "replace" Iwerks with Hand, and that the directing assignment was seen as an attempt to win not only Hand's friendship but his lasting loyalty.

Walt personally supervised every step of production, constantly traveling from workstation to workstation, appraising sketches, revising story elements, giving green lights to proceed only when he felt the essence of what he wanted had been captured. Every day the entire creative team was once again required to watch Chaplin silent comedies, at regular speed'and slowed down, so they could analyze in detail the "magic" Charlie made and try and somehow re-create it in *Snow White*.

As the months wore on and financial pressures rose, Walt increasingly lost patience with his staff, often at the slightest provocation. Hand recalled: "[One time he] was acting out an action of one of the dwarfs. I thought, for the time allotted for that phase, that Walt was taking too long—in other words, the action would have to be cut shorter. I said so. He acted out the action again for me, ending with 'See, no problem.' He stood staring down at me, waiting for my reaction to what he presumed to be his justification. I then did something I regretted later. I had started my stopwatch that was hidden in my pocket when he'd started acting, stopping it as his action ended. I pulled out the watch and held it up for him to see. The watch proved his action was too long. He was boiling mad."

Disney's own ambivalence about his expectations for the staff made work on the film difficult. No one was ever quite sure what it was Disney wanted from them. While specific in his criticism of their work, Walt remained vague as to his overall vision of the film, preferring to let his instincts guide him. Often, in the evenings, many of the animators took to sneaking into each other's studios in the hopes of finding some clue in the next fellow's dailies that would reveal Disney's grand design.

Some animators doubted Disney had any design at all, grand or otherwise. Storyman Joe Grant recalled, "Every time he'd come into a room where the storyboards were, he'd tell the whole goddamn story of the film over again, from beginning to end, to make sure nobody got anything wrong. Each time he retold the story, it seemed to have completely changed."

It got so bad that the animators regularly rotated lookouts to listen for Walt's footsteps or telltale smoker's cough, to make sure he didn't come on without advance warning and catch them idling.

"Yeah, he'd roam the studio, especially at night," recalled animator Ward Kimball. "You could always tell when he was coming because he wore leather heels and you could hear the clickity-clack down the hallway. Of course, everyone would become very busy when they'd hear that sound."

To capture a sense of realism in the physical movements of Snow White, Walt hired a young dancer, Marjorie Belcher, to pose in costume for Arthur Babbitt, the artist charged with animating the character. Disney had previously used Belcher (who became famous later on as Marge Champion, wife and dancing partner of noted choreographer Gower Champion) as a model for the lead in the "Silly Symphonies" *The Goddess of Spring*. One of several pre-*Snow White* "test runs," the primary purpose of *The Goddess of Spring* was to test new animation techniques.

Babbitt shot live-action footage of Belcher dancing and acting out scenes from the script on the studio's soundstage, after which he broke the film down frame by frame to unlock the component parts of Belcher's graceful motions. The two soon became involved in an intense sexual affair that violated one of Disney's strictest "House Rules."

In spite of several discreet warnings from Roy, Babbitt refused to end it. When Walt heard about what was going on, he decided to fire both of them. Their sudden, surprise marriage saved their jobs. Disney reluctantly allowed them to remain at the studio but removed Babbitt from any further work on the character of Snow White, reassigning him instead to the Wicked Queen.

Production dragged on, the already laborious process of animation further slowed by Walt's sometimes maddeningly instinctual perfectionism. Money was never a consideration to him if a sequence didn't look or sound exactly right. By the end of the first year, when the film's original $250,000 budget had doubled, Joseph Rosenberg, of the Bank of America, became alarmed and warned Disney if he didn't control the spending, the studio's line of credit would have to be cut off.

The threat couldn't have come at a worse time. In addition to production costs, the studio owed $1 million in payroll, for a staff that had by now swelled to 1,150 employees, and construction fees to provide enough working space for them. At one point Walt, in a moment of graveyard humor, suggested to Roy they ought to change the title *Snow White* to *Frankenstein*, after the film in which the monster kills its creator.

Rosenberg demanded to see whatever footage the studio had produced before releasing any more of the bank's money. Disney had a reel put together and arranged a private screening for Rosenberg, to be viewed, at Walt's insistence, from the notorious sweatbox. Upon its completion, an overheated Rosenberg immediately agreed to reopen the flow of cash from the bank, telling Walt, almost matter-of-factly, "That thing is going to make you a hatful of money."

Late that evening, after everyone else had gone home, Walt, as he often did, went down to the floor of the main soundstage where he liked to walk in slow circles, munching on saltines or cracking open peanuts from the stash he always kept in his suit pockets, dropping the shells to the floor as he planned his next day's schedule. This night, as he walked, he noticed an unsigned note attached to the projection screen with the words STICK TO SHORTS printed in big letters.

The next morning Walt launched a full-scale investigation to find out who had written it. Although the culprit was never found, rumors persisted for weeks among the staff that the note's author was his brother Roy.

Walt then split his animators into three units and scheduled three daily eight-hour shifts so that production could continue uninterrupted around the clock, seven days a week, until the film's completion. And he planned to remain at the studio for as much of that time as possible.

Part of the reason he preferred his office couch to his own bed was that, during the long and difficult days spent working on *Snow White*, production of another sort had taken place at home: the arrival, on

December 31, 1936, of a second daughter, Sharon Mae. Walt found it impossible to pay full attention to both his imaginary new "daughter" Snow White and his real-life one. He soon made his priorities clear by staying away from home days at a time.

The pressure to complete his film and assume the role of real-life father again caused Disney's nervous condition to flare up. His facial tics returned, worse than ever, and his smoking went back up to three packs a day. His hair started falling out in clumps, and in one of the few trips he made outside the studio's front gates, he visited the same medical specialist who was treating Gary Cooper's thinning problem.

ALL DURING the making of *Snow White*, the Mickey Mouse and "Silly Symphonies" cartoons remained as popular as ever, and Walt continued to receive accolades for them. In January 1937, a month after he turned thirty-six, he was named as the Junior Chamber of Commerce's 1936 "Outstanding Young Man," an annual award presented to the one individual under thirty-five who had made the most valuable contribution to his community. The award, considered among the most prestigious in the country, was given to Walt Disney, according to the inscription on the plaque: "Because of his work among young men and his contributions to the world through his animated cartoons."

Both Will Hays and A. P. Giannini were on the selection committee, and each, for reasons of his own, did what he could to see to it that Disney received the award. While Hays regarded Disney as the best representative of the industry's moral standards, Giannini, the chairman of the Bank of America, hoped Walt's continued popularity would translate into big box-office returns.

In spite of Walt's special request that she attend, Lillian refused to see him accept the award. This only added to the rising tensions between them. After one stretch of several weeks when he didn't go home at all, Lillian let him know in no uncertain terms her opinion of his prolonged absences, particularly with a new child that had to be cared for. Walt promised to come home more often and did, until Sharon's constant all-night crying drove him back to his studio sofa, where he slept for the duration of the making of *Snow White*.

Walt's physical stress intensified after *The Goddess of Spring* received a negative review in the *Hollywood Citizen-News*. A few days later, the paper published a long, rambling, anonymous response to the review that it had received in the mail:

Your dramatic critic, Elizabeth Yeaman, and her vicious article on Walt Disney in the Saturday, April 13th edition are the reasons for this verbal spanking.

I don't mind her tearing one of his pictures apart, though her criticisms were based primarily on the fact that Disney didn't follow the original fairy tale verbatim; and her very generous attitude toward the unknowns behind the scenes were gratifying—but. . . .

Without any reason or any knowledge of Walt Disney—his character, his habits, his attitude toward his work, and his employees—Miss Yeaman sailed into him with a vengeance, casting a number of slurring insinuations about his success going to his head—polo ponies and swimming pools destroying his idealistic incentives and crowding out his work—and more baseless claptrap along the same lines.

I've worked for and with Walt Disney for three years; so I might be in a position to straighten out Miss Yeaman's distorted ideas of him. The man works harder than anyone else in the studio. He gets in at eight and leaves—Lord knows when. He comes back nights and during vacations. All of his social activities, his sports, his family, everyone and everything play second fiddle to his work.

The fact that Walt Disney has doubled his staff and expenditure on pictures in three years, that he maintains classes in story construction and art classes [*sic*] during working hours, that he follows each picture personally from the time a germ of a story first presents itself—somewhat belies Miss Yeaman's intimation that he is just a disinterested bystander.

The men that work with him are artists in their own rights; but without Disney's inspiration and controlling influence, without his stubborn determination to constantly better the pictures, without his ability to draw out of his men more than they themselves feel capable of, these same artists might shine as individuals, but the pictures would be a hodge-podge.

I could go on and on, but I just aim to show that Miss Yeaman rid herself of a grouch without bothering herself about the truth. I would be delighted to show Miss Yeaman just how wrong she is. My sentiments are just a weak reflection of the feelings predominant among the men here.

                                                    —A Disney Artist

The general concensus among artists at the studio was that Walt Disney had written the letter himself.

Then, four days later, another one appeared.

For shame, Miss Yeaman! How dare you write an article criticizing a Disney picture? In fact, how could you have strayed so far from the path of righteousness as to even think a Disney cartoon was less than perfection? Don't you ever read anything? Do you not realize that to write anything other than glowing praise of Mr. Disney smacks of sacrilege?

I can only say that I am stunned: I am spellbound. The old question again arises, "What is the world coming to"? [*sic*] And you were not alone in your wayward jaunt in journalism. You have involved your typewriter. Dear me!

If, in the future, you see a Disney cartoon that is inclined to be just a wee bit "lousee," repeat to yourself one hundred times each day, "It must be good, because it is a Disney cartoon." If you will follow this simple advice you will find it very easy "to fall in line" with "Disney Artist" whose delightful tirade appeared in Friday's paper.

                                                    —Ex Disney Artist

While Disney had no visible reaction to the first letter, the second one threw him into an open rage. Although he was convinced Iwerks had written it, most staffers believed the real author was Art Babbitt, in retaliation for what everyone considered his unfair treatment during the making of *Snow White*.

FINALLY, toward the end of 1937, after nearly four difficult years of trial, experimentation, and artistic and financial crises, production on the film seemed to be nearing completion. At the same time Disney's initial distribution deal with United Artists was about to end. In order to continue their arrangement, UA informed Disney they expected him to sign over all future television rights to his entire inventory. Even though at the time Disney knew absolutely nothing about television, in fact had never even heard of it, he nevertheless held to his longstanding position of retaining all copyrights to his films.

Unable to come to terms, Disney and UA ended their relationship. Walt then accepted an offer from RKO which included increased advances for all shorts and a guarantee to distribute *Snow White* sight unseen. Walt made the switch in spite of RKO's reputation as the worst-managed of the Majors, simply because he had no other options. Still, the loss of UA's financial support had threatened to disrupt final production work on *Snow White* and, conceivably, the studio's entire schedule.

The pressure to find a new distributor had placed an even greater strain on Disney. Roy, worried about his brother's worsening nervous condition, took a cue from Walt's first nervous breakdown. He tried for weeks to lure him away from the studio's day-to-day pressures. Roy finally found a way in the continuing worldwide success of *The Three Little Pigs*, when the film took third prize at the Soviet International Film Festival.

Roy declined the invitation for Walt to come to Moscow for the presentation. However, it did give him the idea for a European working vacation for himself, Walt, Lillian, Walt's brother-in-law Bill Cottrell, and all their wives. With Lillian and Bill's help, Roy convinced Walt the trip was a terrific opportunity to promote worldwide interest in *Snow White*. Believing the film was almost finished, Walt agreed to make the journey overseas.

Throughout Europe, huge crowds greeted Walt wherever he appeared, cheering him as if he were royalty. The mass adulation proved an effective palliative for Walt's nerves. Overnight, it seemed, his twitching stopped, he cut back on his smoking, his hair stopped falling out, and the obliging smile he always reserved for the public eased back onto his face.

Wherever the group traveled, Walt Disney's name appeared in giant letters on movie marquees hailing his arrival. The European press declared Disney the greatest American filmmaker since Charlie Chaplin. The most famous international figures in film, literature, religion, science, and politics lined up for the privilege of meeting him. In England, Disney dined with the royal family and met privately with H. G. Wells. In Rome, he was granted private audiences with both the Pope and Mussolini. In Paris, the League of Nations awarded him a special medal, which Walt accepted using the voice of Mickey Mouse.

Three months later, a revitalized Walt Disney returned to Hollywood ready to kick his staff into overdrive for the ten-week final push on *Snow White*. Finally, in December 1937, production on the film was completed, and the first screening was held in a theater in nearby Pomona, a screening which nearly caused a relapse of Disney's nervous condition.

"That preview was unsettling," recalled Wilfred Jackson, one of the film's sequence directors. "The audience seemed to be enjoying the film, laughing, applauding. But about three quarters of the way through, one-third of them got up and walked out. Everybody else kept responding enthusiastically to *Snow White* right to the end, but we were concerned about that third. Later we found out they were local college students who had to get back for their ten o'clock dormitory curfew."

Snow White and The Seven Dwarfs had its official world premiere on December 21, 1937, at the Carthay Circle in Hollywood. That theater had become Walt's sentimental choice for every premiere since the night they gave Mickey Mouse his first screening. Afterward, Disney hosted a private party for the entire staff on the grounds of the Hyperion studio, where the accumulation of four years of intense, competitive work and personal and professional frustration gave way to the joy of victorious accomplishment. Everyone except a very exhausted Disney was in a happy frame of mind. Several animators decided to play one retaliatory practical joke on Walt, hoping it would serve as an effective release for their long pent-up frustrations.

Recalled one animator, "I remember we framed Walt, who was seated at a table with friends and family. I made an arrangement with the policeman on duty there, without Walt's knowledge, to go over and tell him to quiet down, that he was making too much noise. Walt's reaction was 'I'll have your badge,' that sort of thing. It was finally revealed it was all a joke, and everyone had a good laugh. Except Walt, who I don't think found it very funny."

From its opening night, *Snow White* drew capacity crowds and raves from the critics. The *New York Times* called it one of the ten best films of the year.

The *New York Herald Tribune* critic stated: "After seeing *Snow*

White for the third time, I am more certain than ever that it belongs with the few great masterpieces of the screen . . . one of those rare works of inspired artistry that weaves an irresistible spell around the beholder . . . a memorable and deeply enriching experience."

Time magazine put Disney's picture on its cover, surrounded by the seven dwarfs, and hailed the film as a masterpiece, declaring that "Walt Disney is no more a [mere] cartoonist than Whistler."

By the end of its first week, *Snow White* had become the first must-see film of the new year, and eventually outgrossed notable contemporary works of the time including two of Spencer Tracy's most popular movies, *Captains Courageous* and *Boys Town**; Bette Davis in *Jezebel*; Errol Flynn in *The Adventures of Robin Hood*; and Frank Capra's *You Can't Take It With You*.

In its initial run, *Snow White* played to an audience of more than twenty million ticket buyers and grossed more than $8 million, at a time when the average price of admission was 25 cents. *Snow White and the Seven Dwarfs* souvenirs proved even more profitable than those for *The Three Little Pigs*. The first year after it was released, *Variety* listed *Snow White* among one of Hollywood's "all-time box-office champs."†

At the 1938 Academy ceremonies, Disney was given a second Special Award, a full-size Oscar and seven small ones, for the film's "significant screen innovation which has charmed and pioneered a great new entertainment field for the motion picture cartoon."

Snow White was dubbed into ten languages and distributed in forty-six countries. Foreign audiences proved as enthusiastic as American viewers had been except in England, where the government's censors declared it unfit for children to see, fearing it would give them nightmares. The film produced three hit songs, "Whistle While You Work," "Someday My Prince Will Come," and "Heigh Ho," written by Frank Churchill and Larry Morey.

Twenty years later, an international poll of film scholars was conducted to determine what three films from each year they deemed worthy of preservation. The films that received the most votes for

---

*Tracy won an Academy Award for his performance in 1937's *Captains Courageous*. *Boys Town* was released early in 1938.

† Prior to its highly anticipated 1993 rerelease, the film had grossed more than $100 million.

1937 were Jean Renoir's *Grand Illusion*, Leni Riefenstahl's *Olympiad*, and Walt Disney's *Snow White and the Seven Dwarfs*.

WITH *Snow White*, Walt Disney succeeded in expanding the artistic boundaries of animation and by doing so increased its commercial appeal, a rare achievement in a medium that has always favored the reliability of familiarity over the risks of experimentation.

Like all great artists, Disney's canvas was the battleground for the conflict between his intellect and his emotion. His intellectual adaptation of Snow White's maternal relation to her dwarfs presented an idealized version of his emotional identification with the material, particularly in his self-described paternalistic relation to his employees. In Snow White's struggle to control her own destiny, threatened by the dark forces of evil, Disney found a powerful metaphor for his ongoing struggle to survive in what he perceived as Hollywood's darkly competitive arena.

Disney's faithfulness to the literal surface of his source material allowed his film to find a wide audience among children. It was, however, its classic resonance that also helped project his inner conflicts and made *Snow White* equally alluring, if not more so, to adults. Out of the professional chaos of his work and the emotional insecurities of his life, Disney produced a unified work of enormous depth, at once fundamental and sophisticated, dark and luminescent, tangible and illusory, individual yet universal.

The film's basic theme also managed to strike a critical social nerve. Snow White's struggle against her frightful stepmother became a vivid metaphor identifying the fears of a nation about to enter a world war where the dark forces of evil seemed to threaten America's very existence. On every level, then, *Snow White* was a towering achievement, as compelling as anything yet produced by any American filmmaker or studio.

Its success inspired Disney to begin production on three more features: *Pinocchio, Bambi*, and what would eventually become *Fantasia*. Knowing now it took at least three years to make a cartoon feature, he scheduled the start of these new productions more or less simultaneously, so he could eventually release one new full-length animated feature every year.

Early in 1939, to accommodate the new production schedule and the chronic problem of staff overcrowding—animators' desks were

now lined up four in a row in tiny rooms, mass-production style—
Walt and Roy purchased fifty-one acres of undeveloped land in
Burbank for $100,000 and broke ground on a new $4.5 million
twenty-building studio complex.

And so Walt Disney began the new year on a high note, unaware
that his moment of triumph was about to be overshadowed by people
and events darker and more evil than anything he had ever dreamed
of putting on film.

An extremely rare photo of Elias and Flora Disney, taken in 1934 at the Chicago World's Fair.

RETURN OF A BIRTH.

State of Illinois,
COOK COUNTY.

The Physician, Accoucheur or person in compliance should immediately upon this Certificate, separately filled out, to the County Clerk. Penalty $10 if it not so certified and returned within thirty days.

VITAL STATISTICS DEPARTMENT. COUNTY CLERK'S OFFICE.

1. *Full Name of Child (if any)* .... *Walter Disney*
2. *Sex* .... *Boy* Race or Color (if not of the white race) ....
3. *Number of Child of this Mother* .... *2 Child*
4. *Date of this Birth* .... *20 December 90*
5. †*Place of Birth.* No. *3515 Vernon As.* Street ....
6. *Residence of Mother,* .... " " ....
7. Nationality: Place of Birth: Age of:
   a. *Father* .... *American* .... *Canada America* *34* *26*
   b. *Mother* ....
8. *Full Name of Mother* .... *Flora Disney*
9. *Maiden Name of Mother* .... *Flora Call*
10. *Full Name of Father* .... *Elis Disney*
11. *Occupation of Father* .... *Carpenter*

Name and Address of other Attendants, if any .... Returned by *Mrs. S. Apple* } M.D. Midwife

Dated *8 January* 1891.   Residence *2946 South Park As.*

* The above name of the child should be certified, if possible, when this Certificate is made, and should in any case, be certified and registered within a year.
† City, number, street and ward; same in towns that have them; township or precinct.

An official photostat of a Return of Birth record for Walter Disney, born January 8, 1891, ten years before his "actual" birth. Were the records tampered with? Was Disney's name entered on in the wrong year?

Irrefutable evidence that no birth certificate exists for Walt Disney in Chicago for December 5, 1901.

The application must be in duplicate and accompanied by three unmounted photographs of the applicant, not larger than three by three inches in size, one of which is to be affixed to the passport by the Department; the other two must be attached to the application and its duplicate, respectively. The photographs must be on thin paper and should have a light background. The one not affixed to the application should be signed by the applicant across its face, so as not to obscure the features.

Filed on the 1975 filer block.

[FORM FOR NATIVE CITIZEN.]

[Act of June 4, 1917.]

The fee of one dollar, either in currency or postal money order, must accompany the application.

A widow's application must state whether she is married or not, and a married woman must state whether her husband is a native citizen.

The rules should be carefully read before mailing the application to the Department of State, Bureau of Citizenship, Washington, D. C.

UNITED STATES OF AMERICA.

STATE OF .... } ss:

COUNTY OF ....

NOV 14 1918

I, WALTER E. DISNEY ...., A NATIVE AND LOYAL CITIZEN OF THE UNITED STATES, hereby apply to the Department of State, at Washington, for a passport.

I solemnly swear that I was born at ...... CHICAGO ...., in the State of ILLINOIS ...., on or about the ...5... day of ...December..., 1...909...; that my {father / husband} ...Elias Disney..................., was born in ...Canada..............., and is now residing at ...1523 Ogden Ave....Chicago, Ill.............................

†[that he emigrated to the United States from the port of ...., on or about ...the year 1878, 1........; that he resided ...40...... years, uninterruptedly, in the United States, from 1...878...to 1...918... at ......Chicago, Illinois.............; that he was naturalized as a citizen of the United States before the ...../.......... Court of ...., at ......I do not know..., on ...., 1..., X,as shown by the accompanying Certificate of Naturalization]; that I have resided outside the United States at the following places for the following periods: ...never have............. from .... to .... from .... to ...1523 Ogden Ave.. and that I am domiciled in the United States, my permanent residence being at ...Chicago,........ in the State of ...Illinois..............., where I follow the occupation of ...Chauffeur, U.S. Post My last passport was obtained from ......never have................, on .... and was .... (Disposition of passport.) I am about to go abroad temporarily; and I intend to return to the United States within ...one... {months / years} with the purpose of residing and performing the duties of citizenship therein; and I desire a passport for use in visiting the countries hereinafter named for the following purpose:

...Great Britain............. .....American Red Cross......
(Name of country.)   (Object of visit.)
...France................... .....American Red Cross......
(Name of country.)   (Object of visit.)
....American Red Cross......
(Name of country.)   (Object of visit.)

I intend to leave the United States from the port of ....New York City.............. sailing on board the .... on ...., 191 (Name of vessel.)   (Date of departure.)

OATH OF ALLEGIANCE.

Further, I do solemnly swear that I will support and defend the Constitution of the United States against all enemies, foreign and domestic; that I will bear true faith and allegiance to the same; and that I take this obligation freely, without any mental reservation or purpose of evasion: So help me God.

Walter E. Disney
(Signature of applicant.)

Sworn to before me this ...29th.... day of ...August......... 19..18.

Blanche L. Adrian

Deputy Clerk of the ...U. S. Dist.... Court at ...Chicago..

†A person born in the United States should submit a birth certificate with his application, or if the birth was not legally recorded, affidavits from the attending physician, parents, or other persons having actual knowledge ...

If the applicant's father was born in this country, lines should be drawn through the blanks in bracket.

[OVER.]

Still another date of birth for Disney, this one faked by Walt himself to get into the Red Cross. Note the actual "Disney" signature as opposed to the later famous "curlicue" drawn by artists on his staff.

Former Disney staffer Leo Salkin demonstrated how any rabbit can be turned into any mouse, an object lesson Disney learned doing battle with Universal over the rights to Oswald the Rabbit, and the subsequent creation of Mickey Mouse. (Leo Salkin)

Disney's brother-in-law, William Cottrell, as drawn by former Disney staffer Joe Grant in 1991. (Joe Grant)

A supermarket stands where the original Hyperion Studio was built. A plaque commemorating the site was stolen several years ago and has never been replaced. (Marc Eliot)

The "Rancheros Visitadores" 1931 annual ride over the Santa Ynez Range. Dave Hand (third from left) followed by Walt (center, black hat. (Martha Hand)

Walt (left) and Roy, in 1932. (Joe Grant)

Walter entertaining the Barrymores on their visit to the studio. (Joe Grant/Bill Cottrell)

Joe Grant (left) and Walt, at the studio. A rare shot of Disney with a drink and a bottle of scotch in his hands. (Joe Grant)

Walt Disney "auditioning" the studio's female employees. By suggesting he was shifting to "live action" movies, he hoped to intimidate his animators into not striking. June Paterson is second from the left. (June Paterson)

The controversial cartoon panel with the "swastika" imbedded in the musical notes. (FBI document 61-7560-9276)

Arthur Babbitt, standing, and Dave Hilberman, seated immediately to his right, at a pre-strike meeting. (Leo Salkin)

Babbitt (left) and Hilberman during the strike. (Leo Salkin)

Two views of the picket line. (June Paterson)

EIGHT

A New Language of Art, An Old Sense of Rage

SNOW WHITE'S SUCCESS convinced Hollywood that Disney not only was its best moral figurehead but, because his first feature actually made money, a commercially viable filmmaker as well. To the academic world, however, the film signaled the arrival of an important new American artist. In 1938, Disney received an honorary Master of Arts degree from Harvard University for his work in the field of cinematography and animated cartooning, and an honorary Master of Fine Arts degree from Yale for having "created a new language of art."

Every newspaper in the country continued to want to interview Walt, eager to learn about Disney the man. As always, he cannily kept the press focused on his work, to protect the smooth façade of his public persona from any blemishes of reality.

This was a strategy that had always worked well for Walt. For instance, when it was widely reported in 1936 during the making of *Snow White* that Lillian had given birth to a second child, the story proved an easy sell. Few people outside the immediate family ever had any personal contact with Lillian and would therefore have no way of knowing she hadn't given birth. In truth, she hadn't even been pregnant. The whole story was a lie intended to cover up the fact that the Disneys' new baby was adopted.

Walt's inability to successfully impregnate Lillian had pushed their already tenuous relationship closer to the edge when Lillian, during the making of *Snow White*, threatened to file for divorce. To save his marriage, Walt agreed to her ultimatum they either adopt a baby or go their separate ways.

While this solution may have solved one problem for Lillian, it raised another for Walt. The act of adoption intensified his childhood fear that he himself might have been secretly adopted, made worse by Lillian's insistence they pretend the child was their own.

Lillian's choice of Sharon Mae as their new daughter further upset Walt, who had often expressed a desire to have a son. He had long envied his brother's having been blessed with a son, Roy Edward, nine years earlier, after which Walt longed for a boy of his own. When the opportunity finally came, however, Lillian insisted a girl was a better childhood companion for three-year-old Diane.

Once she brought Sharon home from the private adoption agency, Lillian focused all her energies and attention on her new baby. To Walt, the infant's all-night crying seemed to echo the stridency of their discordant marriage. He finally retreated to the sanctuary of his studio, the castle where he reigned as king, able to exert the kind of absolute control over his professional family he couldn't manage over his real one.

In part, the failure of his home life may explain why Disney took it so personally whenever his studio "children" misbehaved. One such incident occurred upon *Snow White*'s completion. As a way to express his thanks to the entire staff for all their hard work, Disney offered a free "Thank You" weekend at Lake Narco, in northern California. Every employee who had worked on the film was invited to join Mr. and Mrs. Disney and their two children for what Walt envisioned as a two-day mini-retreat filled with hiking, swimming, barbecues, and church services.

What actually took place more closely resembled a Roman orgy. After nearly four years of high-pressure performance, the mostly single young men and women—the average age of the staff was twenty-six—were ready to release a little steam. Walt's number-one rule that no alcohol be consumed was totally ignored, and under the full moon, passions unbridled as quickly as belts and buckles. By midnight, models, inkers, painters, secretaries, and personal assistants eagerly hopped from the tents and cabins of one animator after another, until by dawn most everyone wound up the night with a naked group skinny-dip in the lake.

Predictably, Disney was outraged. Early Saturday morning, without saying a word, Walt packed his car and, with Lillian and children in tow, drove back to Los Angeles. He never again made any reference to the incident at Lake Narco, and nobody ever dared to bring it up in his presence.

As far as Disney was concerned, his staff's behavior had been unforgivable, and he planned dozens of dismissals. A wholesale bloodletting might very well have taken place had Roy not convinced Disney that with three new features in various stages of production, the studio couldn't afford to lose so much as a single animator. Roy knew what Walt didn't, that the employees had decided among themselves if even a single person was fired as a result of what had taken place at the lake, they would all quit.

Again, because he reacted emotionally, Disney missed the deeper significance of the message his workers had sent that weekend. This was a staff exhausted by four years of work on the most difficult project of their young careers, frustrated by the lack of individual recognition, angered by an unfair salary structure that rewarded those Walt personally favored, and fed up by the studio's parochial code of behavior in a town that thrived on social gaiety and sexual abandon.

While the time, place, and manner of Disney's staff protest was unique, the sentiment behind it wasn't. The conflict between Hollywood's workers and management that had existed for the better part of the decade threatened to crack wide open after the 1934 California gubernatorial campaign. This election pitted Upton Sinclair, the Pulitzer Prize–winning novelist, an End-Poverty-In-California (EPIC) Democrat and Socialist sympathizer, against conservative Republican Frank Merriam. The contest helped coalesce the film industry's individual trade unions to form a united front in support of Sinclair.

One of their prime issues focused on the actions of several studios, including Disney's, which had, at Gunther Lessing's urging, followed MGM's lead of mandatory contributions to the Merriam campaign. All employees, regardless of personal preference or political affiliation, provided donations deducted in advance from their paycheck. Lessing was convinced that left unchecked it was only a matter of time before the "subversive" unions would destroy Disney's studio. Despite the studios' outrageous actions, again, little direct protest was heard from the workers. According to Ward Kimball, at Disney, the reason was simply that "you took it, because if you didn't, you were fired."

In a move to counteract the growing momentum of the guilds, most studios granted workers the right to join "house" unions, set up, run, and regulated by management. Disney, however, in spite of repeated warnings from Lessing and the Academy, remained convinced his employees were content with their working conditions and that no additional action was necessary.

Joe Grant recalled, "This one Saturday I came to work, and Walt happened to be there. He came out of the soundstage and saw me working at the desk. 'You know, Joe,' he said, with a sense of pride at the way things were going, 'this whole place runs on a kind of Jesus Christ communism.' "

In that moment of distorted pride, Walt sounded eerily like the Elias he remembered from his childhood.

DISNEY TOOK great pride in the new Burbank studio, which had its official opening in the fall of 1939, what he liked to call "the house that *Snow White* built." Walt considered the studio both a reflection of his success and his gift of gratitude to the more than one thousand employees now on the payroll. Like the new house he had built for Lillian and the two children, the studio was a reflection of his sense of the paternal: Disney as the provider for both his families.

The main animation building was completely air-conditioned, still a rare luxury in the thirties. Every office in it had, at Walt's insistence, a private bathroom. There was also a private coffee shop; private lounge; completely equipped gymnasium; four soundstages; an orchestra stage; a modern theater for studio previews; and a rooftop penthouse club with sun decks, umbrellas, tables, chairs, and sunning mattresses.

Disney took great pleasure in a studio press release describing the club as a "womanless paradise for the recreational use of the Disney male employees. The women may have taken over the bars and the barber shops, but they still can't crash the profession of animation.

The only skirted artists in the studio are the girls who trace the animators' drawings onto celluloid and paint them."

The rest of the sprawling complex included an administration building; an art school; a picnic area for employees; a baseball diamond; a small, well-kept zoo where animators could study the movements of live animals; and a girls' cafeteria "enabling the inkers and painters to buy delicious lunches at minimum prices."

Disney kept an eye on every operational aspect of the complex, down to the smallest detail. When Hazel Cottrell was put in charge of the all-girl division of the inkers and painters and instituted a fifteen-minute tea break for her group, every morning and every afternoon, she insisted that with their tea each female employee be given two cookies. Wednesdays the choice of cookies was Lorna Doone. Shortly after, a note appeared from Walt on the studio bulletin board, which read:

> To whom it may concern:
> While self preservation is one of the first instincts of nature, consideration for others is the keystone for civilization. Will those girls who have been taking more than their alloted shares of their cookies, especially on "Lorna Doone Day," please consider their fellow workers.

In a press release that Disney personally wrote for the new studio's official opening, he took the opportunity to express in the third person, which he preferred when writing about himself, his opinion that Burbank was the perfect creative environment, a place where management and workers coexisted in rapturous harmony:

> This new streamlined motion picture city is a dream come true—a dream whose realization was made possible by the faith of Walt Disney and the band of men and women who are proud to work with him. . . . One of Walt Disney's greatest wishes has always been that his employees could work in ideal surroundings, as the Dean of animated cartoons realizes that a happy personnel turns out the best work.

It was as if Walt was trying to convince himself, as much as anyone else, how well he took care of his workers. Walt expressed his concerns to a newspaper reporter over the well-being of his workers:

They strive all their lives to accumulate a lot of money and achieve success, and when they finally reach that success, their physical condition is such that they cannot enjoy it. It is my ambition . . . to [run] my studio on a basis where all the men connected with me can enjoy life while earning their living and storing away for a rainy day.

Disney's skeptical workers may not have taken his words to heart, but there were others who did. Shortly after that nationally syndicated interview appeared, Walt's two eldest brothers, neither of whom he had heard from for several years, suddenly showed up in Hollywood to seek out their now famous sibling, a pilgrimage Roy described as nothing so much as "bees to the honeypot."

Raymond, now forty-nine, had decided to move his marginally successful insurance business from Kansas City to Hollywood, where he hoped to set up an on-site life insurance program for Disney's employees. At the same time, Herbert, fifty, requested and received a transfer from the main branch of the Portland, Oregon, post office, where he had risen to the level of district manager, to Hollywood, hoping to find a job for his daughter at Walt's studio. So eager was Herbert to make the move, he left behind Elias, now in his eighties, and Flora, nearly seventy, alone in the Portland house.

A month after Herbert's arrival, Roy traveled to Oregon to see how his parents were getting along. When he returned, he told Walt they ought to move them to Hollywood. For $8,000 in cash, the two brothers bought a brand-new cottage for Elias and Flora in Toluca Lake, just north of Burbank.

No sooner had he settled in than Elias started to visit the studio every day, dressed in overalls and with hammer in hand, to help out in any way he could. Walt sent him to the scenery shop, where Elias assisted in the building of sets, repairing motor engines, and mounting flats. Elias's hands-on presence instigated a bizarre rumor that spread throughout Hollywood and persists to this day, that his frugal practicality had influenced Walt to have the halls of the new studio made unusually wide, so that in case it failed, the buildings could be sold to the hospital across from the main entrance. According to Bill Cottrell, there is absolutely no truth to the story, even though Disney never denied it and may have in fact started it himself, to please Elias.

A week after his parents moved into their new house, Walt invited his mother, who had turned increasingly frail with age, to tour the studio. Flora, like Lillian, had become something of a recluse and at first refused. After much prodding, a determined Walt finally convinced her to attend a private screening of *Snow White*. Having never been inside a movie theater, Flora feared she wouldn't be able to sit through a full-length feature. Instead, Walt showed her *Steamboat Willie*.

Afterward, he asked his mother what she thought of the film. He was stung by her comment that Mickey Mouse, for whom Walt had done the voice, sounded too much like a little girl. Walt had just given the green light for the next Mickey short, *The Sorcerer's Apprentice*, which eventually became part of the full-length feature *Fantasia*, the only film since the advent of sound in which the little mouse doesn't so much as utter a single word.

A month after Elias and Flora had moved into their new home, Roy's son, Roy Edward (Roy E.), began to pay his grandparents a visit each day after school. On the afternoon of November 29, 1938, Roy E. knocked at Elias and Flora's front door and was let in by a tall stranger, a doctor who quietly informed him that his grandmother had passed way.

When Walt received news of his mother's death, he was seized with grief and locked himself away in his office. He refused to see anyone, including Lillian, until it was time to attend the funeral, after which he returned home and refused to discuss the subject of his mother's passing. Walt's grief was compounded by an overpowering sense of guilt once he learned the results of an autopsy that showed Flora's death was caused by fumes from a defective water boiler in the house *that he had helped pick out for her.*

Although Flora's demise was officially listed on her death certificate as "accidental asphyxiation," there is some question as to the actual circumstances of her passing. With the advancing years, Walt's mother, upset at having to go through yet another uprooting, had become increasingly despondent after an emotionally detached lifetime spent under Elias's unstable domination.

Unanswered questions regarding her death include what she was doing in the basement of the house; how, if her body was reportedly found on the kitchen floor, she succumbed to the "defective" basement boiler's pilot vent; why a new and presumably well-ventilated house would have a defective boiler in the first place; why no one had detected the smell of gas anywhere in the house; and why Elias hadn't succumbed in the days just prior to her death, which he spent setting up his workshop in the basement.

If, in fact, the boiler wasn't defective, another possible scenario emerges, one in which a severely depressed Flora, rather than suffocating in the kitchen, goes down to the basement, blows out the boiler's pilot light, either lies down next to its vent and inhales the poison fumes, or shuts all the windows and returns to the kitchen to die. Whatever the actual motivation, location, and cause, Flora's death inspired not only an intensified feeling of guilt in Disney, but a renewed sense of rage at her having once more let him down with this final, ultimate abandonment.

WHEN Disney was finally able to return to production, the first thing he did was to rework the plot of one of the scheduled animated features, *Pinocchio*. He ordered nearly all completed footage discarded in favor of a new script that eliminated any mention of the puppetmaker Gepetto's wife. Instead, Disney emphasized the little wooden puppet's wish to become the flesh-and-blood son to the kindly old man who had created him.

NINE

A Means of Absolute Identity

To BRING *Pinocchio** to the screen, Disney put together a team of those he considered his most talented artists, among them Ben Sharpsteen, Hamilton Luske, Bill Cottrell, Fred Moore, Frank Thomas, Bill Tytla, Ward Kimball, Wolfgang Reitherman, Marjorie Belcher (the live model for the Blue Fairy), and Arthur Babbitt.

There was a last-minute addition that surprised everyone, perhaps none more than Disney himself. Early in 1940, just before production actually began, Walt learned that in spite of the modest success of the "Flip the Frog" series he did for MGM, Ub Iwerks had lost the long struggle to keep his independent Hollywood animation studio alive.

When Iwerks, through mutual friends, let it be known he was interested in returning to the Disney studio, Ben Sharpsteen arranged what proved to be an awkward meeting. Over drinks one evening in the Polo Lounge of the Beverly Hills Hotel, Iwerks and Disney kept a polite verbal distance, avoiding any talk of defections and broken promises.

---

*No one was quite sure why Disney chose *Pinocchio* to follow *Snow White*. One of his animators, Norm Ferguson, claimed he passed along a copy of the original fable to Walt. Disney, however, insisted he found it himself, quite by accident, at the children's branch of his local library, where he liked to search for stories to make into movies.

It wasn't until the next day that Walt offered Iwerks the job of heading the studio's technical research division. Iwerks accepted, a position he would hold for the next thirty years. He immediately began working on refining the multiplane system, a process whereby cels could be photographed in layers to create the illusion of physical depth, a technique that would prove crucial to *Pinocchio*'s visual style.

According to Iwerks's son, in spite of their professional reconciliation, there was no rekindling of the personal friendship between Walt and Ub. Contrary to what has been written elsewhere, they rarely, if ever, socialized away from the studio and hardly spoke to one another during the day. To be rehired, Iwerks had to agree to accept no percentage of what would prove to be enormous licensing profits from any technical achievements, including the multiplane system.

DISNEY ALLOWED for few artistic compromises during the making of *Pinocchio*. Aiming for a 1939 Christmas release, Walt, as he had with *Snow White*, once again pushed everyone to work to their maximum potential. As the holidays approached, Disney tried his best to keep the spirits of his workers up, even on Christmas eve, in spite of the fact it was now too late to release the picture before January at the earliest.

One of the studio's painters, June Paterson, remembered what those days were like:

"We worked every night all through the preceding months, and we were all just absolutely exhausted. Well, we worked right up to Christmas Eve from 8:00 in the morning until 10:30 at night, with lunch and dinner breaks. It was very grueling, and we were all just killing ourselves trying to finish this picture, and all of a sudden the door opened, this is about 9:30 at night, and here came Walt, unsmiling, in a porkpie hat pushed back on his head, wheeling a cloth laundry cart. I remember he didn't say a word but just started down the isle, and we all couldn't imagine what in the world he was up to.

"The laundry cart, as it turned out, was filled with beautifully wrapped Christmas presents, compacts or cigarette cases for all the ladies. Walt didn't wish anyone a merry Christmas. He didn't chat. He didn't talk. He just passed the presents out to all the girls and left. What it did to our spirits you can't imagine."

Pinocchio opened in February of 1940, at a final cost of more than

$3 million, which made it then the most expensive animated film ever produced. The extensive use of Iwerks's modified multiplane alone significantly escalated the budget, since it was capable of only processing four feet of film an hour. As he always did, Disney disregarded cost to achieve an effect he wanted. The film's opening sequence alone, a forty-five-second multiplane shot, cost $45,000— $1,000 *a second*.

If Disney's focus in *Snow White* had been the struggle of two maternal figures, the "good" Snow White, the "adopted" mother to the seven dwarfs, versus "evil," her stepmother, the imperious evil Queen, in *Pinocchio* it shifted to a conflict between two opposing father figures, the "good" puppetmaker Gepetto and the "evil" puppeteer Stromboli. By reducing the choruslike seven dwarfs to a single essential character, Pinocchio, and unspooling the conflict through his eyes, Disney had found a way to sharpen the focus of the struggle.

The plot of *Pinocchio* focuses on a lonely old puppetmaker, Gepetto, and his little wooden puppet who wishes to become a "real" boy. One night, Pinocchio is visited by the Blue Fairy, who grants his wish but only partially. She allows him to exist, with some strings attached. He has no "soul," and therefore, although he breathes, he does not live. She tells him that if he works hard, goes to school, and behaves like a good little boy, he will earn the right to become one.

Although he tries to do just that, Pinocchio is soon led astray by a series of evil characters, unable to resist, presumably, because he lacks human moral conviction, a soul. He eventually escapes from the clutches of Stromboli, who had enslaved him and forced him to perform as a freak-show attraction. Pinocchio eventually returns home, only to find Gepetto has disappeared. When he discovers his creator has been swallowed by a great whale, Pinocchio helps rescue him and is rewarded for his valor by the Blue Fairy, who turns him at last into a real boy.

Disney's idea to introduce Pinocchio's "living" conscience as the character of Jiminy Cricket, the story's narrator and the personification of Pinocchio's nascent soul, was one of the more strikingly didactic aspects of the film's entirely original script. Nothing like him appears in the original nineteenth-century Italian fable by Carlo Lorenzini, the closest character to it being a grasshopper who admonishes Pinocchio for his bad behavior before being squashed under the puppet's foot. Indeed, Disney made so many changes to the original fable the author's surviving nephew, Paolo Lorenzini, tried and failed to sue the studio for libel.

Indeed, when projected through the lens of Disney's psyche, *Pinocchio* reveals a powerful Fundamentalist underpinning: the quest for self-redemption and the hellish fate that awaits those who lack the inner strength to resist the inherent evils of pleasure. Ultimately, the film becomes a journey through Disney's inner terrain over the involved question of his own parentage and, therefore, his "real" self. When Pinocchio lies to the Blue Fairy, for example, his "mother," his nose grows longer. Later he pays a penalty for this shameful display of moral imperfection, dramatized with striking Oedipal overtones, when, ironically, he "dies" and is placed in a coffinlike environ. This tragic moment is followed, as it was in *Snow White* when *she* "died," by a miraculous rebirth, a symbolic passage to a far better life than the one left behind.

The most primal of Fundamentalist beliefs, that one will be rewarded in the next life for the abstinence, hard work, and loyal devotion in this one, resolved for Pinocchio on film what this conviction had failed to do for Walt in real life. Unfortunately for him, there were no Blue Fairies beyond the walls of the Burbank studio to absolve him of the guilt he continued to feel over Flora's death, which included the question of whether, in fact, she had been his mother at all. For Disney, unlike his wooden counterpart, the search for a "real" identity would continue.

FOR THE FILM'S New York premiere, Walt hired eleven midgets dressed in Pinocchio outfits and ordered them to frisk about on the roof of the theater marquee. At lunchtime, food and refreshments were passed up to them, including, without Disney's knowledge, a couple of quarts of liquor. By three o'clock that afternoon things got so out of hand an amused crowd was regaled by the spectacle of eleven stark-naked midgets belching noisily and enjoying a crap game atop the Broadway marquee. Police with ladders were called to remove them in pillowcases. Walt decided not to duplicate these festivities in other cities.

In spite of that inauspicious start, the film received excellent reviews. Otis Ferguson in the *New Republic* called *Pinocchio* "a delight that will take your breath away . . . . the limits of the animated cartoon have been blown . . . wide open." And Archer Winsten of the *New York Post* described it as "fantastically delightful, absolutely perfect, and a work of pure unadulterated genius." *Pinocchio* went on to become the second highest-grossing film of the year, with *Gone With the Wind* the only one to take in more money at the box office.

Still, because of its $2.6 million cost, *Pinocchio* failed to generate the kind of instant profits *Snow White* had. The huge thousand-plus staff, the scheduled production of a full roster of shorts, two additional full-length features, and the opening of the new Burbank headquarters, all forced the Disney studio back into the mire of financial chaos Walt and Roy had worked so hard to escape.

Six months after *Snow White's* December 1937 release, Walt had managed to pay off every cent the studio owed, including its bank notes, with several million dollars left over. However, by the time *Pinocchio* opened two years and two months later, the studio was back in debt, over $4.5 million and counting.

As a result, work on the third and fourth features, *Fantasia* and *Bambi*, had to be temporarily halted when the Bank of America, concerned by the studio's alarming financial downturn, froze its line of credit. At this point Roy told Walt they had no choice but to go public.

As Walt recalled years later: "I remember Roy calling me in and his opening remark was 'I've got to talk to you, kid. This is serious. . . .' We had to get capital. We had had no outside stockholders up until then, but Roy said, 'I guess we'll have to let some outsiders in, kid.' "

Roy arranged for the issuance of $4 million worth of nonvoting stock, which quickly found a price of $25 a share. To facilitate the offering, in December of 1939 Disney and his brothers officially incorporated under the umbrella of Walt Disney Productions, an amalgam of Walt Disney Productions, Ltd., which produced motion pictures; Walt Disney Enterprises, which specialized in ancillary activities such as the licensing of the use of names and characters created or developed in connection with the motion picture activities of Walt Disney Productions, Ltd.; and Liled Realty and Investment Company, Ltd., which owned or held real estate used or occupied by Walt Disney Productions, Ltd.

At the age of thirty-eight, Walt found himself the head of a burgeoning financial empire. While this might have made most young venture artists feel they had achieved something quite extraordinary,

to Walt it was a depressing circumstance quite unlike anything re-
sembling success. Instead, it was as if his only child were being taken
away from him. From this point on, he knew he would have eighteen
hundred shareholders to deal with, rather than just one, Roy, who
most of the time felt like one too many.

Further, while going public alleviated the immediate cash-flow
crisis and allowed the studio to return to full production, it by no
means ended its financial troubles. Gaining control over internal
operations was one thing. Events that affected the studio from beyond the gates were quite another. The growing unrest overseas had
effectively cut off Disney's lucrative world market that had by 1940
accounted for more than half the studio's total profits. According to
the corporation's first annual report to the stockholders:

> The effect of the war in Europe upon the affairs of your Compa-
> ny has been serious and the full measure thereof cannot yet be
> determined. It has been impossible to effect an orderly release
> of the Company's pictures in any of the countries at war and in
> many countries it has been impossible to effect any release
> whatsoever. In fact, in most of the territories dominated by the
> Axis Powers, the release of American pictures has been forbid-
> den. In addition, currency restrictions and regulations, as well
> as the fluctuations in foreign exchange rates, have served to
> reduce further the Company's income from such pictures as
> were already released in foreign countries.

As late as 1940, Walt still refused to acknowledge the growing
threat of unionism at the studio, even after his staff formally sought
affiliation with the newly formed independent Cartoonists Guild. In
spite of staff attorney Gunther Lessing's repeated warnings, and the
experience of other heads of animation studios who in the past few
years had failed to embrace the union movement, Disney could not
imagine his "family" would ever turn against him. He held to this
belief in spite of a number of recent events which might have
convinced him otherwise.

Indeed, in 1935, after a series of disruptive demonstrations by
house artists hoping to form an independent animators' union at the
Van Beuren Studios, known for its "Little King" series and currently

riding the crest of a revival of Felix the Cat, Van Beuren closed his studio rather than accept staff unionization.

Then, early in 1937, the industry's first formal animation strike took place, at the Fleischers' New York studio. Strengthened by the passage of the Wagner Act (the Labor Relations Act of 1935), which legalized the formation of independent unions, a number of new unions were quickly chartered. One of these, the Film and Photo League, announced its intention to incorporate animators into its membership.

Fleischers' animators were the first to join. Fifteen members of the animation staff were elected as union representatives and were immediately fired. The Fleischers then demanded their remaining animators sign a document stating they wouldn't join the independent union. If they didn't, they faced instant dismissal. In response the studio's animators walked out.

The National Labor Relations Board (NLRB) was unable to mediate a quick settlement, and the strike lasted for six months. Finally, Paramount, the Fleischers' distributor, impatient for new product, pressured both sides into an agreement. Shortly after, Max and Dave Fleischer moved the entire studio to Florida, one of the most virulent antiunion states, and actively worked to rid themselves of those animators they felt had been behind the strike. Unable to do so, the Fleischers, like Van Beuren, decided to close their doors for good.

When word of the Fleischers' demise reached Disney, his only reaction was delight at the possibility their full-length animated version of *Gulliver's Travels* might not be released.*

At the same time Walt believed there was no reason his staff would rebel against him. He, in turn, "rebelled" against the industry. In 1938, Disney joined an organization of independent filmmakers determined to challenge the Majors' monopolistic hold on the industry. Besides Disney, the group included Hollywood's most successful

---

*The studio was first taken over by its distributor Paramount, which released *Gulliver's Travels* in 1939. In 1941, the Fleischer studio, unable to rid itself of the animators' union, and pressured by Paramount to produce product that more closely resembled the kind of animated films Disney was making, officially ceased operations.

independent studio executives and filmmakers: William Cagney, Charlie Chaplin, Mary Pickford, Sol Lesser, David O. Selznick, Edward Small, Hunt Stromberg, Walter Wanger, Orson Welles, and Sam Goldwyn. The Society of Independent Motion Picture Producers (SIMPP) was created to challenge the Majors' domination of the three main phases of the business: production, distribution, and exhibition.

For the most part, the Majors were still controlled by the same group of men who had first broken the iron grip of the old Edison Trust. Ironically, a quarter of a century later, their success had led them to create an even more anticompetitive environment than the one from which they had so desperately fled. So much so that no independent film could gain national distribution unless the filmmaker or studio dealt with one of the Majors, who not only controlled all the distribution networks but owned virtually every first-run theater in the country. The only deal to be had was their deal, on their terms. In 1938, the society brought formal suit against Paramount Pictures (*United States of America* v. *Paramount Pictures, Inc.*, *et al.*—MGM, Fox, Universal, Warner Bros., Columbia, United Artists, and RKO all named as codefendents).*

Disney's membership in SIMPP signaled his formal entrance into political activism, which had long been nurtured by Gunther Lessing. One of Lessing's primary "Laws of the Jungle" was an allegiance to the politics of opportunism: the principle of personal gain over political idealism. During the time Disney helped organize the independent filmmakers against the industry's mainstream, he also was accompanying Lessing to American Nazi party meetings and rallies.

According to Arthur Babbitt, "In the immediate years before we entered the war, there was a small but fiercely loyal, I suppose legal, following of the Nazi party. You could buy a copy of *Mein Kampf* on any newsstand in Hollywood. Nobody asked me to go to any meetings, but I did, out of curiosity. They were open meetings, anybody could attend, and I wanted to see what was going on for myself.

"On more than one occasion I observed Walt Disney and Gunther Lessing there, along with a lot of other prominent Nazi-afflicted [sic] Hollywood personalities. Disney was going to meetings all the time. I

---

*SIMPP's challenge took more than a decade to reach the Supreme Court. Disney's ongoing involvement with SIMPP is detailed in chapters 12 and 14.

was invited to the homes of several prominent actors and musicians, all of whom were actively working for the American Nazi party. I told a girlfriend of mine who was an editor at the time with *Coronet* magazine who encouraged me to write down what I observed. She had some connections to the FBI and turned in my reports."*

If Disney and Lessing were sympathetic to the American Nazi movement, their interest was most likely motivated by the desire to regain favor with the once-lucrative, Nazi-occupied countries where Disney films were now banned. To that end Walt was also committed to the "America First" movement and became one of Hollywood's most active prewar isolationists. Under Lessing's tutelage, Disney discovered how the passions and power of political activism could be used as weapons for personal gain. And later on, for revenge.

BILL LITTLEJOHN, a tall, pale, lanky "inbetweener" at Fleischer who chose to remain in New York when the studio relocated to Florida, became one of the chief organizers of the independent Cartoonists Guild. Elected its president in 1939, one of the first things Littlejohn did was to affiliate the guild with the much stronger and more powerful Painters Union (A. F. of L. Painters and Paperhangers Union). The newly strengthened guild succeeded in unionizing the animation departments of the Terry studios, MGM, Warner Bros., Screen Gems, and Lantz, after which the Guild set its sights on the big prize, the Disney studio.

To counteract Littlejohn, Lessing continued to urge Walt to form a company union. Finally, late in 1939, with Disney's still reluctant approval, Lessing composed the proclamation that officially established the Disney Studio Federation.

According to Bill Littlejohn, "A company union is always created to keep out legitimate unions. They're seldom organized by the employees and really fall under the heading of antiunion activity. It was ironic that one of the Disney animators involved with the organization

---

*The existence of these reports has been neither confirmed nor denied by the FBI.

In her memoirs German filmmaker Leni Riefenstahl claims that after *Kristallnacht* she approached every studio in Hollywood looking for work. No studio head would even screen her movies except Walt Disney. He told her that he admired her work but if it became known that he was considering hiring her, it would damage his reputation.

of Disney's and Lessing's company union was Arthur Babbitt. For a while he actually represented the Federation."

The irony of Babbitt championing the company union in 1939 was that he eventually became one of the most enthusiastic proponents of the independent Cartoonists Guild. In a 1980 interview Babbitt explained, "I felt that since businessmen have their chambers of commerce, merchants have their manufacturers assocations, churches have their organizations, even country clubs have member groups, why not a group of animators getting together for the benefit of each other? Things like getting raises for people was not the fundamental aim of the organization. It was just to give the workers some sort of way to improve their conditions and maintain their work standards. I was very naive. I knew nothing about unions. My baptism by fire was still to come."

Babbitt soon found himself being pressured into getting the animators to support the Federation. He recalled: "One day Gunther Lessing called me down to his office. 'Now you've really got to get this thing going.' I asked him why, and that was the first time I heard him mention the name Willie Bioff."

Although Lessing and Bioff were close friends, both professionally and personally, Lessing tried to make it sound to Babbitt as if Bioff were the real enemy.

Babbitt said, "He actually told me that Bioff was threatening to come in and make the studio's cartoonists join IATSE, that Bioff was a gangster, and that if we had a union of our own, a company union, we could thwart him. Well, I thought to myself, what more noble reason to help form a company union than to keep the gangsters out."

According to Littlejohn: "Our man at Disney came from the painters. His name was Herb Sorrell, and when he tried to bring the affiliated painters and cartoonists union into the Disney studio, that's when the real trouble began."

Herb Sorrell was one of the most colorful and controversial pro-unionists in Hollywood. Not particularly sophisticated or intrinsically political, Sorrell's activism had come about as the result of firsthand experience rather than the doctrinaire teachings of others. An amateur boxer in his youth, Sorrell was one of the few in Hollywood not intimidated by the antiunionists' "goons." When, in 1939, he became one of the most popular leaders of the painters union, he also came to the attention of Willie Bioff.

Bioff, who had personally guaranteed the heads of the Majors that for the right price he would see to it their labor costs would be kept to an absolute minimum, wasn't about to let anyone stand in the way of what had become for him a very sweet deal.

According to Hollywood labor-relations authority Dan E. Moldea:

> The studios made payoffs to the underworld for labor peace—and to keep their workers' wages and benefits to a minimum. By 1937, Bioff and the Chicago Mafia had started shaking down the major film studios, including Twentieth Century-Fox, Paramount, MGM, and Warner Bros., for $50,000 a year each, and the smaller studios—like RKO and Harry Cohn's Columbia Pictures—for $25,000. According to Bioff, "It was like taking candy from babies. When I snapped my fingers, them producers jumped."

In 1938, a studio craftsman by the name of Jeff Kibre filed a formal complaint with the NLRB claiming Joseph Schenck, the head of Fox, had made a $100,000 payoff to Willie Bioff. In return, Bioff had formed several company unions to counter the employees' movement to join an independent union.

Shortly after Kibre filed his complaint, Bioff had one of his goon squads beat Kibre nearly to death. Sorrell, a close friend of Kibre's, was outraged. He retaliated by taking Kibre's story to the press. An infuriated Bioff requested permission from his immediate superior, John Rosselli, to have Sorrell killed.

Rosselli took Bioff's request back to Chicago, where Frank Nitti decided to handle the Sorrell situation personally, with a show of force that would make anyone else think twice about going up against the mob.

According to Bill Littlejohn, "Sorrell, among other things, was a pretty good pugilist, one hell of a boxer really, and spent a lot of time in the local gyms. One day he got a call from one of the guys who told him, Herb, you wouldn't know who I am, but I know you from coming down to the gym, and I just got a call from Frank Nitti. He's in town to enforce a contract out on you. They hired me as one of the boys to go over with him and do you in. We're all meeting at the Taft Hotel [the corner of Hollywood and Vine, where Sorrell's union office was located], and I just wanted to let you know.

Sorrell told the guy he'd be down in the lobby at 3:00, just standing there. 'When I see some guy put a hand on somebody, I'll know it's you putting your hand on Frank Nitti, 'cause I don't know him. But this'll be a signal, and I'll know what to do.' So Herb was in the lobby at 3:00, the hand went on the shoulder, and Herb went over and without saying a word beat the shit out of Frank Nitti."

Two things happened as a result of that confrontation. First, Sorrell solidified his reputation as a union leader not afraid to stand up to the mob, which in turn made the entire painters union seem that much stronger. Second, he was branded a Communist by J. Edgar Hoover, who believed the American Labor movement that had blossomed under Roosevelt had been thoroughly infiltrated by political subversives who now posed a major threat to the nation's security.

Hoover had became aware of Sorrell and his "political persuasion" through Bioff's Hollywood crony, Gunther Lessing. Lessing, the political pragmatist, was equally at home among mob figures and federal agents, and as such was the perfect intermediary between Bioff and Hoover. The result was a double "marking" of Sorrell, by both the mob and the FBI.

Lessing also helped persuade Disney to become an official Hollywood informant for the Bureau. While the FBI refuses to confirm or deny certain facts regarding its relationship with Disney, Walt's twenty-five-year association with the Bureau—first as an informant, and later as a "Special Agent in Charge" —is irrefutable, supported by a wealth of official documentation and testimony.

Further, there is ample circumstantial evidence to suggest that Hoover was aware of Disney years before Lessing's official introduction, certainly in 1936 and possibly as early as the fall of 1918. That year, Hoover, in his first months in the FBI, became involved with the government's prosecution of anarchists Emma Goldman and Alexander Berkman, who had encouraged the nation's young men to resist the draft. Part of Hoover's assignment was to familiarize himself with the names of draft dodgers. In keeping with the logic of the Bureau, he would also get to know the names of those volunteers like Disney who were so eager to serve they would do anything to get *in* the army.

Disney's attempts to join the military while still underage might very well have brought him to Hoover's attention as having prime

Bureau potential. Among the most common methods of recruitment by the FBI then (and now) were personal recommendation and unsolicited investigation of those the Bureau believed fit its requisite profile.

In July 1936, Hoover sent the now-famous Disney a letter, one of many attempts the Bureau had made as part of an ongoing campaign to recruit him. The last paragraph of the letter (the rest remains classified by the FBI) reads as follows: ". . . I am indeed pleased that we can be of service to you in *affording you a means of absolute identity throughout your lifetime. . . .*" [Italics added]

On November 10, 1940, Disney apparently struck the following deal with the Bureau. It appears that in exchange for its continuing assistance in his personal search to find out the truth of his parentage, Walt agreed to assist Hoover's crusade against the spread of communism in Hollywood by becoming an official informant of the FBI. His initial contact was Special Agent in Charge (SAC) E.E. Conroy.*

That same day the *Washington Post* ran a story that began with the headline WALT DISNEY STROLLS TWO DAYS UNRECOGNIZED IN WASH-INGTON, in which Walt was quoted as stating he'd come to the nation's capital "simply to see the sights."

LESSING'S PLAN to thwart the Cartoonists Guild included a massive public relations campaign to inform the public just how good things really were at the studio. In a lengthy 1940 profile published in the prestigious *Atlantic Monthly*, Disney stated the average pay of his workers was higher than the average at any other studio, excluding star salaries. The highest paid members of his staff made the princely sum of more than $300 a week. Walt did not include in the interview his own weekly salary, which had risen to $2,000 a week, or Roy's, $1,000, with all their travel and other related expenses paid by the studio.

In private, Walt continued to complain to his brother about the way his men wasted company time and money. According to his calculations, nearly half the working time of his animators was spent sharpening pencils, for which he was paying top dollar.

*How the FBI worked on Disney's behalf is examined in chapter 12.

On more than one occasion Walt threatened to follow the Fleischers' lead and move his entire operation to Florida. While he never followed through on that threat, he did begin to institute certain changes in Burbank's daily operation. One was the introduction of time clocks and the requirement that every member of the staff, from the lowest part-time manual laborers to the top artists, punch in and out. They had to do so even if they left their stations for so short a time as a drink of water or a trip to the lavatory. Or to sharpen a pencil.

Despite numerous promises from Lessing, the studio Federation made no concessions to the workers on wages, hours, benefits, or working conditions. Finally, early in 1940, Littlejohn enlisted the aid of David Hilberman, one of Walt's top animators, to help strengthen the Guild's foothold at Disney.

Hilberman had first joined Disney on July 4, 1936. A former high school art teacher, he was one of forty artists chosen out of thousands that had applied during a nationwide Disney talent hunt. Like all beginners at the studio, Hilberman served his apprenticeship as an "inbetweener" before being promoted by Bill Tytla to work as a second layout assistant.

Hilberman recalled, "I knew the Federation was a company union, but I wasn't interested either way. I was moving along in my career, making major advancements, and had no quarrel with the studio. I was then contacted [at Littlejohn's directive] by Charlotte Darling, one of the girls at Warners, which was about to become part of the Cartoonists Guild, as was MGM. Charlotte kept after me to do something about Disney, and I told her that I didn't think our people were interested in a union. At any rate I said, well, look, I'll call a bunch of friends together and sound it out.

"After the first meeting, about a week later we got together again at the same house, and I was floored when the sentiment was so strongly in favor of an independent union."

At Littlejohn's directive, Hilberman asked for a meeting with Babbitt, who at this time still represented the company union.

According to Babbitt, "The first formal meeting we had was held in Charlotte Darling's private home, where [Hilberman] pointed out to me the evil of my ways, and that to really be able to accomplish what I wanted to accomplish, I should join them in a legitimate union. I attended several meetings with Hilberman, Littlejohn, and others, and quickly came to see that yes, what I really wanted was to be a part of a legitimate union, rather than serve as the company ploy. That was when I began to work actively at converting as many people as I could from the Disney Federation to the Guild."

Hilberman and the others then met with an official from the NLRB to find out what had to be done to qualify Disney's animators for membership in the Guild. Pledge cards were made up, and Charlotte Darling became the official go-between for the Disney animators. Along with Herb Sorrell, she helped coordinate the operation so that affiliation with the Guild might occur the same time at Disney, Warners, and MGM. Once Hilberman had the requisite four hundred signatures, Sorrell called an open meeting for all Disney artists at the Hotel Roosevelt on Hollywood Boulevard.

When Disney heard about the gathering, he became furious and instructed Lessing to call a mandatory meeting just before Sorrell's. Lessing, in no uncertain terms, warned of serious reprisals for anyone who attended the Guild meeting. What particularly enraged Disney was that those who appeared to be leading the movement to unionize, Hilberman and Babbitt, were among his highest-paid pencil-sharpeners. Babbitt recalled, "Disney was paying $16 a week to beginners and $18 to experienced inkers and painters. One of the reasons I decided to join Hilberman's movement was because one of the inkers fainted one day during lunchtime at the studio. She couldn't afford to buy lunch, and some hardhearted character was charging her $2 a week transportation from her home on Wilcox Avenue in Hollywood to the Burbank studio.

"At the same time I was earning an average of $15,000 a year. My bonus and stock dividends amounted to another $5,000, a fortune in those days. But my top assistant, Bill Hurtz, was only earning $25 a week. I tried to get him a $2.50 raise. Roy put on a real tough air and told me, 'If he was worth it, he'd be getting it.' I decided to go directly to Walt.

"'Walt,' I said, 'I want to see about getting Bill Hurtz a $2.50 raise.' And he said to me, 'Why don't you mind your own goddamn business. You and your goddamn Communist friends, you sit down there and you don't know what the hell is going on in this world! That's why nobody likes you!' I looked at Walt and said quietly, 'If you can't afford to give Bill Hurtz the $2.50 a week raise, I'll give it to him out of my own pocket.' The next day not only did Walt give Bill Hurtz a two-and-a-half-dollar raise but a dozen other assistants as well, I guess to show me that he could afford it.

"I was then warned [by Gunther Lessing] not to do any organizing on the company grounds on company time or I would be fired on the spot. However, the Wagner Act granted organizers certain rights, and I followed all the legal rules. I just went as far as I legally could."

Hilberman added, "It's important to remember that we'd organized ourselves as a union committee, not a strike committee. At the big meeting in the Roosevelt Hotel right after Lessing read the riot act to the staff, we began by telling everyone once they signed their cards not to tell anyone else they'd done so, for their own personal safety and job protection. Then Herb Sorrell, who up until that time had stayed mostly in the background, got up to speak. His language was designed for studio painters, old-timers and so on. I winced because he cussed and swore and, you know, said things like we ought to 'Squeeze [Disney's] balls 'til he screams.' Well, I guess his message got across, because by the end of the evening we had all the cards we needed."

When Babbitt and Hilberman presented the signature cards to Disney, he refused to recognize their legitimacy and fired twenty of the strike's leaders on the spot, first and foremost among them Babbitt. Disney's action was a blatant violation of the Wagner Act and outraged the staff. For the first time there was talk of a strike. Hilberman recalled, "When the firings came, I had a friend, Zack Schwartz, who was laid off immediately following his work on the 'Sorcerer's Apprentice' episode of *Fantasia*. I couldn't understand why Zack was fired, in spite of his being in favor of the Guild. For what little he was getting paid, Walt could have laid off three of the many novices who'd come aboard and saved more money. Plus, I wouldn't have to work weekends for overtime, and we'd have the advantage of a guy who was completely familiar with the characters, the stories, and everything else.

"That's when I realized how no-good the situation really was. If Zack's job was gone, then no one's job was secure at the studio. People's livelihoods were at the capricious mercy of Walt Disney and his executives. The Federation, of course, did nothing to protect Zack, and that was precisely why we needed an independent union.

"Why was Zack fired? Well, let me put it this way. He wasn't a troublemaker, he was a good artist and didn't give anybody a hard time. What he did have was the last name of Schwartz and a big nose."

According to Babbitt, "Mr. Lessing brilliantly had two company policemen present me with a letter written by him [Lessing] stating that they had warned me numerous times not to do any organizing on the company grounds, and as I had disobeyed, I was being fired. This in spite of the fact I had a three-year contract and firing me was a direct violation of the Wagner Act.

"I asked the policemen if they minded if I went to my office and got my pencils and things. They said all right. It took me a half hour to gather up about three pencils. In the meantime quite a crowd gathered at the door of the building, and I was marched off the grounds with a policeman holding me at each elbow."

Babbitt appealed his firing to the labor board. On the day he was supposed to give his deposition, two Burbank policemen paid a visit to his home and charged him with carrying a concealed weapon.

Babbitt said, "They were so concealed they still haven't found them. I did have a weapon hidden somewhere for my own protection, because I'd been threatened several times. It got so bad I had to sleep in other people's houses. I'd get a phone call telling me it'd be a good idea not to go home that particular night. So I was taken to the Burbank jail, and of course it was just a coincidence that the chief of police of Burbank was the brother-in-law of Disney's in-house chief of security. I was not allowed to make any phone calls.

"Because I didn't have the weapon actually on my person, I was fingerprinted and put into the drunk tank. I had a two o'clock appointment with the labor board, which of course, I missed. When I didn't show up at the hearing, one of the sympathetic vice-presidents at the studio, Phyllis Lambertson, somehow found out where I was and had my hearing postponed from two to seven.

"In the meantime the Burbank police department received a call around five in the afternoon that it was okay to release me. Which they did, whereupon I was brought directly to Walt Disney's studio. 'Uncle' Walt and I had a little conversation. He told me how foolishly I'd been behaving and how things could be so good for me if I just understood things from his point of view."

As a result of his labor board hearing, Babbitt was reinstated. He returned to the studio and immediately resumed his union activities.

As 1940 CAME TO A CLOSE, *Fantasia*, Walt's Gothic meditation bathed in heavy classical music and awash in dark visions of fear, isolation, repentence, and mourning, opened in theaters across the country. Although no one could know at the time, *Fantasia* would prove the funeral pyre for Disney's dreams, out of whose charred ruins would emerge a fiery nightmare of terrible vengeance.

Strike!

Most evenings after leaving the studio, Disney liked to stop at one of his favorite watering holes, the bar at Hollywood's Musso and Frank, or Chasen's in Beverly Hills. As Lillian rarely cooked, after a few cocktails he often took a table for himself and had his dinner while the industry's most popular actors, writers, and directors regularly genuflected before him, to pay their respects to the man they now considered one of Hollywood's resident geniuses.

During the final days of postproduction on *Snow White*, Walt had thought about "guest-starring" Mickey in the still very popular "Silly Symphonies" series, which he hoped would revitalize the little mouse's fading box-office appeal. One night, not long after, according to animation historian Charles Solomon:

While dining alone at Chasen's in Beverly Hills, Disney saw Leopold Stokowski, also alone, and invited the conductor to join him. During the course of a three-hour conversation, Disney mentioned his plans for [starring Mickey Mouse in the "Silly Symphonies"] *The Sorcerer's Apprentice*. Stokowski offered to waive any fee and conduct the recording of the [film's original Paul Dukas] score.

The conductor [Leopold Stokowski] also suggested that he and Disney join forces to create "a fanta-zee-ah," a [full-length] feature that would illustrate several pieces of classical music.

Thus, *Fantasia* began as an extension of *The Sorcerer's Apprentice*. The idea appealed to Disney for several reasons. Economics was certainly one, for the cost of making *The Sorcerer's Apprentice* had already escalated to $125,000. As a short subject, Walt knew, it stood little, if any chance of recouping its investment. The disappointing returns from *Pinocchio* had helped deplete the profits from *Snow White*. The Bank of America and his stockholders were now watching Walt's every move with as much interest as they did his movies. The opportunity to keep Mickey Mouse alive and make a financial killing always appealed to Walt. However, what really excited him about working with Stokowski was the chance to produce a major work of "art."

Curiously, although Walt loved it when newspapers, magazines, and academic journals described him as an artist, he continued to reject any suggestion of "artistry" in his films. He dismissed as "hogwash" what a growing number of serious film critics and social commentators were beginning to suggest, that there was a dark side to Disney's films which not only deepened their meaning but identified them as more than merely cartoons for children.

Indeed, *The Three Little Pigs* and *Snow White* were among the more complex and provocative films to come out of Hollywood, animated or otherwise. Unlike most studio films, which conformed to preset commercial guidelines, Disney's were unfettered picture-window views into his inner conflicts and emotions. In that sense, *Snow White* in particular resembled Chaplin's *Modern Times* (1936) and, in the world of art, Picasso's *Femme Qui Pleure* (1936), all three of which appeared within a year of each other. Like Chaplin's film, in which Charlie gets entangled in the internal works of the machinery that symbolizes man's mental destiny, and Picasso's portrait of the inner emotions of his weeping woman, Disney's most recent work alerted the intelligentsia that Walt's films were essentially theoretical, psychologically rooted rather than literal-minded. To paraphrase T. S. Eliot on D. H. Lawrence, it was becoming increasingly apparent to a growing number of critics that Disney's insistence upon creating perfect worlds in his films for children reflected nothing so much as what they suspected was his own nightmarish childhood. While his filmed fairy tales may have appeared at first glance to be light and dreamlike, upon closer examination they seemed more nightmares of deconstructed reality in a league with the era's leading neo-Freudian Modernists.

In the company of the great conductor, Walt, for the first time, felt obligated to make an "artistic" film. With *Snow White* and *Pinocchio*, Disney had taken what were, in his view, literal fairy tales and turned them into great movies. Now he began with the intention of making a "great film." Whereas in his two earlier features he had succeeded in projecting his emotions onto the screen, *Fantasia* was, essentially, an exercise in intellect. As such, it was overwhelmed by excessive self-consciousness. With neither the frame of recognizable form or the anchor of linear narrative, the film came across as inherently false as the celebrated Walt Disney signature. Hollywood historian Otto Friedrich was one among several critics who recognized the film's pretentious exercise in "art" for Walt's sake when he described it as Disney's "grandiose venture into culture."

The film's unrelated sections left audiences, for the most part, dumbfounded. From the film's live-action opening, featuring music critic Deems Taylor as narrator in black tie and tails and the shortcut visual vernacular meant to telegraph cultural significance, the film unspooled a series of discombobulated vignettes.

In its purely expressionistic first "movement," abstract visuals "illustrate" the sounds of discordant music. This is followed by the muted oddity of "The Sorcerer's Apprentice," in which a silent Mickey Mouse serves a Merlinlike sorcerer. Next, one sees excerpts of *The Nutcracker Suite*, *The Rite of Spring*, and *The Pastoral Symphony* visualized with an air of portentousness that managed to smother their few wondrously light and sweetly entertaining moments.

In *Fantasia's* penultimate sequence, "A Night on Bald Mountain," Disney startlingly and unexpectedly shifted the film's mood as he attempted to visualize the "God of Evil and Death," the gargoylish Chernobog. This was followed by "Ave Maria," the film's final "movement," in which a candlelit procession of those who worshipped the God of Light celebrated the coming of dawn.

Because of *Snow White*, *Fantasia* was one of the most highly anticipated films of 1940. The advance word was unerringly positive, not surprising since most of it came from Walt himself. Disney personally approved the daily "leaks" to the press that Stokowski had become completely enchanted working at the Disney studio surrounded by a wealth of the latest available sound equipment, as well as a resident symphonic orchestra at his disposal.

Walt basked in what he believed was his guilt by association with

Stokowski, believing *this* was what it meant to be an artist. At one point, while listening to Bach's *Improvisations*, Disney claimed he "saw" the accompanying visual sequence as somehow "orange" in nature.

"Oh, no," Stokowski replied, "I see it as purple," an opinion to which Walt immediately acquiesced.

Disney's awed reaction to the first footage for the *Pastoral Symphony*, with its nymphlike fawns and centaurs, was a gushing "Gee, this'll *make* Beethoven."

For financial purposes, Disney intended to include only the music of dead composers to whom he would have to pay no royalties. However, at Stokowski's insistence, Walt agreed to seek out the great, and still living, Stravinsky for permission to use *Le Sacre du Printemps* (*Rite of Spring*). Disney had no idea the piece had been originally conceived as a pagan ritual meant to evoke a sacrificial virgin dancing herself to death, or that its 1913 Paris premiere had caused a near riot. He believed it made the perfect accompaniment for a planned battle sequence between two dinosaurs.

Disney wired Stravinsky, in Paris, with an offer of $5,000 for the use of the music. The inquiry infuriated Stravinsky because, as he later claimed, it "was accompanied by a gentle warning that if permission were withheld the music would be used anyway." Gunther Lessing had put the offer that way, after he discovered the original copyrights had been taken in prerevolutionary Russia and were most likely unenforceable.

Stravinsky, fearing his music might be stolen outright if he didn't agree to its use, reluctantly signed and returned an accompanying contract to Disney.*

During the making of *Fantasia*, the Disney studio became an obligatory stop for many of the world's renowned *artistes*, all eager to meet America's newest master animator. Among the notables were

---

*According to the *New York Times* of January 23, 1993: The publishing company of Boosey and Hawkes bought the rights to *Rite of Spring* from Stravinsky in 1947. When *Fantasia* was released on videotape cassettes and laser disc in 1991, they sued the Disney studio, insisting "Stravinsky never granted the right to use [*Rite of Spring*] in any medium or by any other form of distribution" other than theatrically exhibited film. In 1992, the Philadelphia Orchestra, which recorded the sound track for the film, also sued the studio, demanding half the profits, as "co-creator" of the sound-track score, and videocassette and compact disc royalties. Both cases are pending.

Thomas Hart Benton, who posed with a centaur model from the *Pastoral Symphony* segment of the film; Kirsten Flagstad, the legendary Wagnerian soprano, who insisted on having her photograph taken with Walt; the actress Katharine Cornell, who had hers taken with one of *Fantasia*'s "characters," Hyacinth Hippo; George Balanchine; Dr. Edwin Hubble; Dr. Julian Huxley; and Thomas Mann. Journalists too continued to write with glowing fascination about Walt Disney. Paul Hollister shadowed Walt day and night for weeks, after which he wrote a tony *Atlantic Monthly* profile, with Walt's preapproval part of the deal, entitled "Walt Disney: Genius at Work."

Not all distinguished visitors to the studio were as taken with Disney. When Frank Lloyd Wright passed through Hollywood, Walt invited the famed architect for a personal tour and to guest-lecture at the in-house film school. Wright accepted both offers and as part of his preparation screened some of *Fantasia*'s completed sequences.

When Walt asked him his opinion, Wright, without hesitation, expressed his strong dislike for what he had seen. Labeling the film absurd, he changed his mind about lecturing and advised Disney it was time for him to take a long vacation. His opinion, while in the critical minority, was echoed by Lillian. She had become by now an astute if somewhat cynical evaluator of Walt's work. From the time of his first meeting with Stokowski until *Fantasia* opened, Lillian expressed her strong dislike for the whole project. Time and again she warned Walt that the film would be a disaster, that he should abandon it and return to making simple cartoons.

Walt dismissed both her and Wright's opinions, preferring those of the growing number of professional pop culturists who saw in Disney's movies nothing more than a bit of enjoyable, if somewhat simplistic, entertainment. No less an aesthete than Alexander Woollcott had become a great fan of Disney's, marking him no more low to middlebrow than that Hollywood mascot of the legendary Algonquin Round Tablers, Harpo Marx.

Still others with no direct connection to the arts had come to admire Disney. Among these was Henry Ford, whom Walt had first met while on a promotional trip through Detroit during the showing of *Snow White*. Ford admired both Mickey Mouse and his creator. Walt held Ford in equally high esteem, and the two men developed a lasting friendship. At one point just before taking the studio public, Disney had asked the automotive legend his opinion of the move.

Ford replied that he admired Disney because he was a successful self-made Protestant in a field dominated by Jews. Still, Ford explained, because the stock market, like the film business, was controlled by Jews, Disney ought to sell his entire company outright before losing it to "them," piece by piece. Disney took Ford's advice quite seriously and thanked him profusely for his words of wisdom.

It took three years to complete *Fantasia*, with work on the final "Ava Maria" segment continuing right up until *two days* before the film's extravaganza world premiere. *Fantasia's* first public showing was scheduled for November 13, 1940, at the Colony, the same New York theater where *Steamboat Willie* had debuted twelve years earlier.

Based on the reaction to a special advance screening just prior to its premiere, Disney felt confident he had accomplished his goal of making a great art film. Shortly after the screening, New York's Metropolitan Museum of Art requested individual *Fantasia* cels for inclusion in its permanent collection. Critic Philip Hartung, in *Commonweal*, reported that the film represented "a new artistic experience of great beauty."

Encouraged by the advance reviews and in spite of *Fantasia's* budget having swelled to $2.28 million, Disney now insisted the film had to be exhibited *only* in its original wide-screen format and "Fantasound," Iwerks's patented ninety-six-speaker stereophonic system that cost the studio an additional $85,000 per theater to install. Certain he had created a great work of art, Disney hoped to mark the occasion with the introduction of his latest technological "miracle." What sound and color had done for Mickey Mouse, Walt predicted, wide-screen and Fantasound would do for *Fantasia*.

Ironically, Fantasound nearly caused the film not to open. A conflict over the rights to handle the installation broke out between hostile New York branches of IATSE and the International Brotherhood of Electrical Workers (IBEW). The latter had openly supported the Disney cartoonists' quest to join the independent Cartoonists Guild. To settle the dispute, Disney offered to pay for the services of both unions, which doubled the cost of installing Fantasound. The incident proved only the first of a series of union grievances and delays that occurred at nearly every scheduled first-run theater as part of an organized series of disruptions by those unions sympathetic to Disney's animators.

After a dozen mostly unsuccessful attempts, Disney reluctantly gave up on Fantasound when the government insisted RCA, Fanta-sound's manufacturer, had to cease all further production of the sound system's essential component parts. The reason given was the need to conserve raw materials in anticipation of America's entrance into the war.

The actions of the Defense Department outraged Disney, who at this point thought about postponing the film's run altogether, and may have done just that if the Bank of America's Joseph Rosenberg had not warned him of the certain economic disaster such a decision would cause. Instead, Disney angrily "dumped" the film into general distribution, where it turned up more often than not on the bottom half of double features.

Nevertheless, critical praise for *Fantasia* continued after it opened. Otis Ferguson of the *New Republic* declared it "one of the strange and beautiful things that have happened in the world." The prestigious *Art Digest* ran a signed editorial by its publisher, Peyton Boswell, who described *Fantasia* as "an aesthetic experience never to be forgotten." Bosley Crowther of the *New York Times* proclaimed the film "dumps conventional formulas overboard and reveals the scope of films for imaginative excursion . . . [and is] simply terrific."

The film, however, did poorly at the box office, and it soon became apparent that *Fantasia* was going to be the studio's first major box-office bomb. Rather than accept the fact that audiences simply didn't like his movie, Disney blamed the film's failure on everyone and everything but himself. First it was the conspiracy of the pro-unionists that had effectively killed his picture. Then it was the government's refusal to allow the use of the necessary equipment, followed by that favorite excuse of *nouveaux artistes*, that the general audience wasn't capable of understanding what he was trying to do. At one point he even claimed that the unusually bad weather that had swept across the country the week of *Fantasia's* opening had kept audiences away. When he asked Roy what he thought, his brother decided *Fantasia* had done poorly because of its "unfortunate" choice of music. "I'll never understand why we couldn't have sneaked a little Tommy Dorsey in there," he remarked to Walt after studying the film's receipts. That was the last time Walt ever asked his brother for his opinion about anything.

PERHAPS EVEN WORSE than having to deal with *Fantasia's* financial failure, Walt now found himself being praised for work actually done by Arthur Babbitt, particularly the "dancing mushrooms," considered by everyone, critics and audiences alike, among the few genuine diamonds in a film loaded with rhinestones.

Ironically, such praise didn't make life easier for Babbitt. Shortly after *Fantasia* opened, "Roy called me into his office," the animator recalled, "and told me if I didn't stop sticking my nose into other people's business I was going to get it cut off."

While Roy preferred to make his threats in private, Walt chose to humiliate Babbitt in front of his fellow workers, a strategy that invariably backfired. The diminutive animator stood barely five-foot-six, at least six inches shorter, and weighed in at a hundred and thirty in his shoes and socks, fifty pounds lighter, than Walt. As a result Disney came off as nothing so much as an ineffective bully.

"During the course of *Fantasia*," Babbitt recalled, "I started taking piano lessons. After the film opened, Walt heard about it, and in the presence of maybe fifty people at a story meeting, he said, 'I understand you're studying the piano.' I said, 'Yeah, that's true.' He said, 'Well, what the hell's the matter with you; are you some kind of faggot?' "

Babbitt responded by declaring that "*Fantasia* lacked balls." The phrase became an instant rallying cry among Disney's increasingly discontented animators, which further infuriated Walt.

THE UNION DISRUPTION of the opening of *Fantasia* and the incident with Babbitt were two clear signals of the growing discontent among Disney's staff over his refusal to recognize the Cartoonists Guild. In January 1941, two months after the film opened, the situation grew more intense when Herb Sorrell met with the Disney brothers and presented them with the required number of signature cards to permit Guild representation. Refusing to believe his animators had actually signed the cards themselves, Disney requested a one-day delay and used the time to call a last-chance meeting with his entire staff. During the meeting he made an impassioned plea for understanding and appreciation for all he had done for them.

"Everything that you are going to hear is entirely from me," Walt began, "and to doubly insure not having things credited to me I did not say, I have arranged to have this whole affair recorded on records. In addition, I have three impartial witnesses present in the recording room to verify the authenticity of the recordings."

Initially Disney hoped to appeal to his staff's loyalty. Before long, however, Walt lapsed into a nearly incoherent tirade and began scolding his staff. According to one employee, toward the end Walt actually choked with tears as he reminded everyone how he felt like a father toward them and that he considered each his own son. Walt then bowed his head, and the room grew still, until someone in the audience loudly booed, effectively shattering the moment.

The following day, Walt and Roy, now joined by Lessing, met with Sorrell and this time insisted on a secret vote. Sorrell, who had tolerated endless delays and excuses, was absolutely opposed to the idea of any more ballots, secret or otherwise, and threatened to call the staff out on strike immediately if Disney didn't accept the validity of the cards. The meeting ended with Walt insisting he be allowed to call the Labor Relations Board in Washington, D.C., to check the legality of Sorrell's actions.

That call began another five months of legal challenges, during which time the studio finished production on *The Reluctant Dragon*, a minor, impersonal combination live-action–animated production that offered a highly controlled peek behind the front gates of the Disney studio.

In a move intended to intimidate his animators, Walt announced to the press that he was so pleased with the results he was considering abandoning animation altogether in favor of full-length live-action features. To underscore his seriousness, Disney grandly auditioned his most loyal contingency for roles, the ever-faithful "girls" who worked for the studio. In one of the most bizarre moments of his career, Disney invited the press to attend the auditions in which he encouraged his "girls" to show up in skimpy bathing suits for his personal perusal.

On that day dozens of the studio's hopeful "Hollywood honeys" displayed their charms to their leering boss and an equally leering press. Publicity photos revealed a previously unseen side of Disney that shocked the public and dismayed Roy.

Meanwhile, an increasingly impatient Sorrell acquired the services of the painters union's legal representative, George Bodle. As Bodle recalled, "There was just no negotiating with them. I had to deal mostly with Roy, because Walt simply refused to see me, who just told me what they [the studio] wanted, and that was it. Before the strike, when I was still trying to effect some sort of settlement, I raised questions about salaries for the inkers and painters, the lowest-paid creative staffers. They were making $18.50 a week. We wanted contracts for people so they couldn't get fired at Walt's discretion, without reason or explanation. We wanted recognition for the union. Their only response was 'You're not going to get away with this. . . .' "

On the morning of May 17, 1941, an anonymous memo appeared, informing Disney's twelve hundred employees that only those who qualified as "artists," some nine hundred of them, would be eligible for representation and continued job security. The implication was clear. Any nonanimator who supported the guild would eventually lose his or her job because of it.

That same week, the NLRB declared Disney's own Federation, which covered the studio's entire twelve hundred employees, illegal. The NLRB said the Federation was controlled by management and ordered it disbanded. Disney then attempted to install in its place an organization he called the American Society of Screen Cartoonists, which Bodle immediately and successfully challenged as being nothing more than a name change for the Federation.

Five days later, on May 22, a consent decree officially dissolved the Federation. That same day, Disney released a written statement to the press, declaring: "My position is that the field is clear for my employees to do as they please—I won't permit any of my representatives to take a hand in their organization efforts. They are free to join any organization, and we will bargain collectively with the groups chosen."

In spite of that public proclamation, in private Disney remained adamantly opposed to the Guild and threatened immediate dismissal for anyone who joined it. When Babbitt and five other workers urged the staff to protest the threat, Walt fired them. This was Babbitt's second illegal dismissal. Disney then publicly reiterated his position that under no circumstances would he submit to collective bargaining with the Guild.

The next day leaflets appeared all over Hollywood denouncing Babbitt, Sorrell, and Hilberman as Communists:

> Your leadership STINKS. Do not allow your American courage to be further DUPED with the paralyzing poisons of the RED SPIDERS . . . The freedoms of Democracy must not be misused by Subversionists to destroy our Democracy. . . .

The authors and distributors of the leaflets identified themselves only by their collective number as the "Committee of 21." In subsequent leaflets the Committee of 21 vehemently denied accusations by the Guild's leaders that the committee was, in reality, made up of Willie Bioff, Gunther Lessing, Walt and Roy Disney, and a handful of employee loyalists.

In subsequent leaflets, the Committee of 21 specifically named Littlejohn—"Littleguy" as they called him—Sorrell, and Arthur Babbitt as Communists and warned:

> We are continuing our investigations of your leaders and of some of you. We are not yet ready to disclose our identity or to turn over our findings to the proper authorities. We are not yet willing to report on what you have been doing and saying until you yourself answer the question of your own conscience: "AM I A LOYAL AMERICAN OR A LOYAL DUPE. The COMMITTEE OF 21 holds this conviction that anyone who knows the facts and fails to speak out in this hour of national emergency must be judged as equally guilty with those who are seeking the destruction of DEMOCRACY."

On May 27, Richard Storey, the representative of the Boston banking firm of Kidder, Peabody and Co., the underwriters of the studio's public-stock offering, and Joseph Rosenberg from the Bank of America called for a private meeting with Disney. Working through the night, Storey and Rosenberg tried unsuccessfully to convince Disney to recognize the Guild.

On the morning of May 28, Sorrell called Disney's workers out on strike. Barricades went up around the entrance to the Burbank studios, and more than a thousand picketers appeared the first hour. An arrangement which became known as the "Noah's Ark" agreement was worked out by the strike's leaders with the local police to allow cars to enter the studio two by two, with time for picketing between each pair.

When Walt arrived in his car at the front gates, he smiled and waved, as if he couldn't care less about the strike. Babbitt recalled: "As he slowly drove through the line in his fancy Packard, waving to everybody and having a great time, I grabbed a megaphone from John Garfield, one of the many Hollywood celebrities who showed up in support of our cause, and shouted through it, 'Walt Disney, you should be ashamed of yourself!' Then I turned to the crowd and shouted, *'There he is, the man who believes in brotherhood for everybody but himself!'* "

With that, the crowd broke out into loud, derisive boos. Walt lost all reserve and, red-faced and heaving, pulled up, got out of his car, ripped off his jacket, started after Babbitt, and was immediately restrained by security guards. He did, however, get close enough to warn the artist he was through, not just at Disney but everywhere in the industry. Walt then got back into his car and drove through the gates.

Once inside the confines of his office, Disney arranged to have a photographer take pictures of the men out on the picket line. They were delivered that afternoon, and he papered the walls of his office with them, after which he walked around the room pointing out individuals to Roy and Lessing he thought would have remained loyal. "Damn, I didn't think *he'd* go against me," he said about one, then another, "That sonofabitch, I trusted him and he went out on me." As for a third, he shrugged and said, "We can get along without him."

Lessing then confidently predicted the strike would last less than twenty-four hours and that the union would be busted. The studio could then hire all the animators it would ever need for fifty bucks a week, tops. In response Walt opened a bottle of Harvey's Bristol Cream and toasted the walkout's anticipated early end.

Lessing had made his prediction based on the fact that, according to his count, only 293 actual Disney employees had joined the strike that first day. The strikers' count was 580. Lessing's confidence gave Disney a false sense of early and inevitable victory. Late that first afternoon, from his office Disney issued the following statement to the press:

I desire that it be made plain to all my employees that they are free to join any union which they may select or prefer. We always have been ready, are now ready, and always will be ready to bargain collectively with any appropriate bargaining unit designated by a majority of the employees by secret ballot in an election held for that purpose.

Disney explained the discrepancy in the number of studio employees actually out on strike and the nearly one thousand picketers outside his Burbank studio by claiming more than half were illegal, outside agitators and Communists. In fact, many were family members of the strikers and recent victors from the MGM and Schlesinger studios, which had accepted the Guild and avoided similar strikes. They had come to lend support to their fellow workers.

Later that night, Walter B. Spreckels, former regional director of the NLRB hired by Disney as the studio's on-site strike counselor, "clarified" Disney's earlier statement. Spreckels explained the studio would recognize only the union that accepted a majority of the *total* staff, as had the defunct Federation, rather than just animators as the Guild intended. And, Spreckels went on, the union would have to be voted in by secret ballot, and until then the studio would make absolutely "no overtures toward stopping the strike."

The issue of the secret ballot remained a nonnegotiable point to the union representatives. The next day, in response Littlejohn told the newspapers that "the union offered on numerous occasions prior to the strike to enter into an election or a cross-check of its membership against the company payroll," and that Disney's request for secret elections was "made only for the purpose of beclouding issues involved in our strike."

Walt countered by vowing to keep "Commies" out of his studio, publicly declaring the strike as part of the growing Communist "conspiracy" threatening Hollywood and the nation. And on this point he was at least partially correct.

Ever since Sinclair's gubernatorial campaign helped unify Hollywood's left, the Communist Party of the United States of America (CPUSA) had made its presence felt by championing the rights of the film industry's workers. The CPUSA played a vital role in the Screen Writers Guild's long battle to exist, thus helping to make legitimate the industry's burgeoning union movement.

In 1937, the same year the studios officially recognized the Guild and its member writers, *Daily Variety* ran the first of a series of front-page articles warning of the growing presence and influence of the Communist party in the film industry. After that, the CPUSA's influence began to fade and was further eroded two years later with the announcement of the 1939 Nazi-Soviet pact. From that point on the party played an increasingly small role in the functioning of the studios and in the structure of the system. The CPUSA also proved unsuccessful in its attempt to gain a lasting power base in any unions, in many instances simply because the mob had gotten there first. It did, however, continue to play an important role in the politicalization of Hollywood's citizenry. The decade-long Depression, participation in several "Popular Front" organizations that fought the American Nazi party, and support for the Loyalists in the Spanish Civil War all helped the CPUSA maintain a significant membership during the thirties and early forties.

In 1941, a popular phrase that caught the ear of Americans was that the CPUSA never met a strike it didn't like. When Disney's staff walked out, a good number of those who came to lend their support were, indeed, members of the CPUSA. As was the party's way, it wasn't content to participate in the walkout; it wanted to control it.

According to one member of the party, a Disney animator and key organizer of the walkout (not Arthur Babbitt):

> I got a call from a reporter from the [Communist party newspaper] *People's World*, who wanted to see me. [The call came about a month into the strike.] I arranged to meet him at a corner and we talked. He'd brought with him a representative of the Communist party. The representative said the time had come to settle up. We'd been out for five weeks and morale was going down the drain and we should settle. I was involved, they were involved, and that's about it.

In the first days of the strike, a party mood had permeated the air as picketers and their wives marched in spirited formation. Utilizing their talents, they carried colorful signs, among the more memorable: MICHELANGELO, RAPHAEL, LEONARDO DA VINCI, REUBENS, REMBRANDT ALL BELONGED TO GUILDS; SNOW WHITE AND THE 600 DWARFS; ONE GENIUS AGAINST 600 GUINEA PIGS; IT'S NOT CRICKET TO PASS A PICKET (with a sketch of Jiminy Cricket); and I'D RATHER BE A DOG THAN A SCAB (Pluto).

Others held aloft caricatures of an angry, bullying Mickey Mouse or an outraged Donald Duck. At night boisterous poker parties took place on the grassy lawn. However, as the weeks dragged on, the hard reality of a long strike settled in.

On June 20, when the walkout had neared the end of its first month, *The Reluctant Dragon* premiered at the Pantages Theater in

Hollywood. The strikers, angered by the film's depiction of life at the studio as one big happy family, turned out en masse to picket the opening. They carried derisive signs and posters of distorted dragons bearing Walt's caricature. Disney was furious and had to be driven away from the theater by Roy before the film began.

Rosenberg and representatives of the stockholders continued to pressure Walt to settle. Finally, on the morning of June 30, Disney appeared ready to negotiate and asked Willie Bioff to call a meeting with the strikers for that night. That same day, before the meeting could take place, however, Bioff was indicted by a federal grand jury. The charge was complicity to extort half a million dollars from several motion picture studios, based on information Kibre and Sorrell had supplied to the authorities regarding Joseph Schenck's $100,000 pay-off to Willie Bioff that had almost caused the murder of Kibre and Sorrell.

The indictment may have been more fortuitous to Disney than he first believed. According to several sources, Bioff, believing he was about to be indicted, had hoped to gain points with the government by demonstrating his role as a legitimate negotiator. He was, therefore, determined to end the strike no matter what it took.

George Bodle remembered this incident that occurred the night before Bioff's indictment was handed down:

> One of the most amazing things happened. We were in a meeting at the union's hall at the corner of Sunset and Highland, and we were told that Disney had requested a meeting with the strike leaders—me, Herb Sorrell, Art Babbitt, Bill Littlejohn, and David Hilberman—to bang out a settlement. We got ready to leave. We all got into one car, except Hilberman, who got into another, and started out for Disney's strike headquarters at the Roosevelt Hotel.
>
> That's when Sorrell realized the address he'd been given wasn't the hotel but Willie Bioff's ranch. That was where Disney had supposedly called the meeting. None of us wanted to walk into that kind of a setup. We knew Bioff's history of intimidation, and we weren't going to put ourselves in a position where, if things got rough, we might not leave standing up.

According to Hilberman, "I didn't particularly want to have anything to do with Bioff, even so much as meet with him, as I knew his background in organized crime. I got into a car he'd sent for me, and we started off and made a turn. 'Wait a minute,' I said, 'the Roosevelt's that way.' He [the driver] said, 'We're not going to the Roosevelt. We're going to Bioff's ranch.' I said the hell I was and told him unless he pulled over I was going to jump out of the car."

The meeting at Bioff's ranch never took place. The next day Bioff was indicted, and two days later Disney ran a full-page ad in the July 2 edition of *Variety* outlining the terms of the settlement he had planned to present personally to the strike leaders at the aborted meeting:

TO MY EMPLOYEES ON STRIKE:

I believe you are entitled to know why you are not working today. I offered your leaders the following terms:

1. All employees to be reinstated to former positions.
2. No discrimination.
3. Recognition of your union.
4. Closed shop.
5. 50 percent retroactive pay for the time on strike—something without precedent in the American Labor movement.
6. Increase in wages to make yours the highest salary scale in the cartoon industry.
7. Two weeks' vacation with pay.

I believe that you have been misled and misinformed about the real issues underlying the strike at the studio. I am positively convinced that Communistic agitation, leadership, and activities have brought about this strike, and has [sic] persuaded you to reject this fair and equitable settlement.

I address you in this manner because I have no other means of reaching you.

Walt Disney
Hollywood, California
July 2, 1941

Disney feared Bioff's indictment might seriously damage the studio's relationship with the Bank of America as well as with the general public. Throughout the strike, Walt had been careful to keep his distance from the corrupt union official. While Bioff's relationship to the mob was an open secret in Hollywood, the general public had most likely never heard of him until now. Any connection between the Disney studio and the mob, no matter how indirect, could result in a public-relations disaster. Walt was now anxious to do whatever it took to settle the strike as quickly as possible.

Had the meeting at Bioff's taken place, the strike leaders were prepared to accept any reasonable offer to settle. However, Bioff's indictment strengthened the resolve of the leaders of the strike, and they called a halt to all further negotiations. The next morning Disney was accused, in a public statement by the strike's spokesmen, of being an "Egocentric paternalist" living off the success of his workers.

By now the walkout had escalated into a full-scale war and gained national attention. Nobody could predict when a settlement might be reached. Many felt the leaders of the strike were out to punish Disney by forcing him out of business, which appeared more likely each day the strike continued. Fallout from Bioff's indictment forced IATSE, the mob-connected union, to withdraw its support from Disney as it, too, sought to put as much distance as it could between itself and Bioff.

By the start of the walkout's second month, the members of the Screen Actors Guild voted to donate $1,000 a week to the strikers' support fund, and the Printing Council forced the withdrawal of the "Mickey Mouse" comic strip from its member newspapers.

The second week in July, the Technicolor Corporation threw its support to the strikers and announced its refusal to process any Disney film until the studio recognized the right of the Guild to exist. The next week, sixteen national AFL unions came out in support of the strikers. The AFL placed all Disney pictures on its "Unfair List," and its five million affiliate members were asked not to patronize the studio's movies.

On July 15, Franklin Roosevelt dispatched Stanley White, a federal labor conciliator, to Hollywood to try to effect a workable settlement.

White met separately with Sorrell and Lessing. Lessing, according to the *Hollywood Citizen News*, informed White:

> We are compelled to withdraw our concessions for a settlement because we find that the representatives of the strikers are not sincere. We learned that they had intended imposing other demands upon us which would have been tantamount to their

taking over the studio. That has been the situation all along in this strike. Every time we offered to concede to their demands they would turn right around and impose others. We are going ahead with the operation of the studio with the employees who refused to walk out.

In the wake of Bioff's indictment, Lessing had taken over as the studio's chief negotiator, and for a very practical reason. Not surprisingly, the ongoing strike had caused Walt's chronic nervous condition to erupt, reducing him to a walking collection of tics and phobias. His hand-washing alone became so obsessive he visited his private studio bathroom sometimes as often as thirty times an hour.

His temper grew shorter, and his willingness to reason with the strikers evaporated. Spontaneous outbursts continued to punctuate his meetings. At home, screaming matches with Lillian could be heard by passersby and neighbors. Rumors that Walt had actually struck his wife so hard he had broken her jaw circulated for weeks. Roy recognized the familiar warning signs and believed his brother was in the early stage of yet another nervous breakdown.

Fearing what a continuing strike might do to the economic foundation of the studio and his brother's rapidly deteriorating condition, Roy began a secret campaign to get his brother out of town until a settlement was reached. While John Jay Whitney, the director of the motion picture division for the Coordination of Inter-American Affairs, is generally credited with conceiving the idea of Disney's 1941 "goodwill" trip to South America, the idea actually originated with Roy, who appealed directly to J. Edgar Hoover for help in making it happen.

Roosevelt's concern over Nazi Germany's growing influence in South America had prompted him to appoint Nelson Rockefeller to the newly created post of Official Coordinator of State Department Inter-American Affairs. Rockefeller had previously sponsored film projects for Darryl F. Zanuck and Orson Welles, and Hoover suggested to Roosevelt that Disney should also be made part of the program. Roosevelt passed on the suggestion to Rockefeller, who then offered to send Disney on the tour.

Walt initially turned down the opportunity, fearing it would look as if he were running away from the strike, which was exactly what Roy wanted him to do. To help persuade him to take the trip, the government agreed to put up $100,000 for Walt to make two films during the tour. In addition, Roy pointed out to Walt, the positive publicity he would receive as America's Ambassador of Goodwill would go a long way to counter new rumors of his pro-Nazi sympathies, sparked by, among other things, Disney's presence alongside Charles Lindbergh at several "America First" rallies in New York and elsewhere around the country.

Inevitably, those who most vehemently opposed the country's involvement in the war, as did Disney, were thought to be sympathetic to the Axis powers. There were those who began seeing "secret signals" in Disney's work, including, in one instance, a swastika in the final panel of a June 19, 1940, "Mickey Mouse" comic strip.

Disney had little direct input with the King Features daily "funny." However, like most everything else, it carried the sole credit "By Walt Disney" at the top of each day's final panel and the familiar curlicue signature at the bottom. The flurry of apprehension surrounding the strip eventually reached the desk of J. Edgar Hoover after one of Disney's "fans" wrote the Bureau chief citing the June 19 edition. The "fan" advised that "in the last section of *Mickey Mouse* by Walt Disney [there is] a very distinct swastika in the form of two crossed musical notes. . . . Perhaps [Disney] is not a Nazi sympathizer at all. . . . If it could mean anything, I know you are the man that should be informed of this." Hoover put the letter in Disney's file and marked the matter closed.

Walt finally agreed to make the trip to South America, and on August 17, Walt, Lillian, Bill Cottrell, Hazel, and a handpicked staff of fourteen loyalists, including Norm Ferguson, Jack Miller, Jim Midrell, Webb Smith, Ted Sears, Larry Landsburg and his wife, and Lee and Mary Blair left Los Angeles for the much-publicized journey. The entourage made several stateside fueling stops in major cities, where they were greeted by the prearranged presence of reporters, whose photos and stories of AMBASSADOR WALT DISNEY— PATRIOTIC AMERICAN WITH A MISSION helped push the story of the strike off the front pages of the nation's newspapers.

Disney's brother-in-law Bill Cottrell recalled, "Rio was the first major stop where we stayed overnight, before going on to Argentina. We stopped for refueling at a little dirt airport somewhere out of Brazil, and there were hundreds of people there, mostly children, waiting for us. How they knew we were coming we couldn't figure, because there were no newspapers or radio. But there they were, all dressed like Mickey Mouse, cheering Walt Disney."

Disney had been instructed by Whitney to specifically avoid public appearances, so it wouldn't seem he was there for any reason other than to make movies. It was the belief of the trip's sponsor, Nelson Rockefeller, that any hint of political motives would destroy Disney's effectiveness as the bearer of "friendship and goodwill." Walt had no objections. The strike had caused the flow of new product to dribble to a near-halt. The chance to make two commercial films at the American government's expense was something Disney didn't need much convincing to do.

Upon arriving in Brazil, he set up a small studio and used his traveling staff to supervise the available local talent. Work went smoothly until someone from his staff casually referred to one of the Brazilian animators as a "native." The incident upset the locals and nearly brought the filming of *The Three Caballeros* to a halt, until Walt personally apologized to the offended party.

Meanwhile, during his brother's absence, Roy worked feverishly to effect a strike settlement. The week after Walt's departure, at Roosevelt's directive, the U.S. Labor Department Conciliation Service sent James F. Dewey to see if he could succeed where the other delegates from Washington had failed.

Before Dewey arrived in Hollywood, Nelson Rockefeller placed a call advising Roy there was no use in continuing a hard line, that the studio simply couldn't win. On September 9, twenty-four hours after Dewey arrived in Hollywood, Roy agreed to submit to binding arbitration.

His actions meant that the Disney studio was ready to recognize the Cartoonists Guild with no further votes, secret or otherwise. Roy also agreed to rehire all the cartoonists who had been fired as a result of union activities, the equalization of pay among staffers, severance pay guarantees, vacations with pay, and closed-shop status. These were the same terms Walt had offered back in July. This time, however, under the terms of binding arbitration, the strike's leaders agreed without condition.

When news of the settlement reached Walt in South America, he became so furious he wrecked his makeshift office and vowed to close down his studio forever, declaring he would sooner sell toys for a living than have to admit the Cartoonists Guild to his studio. He drafted an open letter he paid to have published in as many newspapers as he could afford, in which he stated, in part, that:

> To me, the entire [strike] situation is a catastrophe. The spirit that played such an important part in the building of the cartoon medium has been destroyed. . . .
>
> I am convinced that this entire mess was Communistically inspired and led. . . . I am thoroughly disgusted and would gladly quit and establish myself in another business if it were not for the loyal guys who believe in me—so I guess I'm stuck with it. I have a case of the D.D.s—disillusionment and discouragement.

UPON HIS RETURN to Hollywood, Disney, by now more dejected than angry, received additional bad news. In his absence Elias had passed away.

Disney's obsessive enthusiasm for filmmaking had been fueled, in part, by the phenomenal level of his early, un-Eliaslike success. With the unexpected failure of *Fantasia*, the strike, and the death of his father, Walt, at the age of forty, seemed to have run out of creative energy. Feeling his striking "family" had betrayed him, he reacted as Elias might have, and turned his back on them and the common ground of animation they shared. Except for those films begun before the walkout, from the day of the settlement on, Walt never again achieved anything like what he had during the four-year period between *Snow White* and *Fantasia*.

The year 1941 had begun for Walt with the belief that *Fantasia* would provide the vehicle for Mickey Mouse's rebirth. It ended instead with multiple images of death. The death of his father, the death of his studio, the death of his creative spirit.

SHORTLY AFTER his return from South America, Walt received a call from J. Edgar Hoover regarding the details of a secret journey recently completed by a contingent of special agents to a remote village on the southern tip of Spain. There, Hoover told Walt, the Bureau had traced the origins of the woman who might well be Walt's real mother. This news, coming when it did, finally and completely unnerved Disney.

That day, he locked himself up in his office and refused to talk to or see anybody. From outside his door the unmistakable sounds of sobbing could be heard into the night.

ELEVEN

The Mojacar Connection

IN THE WINTER OF 1940, the same year Walt Disney became an official Hollywood informant for the FBI, two well-dressed Americans in wide-brimmed hats and pin-striped suits went on a mission to Mojacar, a tiny Spanish village east of Almeria, on the Mediterranean coast. Upon their arrival, the two men asked Senor Jacinto Alarcon, the mayor of the village, for assistance in locating the town priest. Their stated objective: to obtain a baptismal certificate for a baby born in or around 1890 to one Señora Isabelle Zamora.

According to Barcelonan journalist Paco Flores, the son of Mojacar's official archivist, the two men were from the FBI. "Going by my [deceased] father's records, I don't believe they took anything, although there are many here who believe their real mission was to erase all evidence that Walt Disney was really born here.

"The story is told that at the end of the past century there lived here a very attractive washerwoman called Isabelle Zamora Ascensio, known to the villagers as *La Bicha*. She was very popular with the men of the village and became pregnant by one.

"It is believed that the father of Señora Zamora's baby was the already married Dr. José Guirao, who conducted the boy's christening himself, naming him José Guirao as well. Dr. Guirao died shortly after the birth of his son, after which Señora Zamora decided to leave Spain and journey by boat to America."

Barcelonan historian Carlos Almendros spent ten years researching

the family origins of Walt Disney, his work underwritten by the
Spanish government. According to Almendros, Señora Zamora left
Spain because she and Dr. Guirao were devout Catholics and wished
to protect both their families. When Señora Zamora, according to
Almendros, arrived on the east coast of the United States she began
another journey, this one overland, heading west to California, where
she was eventually taken in by Franciscan missionaries.

There are no existing records in Spain, and none forthcoming from
the FBI, regarding the identity of the two American men who made
the 1940 trip to Mojacar. Julian Ruiz, nationally known Spanish
journalist, investigated that visit for three years as part of *his* ongoing
study into the origins of Walt Disney. He believes, as does journalist
Paco Flores, that, based on what he has been able to piece together,
the men were indeed Special Agents of the Federal Bureau of
Investigation.

However, Jacinto Alarcon, Mojacar's former mayor, insists that
when he personally greeted the two men, they identified themselves
as being from the "Walt Disney Studios." Flores, Ruiz, and Alarcon
all agree on one thing: The men had come to Mojacar to obtain
information on the birth of José Guirao in the hopes of discovering if
he was, in fact, Walt Disney. It is not known if the two men,
whomever they represented, actually found José Cuirao's certificate
of baptism. If they did, and if they were federal agents, they presumably delivered it to J. Edgar Hoover.

According to Flores's archives, another visit was made to Mojacar
in 1954, this one on record by a group of California-based Franciscans
inquiring about birth records for José Guirao and/or Walt Disney.
The Franciscans visited the schoolhouse, dined with the mayor, and
spent a great deal of time at the courthouse searching through birth
records that might have survived the ravages of the Spanish Civil War
that nearly destroyed Mojacar.

In 1966, one year after Walt Disney's death, still another contingent of investigators came to Mojacar in search of any documents to
link Isabelle Zamora Ascensio to Walt Disney. There are literally
hundreds of corroborating witnesses to this visit. The sitting judge of
Mojacar at the time, Blas Caparros, authorized the official "American
Search Committee's" papers and granted them full access to whatever
records they might find regarding Isabelle Zamora Ascensio and her
son José Guirao.

Most Mojacans believe this team of investigators came from the Disney studio, and finally did uncover the boy's long-missing baptismal certificate, only to summarily destroy it so as to insure no "outside" claims could be made by Señora Zamora's descendants against the estate of Walt Disney.

There are many among Mojacar's older citizenry who remember quite vividly the Zamora and Guirao families. Stories have survived for generations regarding Señora Zamora's sudden departure for America. Her reputation made her something of a celebrity in Mojacar, the saga she starred in still the subject of many family Sunday get-togethers. Still, the villagers have made no attempt to exploit Disney's name. No Disney memorials exist, no preserved birthplaces, no tours, no souvenir shops. No plaques, no monuments, no statues.

The strange circumstances surrounding the birth and fate of José Guirao have been the subject of intensive research by generations of Spanish journalists for more than fifty years, and it will continue until conclusive evidence is found to provide the answers to one of Spain's strangest and most enduring mysteries.

In 1890, Elias Disney, as he often did, took leave of his wife and children once more, this time to take part in the second wave of the California Gold Rush. Having again failed to find his fortune, Elias returned home early in 1891. His arrival occurred only weeks before the unexplained listing of the birth of a "Walter Disney" on January 8, 1891, in the official records of the Illinois Department of Vital Statistics, *ten years before he was supposed to have actually been born.*

The 1891 listing might lead some to believe that Walt Disney was actually ten years older than has been previously thought. Photos of Walt taken throughout his life amply support what those who knew him have often said, that he seemed to have begun to age quite early, and that his accomplishments, culminating in the heading of his own studio while still in his twenties, were all the more remarkable because he was so young.

While age might be deceptive in later years, it is inconceivable that a boy of thirteen could pass for one of three. There are far more likely explanations for the discrepancy in the birth records. Because Disney was born at home, his name may have been omitted in error by the midwife who delivered him. Midwives were known to be careless about paperwork, and as a result, records from that time were often inaccurate and incomplete.

However, this doesn't adequately explain the listing of Walt's name ten years *before* he was born. The page in question appears to have no late entries or changes, suggesting that either his name was entered in sequence, in 1891, or the entire page was later redone and reinserted into the log. If such a forgery were made, the most logical explanation for Disney's name being entered the wrong year is that whoever did it simply made a mistake and altered the wrong page.

What, then, is the significance of Elias's 1890 journey to California? For one thing, it places him there at exactly the time of Señora Zamora's arrival. One unproven theory posits that Elias, who fancied himself a ladies' man, began an ongoing affair with Señora Zamora. Because he was prominent in the Fundamentalist church, divorcing Flora, the mother of his three children, was impossible. Instead, Elias brought Señora Zamora back to Chicago, where he supported her until Preacher Parr, perhaps discovering Elias's indiscretion, expelled him from the church. This would explain Elias's sudden uprooting of his family to the Midwest.

Then there is the question of the young boy, José Guirao—if he actually existed, and if so, what happened to him. One possible explanation, again unproven, is that he was in fact born out of wedlock in the United States. If this is true, several other pieces of the puzzle fall into place: the falsified placement of Walt Disney's name in the birth records, for example. If Elias had a child with Señora Zamora, he may have convinced, or possibly forced, Flora to raise the boy as their own, to avoid the shame of scandal following them to Marceline, where Elias fled after being discovered by Preacher Parr.

And, if Señora Zamora was in fact Walt Disney's real mother, the unexplained 1940 visit by the FBI might have had an entirely different goal. Rather than looking for evidence that would prove José Guirao was Walt Disney, the team may have actually gone to Mojacar to *plant* such evidence. That way, if any parental link were ever established between Señora Zamora and Elias, the record of her having given birth to a boy in Spain, and the probably altered Chicago birth records for Walt, would prove that José Guirao could not have been Walt Disney.

Finally, what of the so-called family resemblance between Walt and Roy? To begin with, there was virtually no physical resemblance between either Walt or Roy and their two eldest brothers. There was, however, a passing resemblance between Walt, Roy, and Elias. Walt's dark, handsome features were often described in newspaper articles and magazines of the thirties as "Castillian."

His resemblance to Roy is notably less apparent in photos taken of the two together. Roy's features were thick; Walt's aquiline. Roy had large ears and a receding hairline. Walt had small ears and thick, wavy hair. Roy's overall appearance was bookish, accountantlike; Walt's was one of dashing sensuality. The similarities could certainly be accounted for as those between stepbrothers. A darker theory, without much support from any research thus far, suggests that Roy too was born out of wedlock, to Señora Zamora.

There is one final, tantalizing twist. Upon returning to Flora, Elias hired a housekeeper who remained in the family employ for thirty-five years. It is believed this was the same woman Walt Disney hired as *his* housekeeper, after Elias's death. She was said to be of Spanish descent, from a remote village called Mojacar, located in southeast Spain.

ONCE Walt Disney discovered he couldn't conclusively prove where, when, or even to whom he was born, it was the *possibility* rather than the fact he was adopted or born out of wedlock that haunted him the rest of his life and shadowed many of the characters of his greatest films. Notably, there were the abandoned stepchild left in the woods in *Snow White*; the wooden puppet who longs to be Gepetto's real boy in *Pinocchio*; the forest creature who loses his mother and is separated from his father in *Bambi*; the apprentice in fearful servitude in *Fantasia*'s "Sorcerer's Apprentice"; and the baby elephant separated from his real mother in *Dumbo*. In many of Disney's lesser efforts the theme of abandonment emerges with the parentless leader of the Lost Boys in *Peter Pan*; Cinderella and her stepsisters; the homeless street animals in *Lady and the Tramp*; the adopted dogs in *101 Dalmations*; and the idealized father/son relationship between Jim Hawkins and Long John Silver in *Treasure Island*. What these films all have in common is their main characters' quests to find their real parents. Those who interfere with that quest, usually symbols of evil authority, complete a recurring dramatic metaphor in Disney's films for the internal struggle between moral conviction and doubt.

J. Edgar Hoover skillfully exploited Disney's great conundrum to insure his unswerving loyalty to the Bureau, which the FBI then used to maximum advantage. Walt's real loss of Elias, coming as it did at the moment of the symbolic loss of his studio, made Disney even more psychologically vulnerable to Hoover's paternalistic influence.

To assist in his battle against communism in America, Hoover encouraged Disney to unleash what was loyalty's dark antithesis— unwavering vengeance. In the years immediately following the strike, Hoover provided Disney the impetus, the opportunity, and the encouragement to externalize his emotional conflicts by vowing to take unbridled vengeance on those "Communist" strikers he believed had been disloyal and conspired to destroy him and his "family."

TWELVE

Disney Goes to War

THE BLOODLETTING began September 15, 1941, the day after the strike's official end. The first two victims were the men Walt considered to have been the leaders of the walkout, Arthur Babbitt and Dave Hilberman. The diminutive Babbitt, whom Disney now referred to as the Guild's "head sewer rat," was personally stopped at the front gates of the studio the first day after the settlement by Gunther Lessing. The attorney put a finger in Babbitt's face and told him the only way he was ever going to get back on the lot, NLRB or no NLRB, was if he took Disney to court. Disney would sooner shut down his entire operation, Lessing added, before ever allowing Babbitt to spend even one more minute inside the studio's gates.

Babbitt recalled, "I was fired a total of five times. Disney would fire me, conciliators would put me back in. I was determined to take the case all the way to the Supreme Court.

"I knew that would take forever, that Disney and Lessing would throw every legal obstacle in my way, so I decided in the meantime I'd do my bit, and I joined the marines. Or at least I tried to. After being accepted, my enlistment was mysteriously canceled. It took a long time before I was able to get reinstated. Seems the FBI had a file on me that said I was a Communist sympathizer. I had to [win that] battle before I could get back into the marines."

Babbitt reenlisted after proving in court the FBI's charges were totally unfounded. He eventually received top security clearance and served his tour of duty in Corps Intelligence. Upon his honorable discharge he resumed his legal battle for reinstatement with Disney.

Walt had initially justified his refusal to rehire Babbitt after the settlement by claiming the studio had to cut staff due to the ongoing loss of the overseas market. The Cartoonists Guild responded by accusing him of conducting an illegal lockout. Gunther Lessing then threatened to lay off the entire animation staff until the war ended. At this point, with Guild support, Babbitt took his battle to court.

Dave Hilberman was fired by telegram:

ARBITRATION AWARD HAS BEEN MADE. IT IS NECESSARY TO REDUCE OUR STAFF AND WE ARE SORRY WE HAVE TO EXTEND YOUR PRESENT LAYOFF INDEFINITELY.

WALT DISNEY PRODUCTIONS BY GUNTHER R. LESSING, VICE-PRESIDENT

According to Hilberman, "We knew that Walt was going to do his best [once the strike was settled] to get rid of me, so we traded an extra raise for the inkers in exchange for my agreeing not to contest what was a certainty—my firing."

The fate of Babbitt and Hilberman, combined with Lessing's threat of mass, arbitrary and open-ended layoffs, so angered Disney's animators that dozens chose not to return to their jobs at all. Frank Tashlin, the head of Screen Gems (Columbia studios' animation division begun by Harry Cohn after his split with Disney), was able to lure many of Walt's best animators with offers of better working conditions, on-screen credits, and higher pay.

Among the first to sign with Tashlin was David Swift, one of Disney's youngest and most promising animators. When Walt learned of Swift's plans to leave, according to the artist, "He called me in, finally, and putting on a phony Jewish accent he said, 'Okay, Davy boy, off you go to work with those Jews. It's where you belong, with those Jews.'"*

Far from being disturbed by the loss of so many key personnel,

---

*Swift told author Leonard Mosley what happened after he tried to rejoin Disney a few years later: "And when I came back to him later after the war, he was still resentful. 'Well, Bud,' he said, at the first studio meeting I went to, 'You can see we didn't come to any harm while you were away with those Jews. We got on quite well without you. We don't need you—and it looks as if those Jews don't need you either.

Disney seemed altogether delighted with what he described as "the mass defection." He chuckled to Roy that it had produced the very housecleaning of pro-unionists the Guild had fought so hard to prevent.

Thus encouraged, Walt judged that others no longer fit to work at his studio had to forfeit their jobs as well. Such was the case with Dave Hand, Walt's longtime riding partner and director of *Snow White*. Even though Hand had been openly sympathetic to the Guild, he had not gone out on strike. Nevertheless, Disney insisted the director and a handful of other top talent would have to continue to punch a clock. As Walt knew he would, rather than do that, Hand resigned.

The relationship between the two had disintegrated after Disney found out Hand was living with another woman before his divorce was finalized. Walt was disgusted by Hand's behavior, which he characterized to several other staffers as typical of the kind of "Communist-inspired immorality" he wasn't going to tolerate at his studio. This happened at the same time Walt ended his close friendship with Spencer Tracy, after learning the actor had separated from his wife and taken up with Katharine Hepburn. Disney never spoke to him again.

Other firings and departures followed. Within months of the settlement, Disney faced a serious manpower shortage for the heavy backlog of animated pictures that had been delayed by the strike. At the same time Roy was alarmed by his brother's decimation of a hand-picked staff that had taken years to put together and had produced the studio's greatest films. Gunther Lessing was also concerned and let Walt know it. However, ever since Lessing's prediction of a quick victory in the strike proved so disastrously incorrect, Walt had lost faith in him. "Gunny doesn't know his ass," Walt angrily told Roy, in response to what Disney described as Lessing's "hand wringing."*

With production drastically reduced and few completed films avail-

---

*According to Ward Kimball: "[Lessing] was a broken man. Once Walt said, 'Gunny doesn't know his ass.' Many times Walt would remark, 'Well, you know Lessing.' Walt kept him on, but only out of pure sympathy. Lessing still had his office, and had his secretary, but he no longer had any power. Nobody would listen to him anymore. There was a new man heading the legal department. Lessing would come to work every day with his umbrella and his hat. He'd sit down and fall asleep at his desk. Lessing died an outcast, of old age, a brokenhearted old man." From an interview in *The Comics Journal*, #120, March, 1988, by Klaus Strzyz, p. 94.

able for release, the studio slipped dangerously close to bankruptcy. What saved it from going under was the success of the animated feature *Dumbo*. The film, begun shortly before the strike began and completed before it was settled, was ready for release in October 1941.

About a month before its opening in late November, a major rift developed between Disney and his distributor, RKO, over the film's running time (sixty-four minutes). RKO wanted another ten minutes added to the film's length to qualify it for distribution as a full-length feature. Walt refused, insisting the film was perfect the way it was. Although he adamantly denied it, the film's shortness had less to do with art than economics. Animation's production costs rose by the literal minute. Because of its short running time, Disney was able to complete *Dumbo* for just under $1 million, as compared to the $2 to $3 million his other animated features had averaged.

Disney came up with the idea to film *Dumbo* after finding it in a collection of contemporary children's short stories. He intended to make it a "Silly Symphonies" until the story team of Norm Ferguson and Ham Luske developed it into a full-length feature, revised by the team Joe Grant and Dick Huemer while Disney was in South America. The story concerns the relationship between a baby elephant, Dumbo, and his mother, who travel with the circus. Dumbo's big ears mark him as different and funny-looking, causing his mother to be overprotective of her baby's feelings. One day a little boy comes to the circus and makes fun of Dumbo, sparking a near riot. Dumbo's mother is blamed, and as a result is separated from her baby and locked in a cage.

In his grief Dumbo is befriended by a little mouse, Timothy, who helps him discover that by flapping his ears he can fly. An aberration now becomes a blessing, and Dumbo winds up the circus's newest, brightest star, while his reinstated mother proudly watches from the sidelines.

The film's two set pieces—the trunk-touching scene between Dumbo and his imprisoned mother, and the "pink elephant" scene in which Dumbo accidentally drinks some alcohol, falls asleep, and has a nightmare leading him to discover he can fly—were highly entertaining, visually striking, and emotionally effective. The main problem with the film was that Disney had essentially done it before, and better.

Dumbo's big ears recalled perhaps a bit too vividly Pinocchio's wooden awkwardness. Jiminy Cricket's mission of moral rectitude made him a metaphor for Pinocchio's *conscience*, a more vivid image than Timothy's sidekick, who functioned as Dumbo's *subconscience* (the elephant's ultimate flight of fancy was the result of a dream). And the "pink elephant" sequence's bubbly visuals resembled nothing so much as an outtake from *Fantasia. Dumbo*'s retread themes and characters, increasingly familiar style of animation and noticeable lack of new technical wizardry, left some critics with a heavy sense of Disney Vu.

Walt actually had very little to do with the production, the bulk of which was completed in the summer of 1941, before he returned from South America. In his absence the studio's nonstriking artists and storymen tried to make a "Disney" movie without him. An expertly crafted, highly commercial *imitation* of a Disney film, *Dumbo*'s limitations demonstrated little of the originality, ingeniousness, and complexity of Walt's great cinematic vision.

Still, as he felt sure, because of its short running time, *Dumbo* proved a substantial commercial and popular success. The picture not only saved the studio from certain financial disaster, the little elephant seemed about to inspire a reawakening of Walt's creative spirit when, a week after the film's premiere, on Sunday morning, December 7, 1941, the Japanese attacked Pearl Harbor and the United States officially entered World War II.

The very next morning Walt was prevented from passing through the front gates of his own studio by U.S. military personnel until, with some difficulty, he was able to confirm his identity. Only then did a satisfied guard escort him to his captain's makeshift headquarters. He informed Disney, now in shock, that his studio was being commandeered as a primary defense station to guard the nearby Lockheed plant against a possible enemy air strike. Indeed, by Monday evening, all film equipment at the studio had been replaced by anti-aircraft weaponry, the parking lot was filled to capacity with stacked crates of ammunition, the grass lawn was covered by Jeeps.

Disney's shock turned to outrage when he discovered that his studio was the only one the army had commandeered. He attributed this intrusion to his lack of power within the hierarchy of Hollywood. Would the government have dared to take over Paramount, he wondered? Or Universal?

A WEEK LATER, still enraged and having just turned forty, Disney announced to his family he had decided to retire from the business of making movies. As if to emphasize his decision to make some real changes in his life, he decided it was time for the family to move. Now, however, instead of purchasing a house, he had plans drawn to have one built. He purchased a piece of property in the Holmby Hills, one of the most exclusive sections of Los Angeles, between the hills and canyons of Bel-Air and Beverly Hills, where every house, it seemed, was occupied by a show-business family.

Early in 1942, upon its completion, Disney moved his family and all their possessions into their new home. For the first time since he had been forced to do so as a child, Walt attended weekly church services, accompanied by his wife and two daughters. Often, after Sunday school classes, he spent the entire afternoon with nine-year-old Diane and six-year-old Sharon, taking them for rides on the carousel in Griffith Park or for horseback-riding lessons.

During the week he became the family chauffeur, driving the children to their respective schools: Diane to the Marlborough Middle School in the Wilshire district, Sharon to the more exclusive Westlake School for Girls in Holmby Hills. He was determined to spend as much time with his daughters as possible. And because he believed as everyone else, that the Japanese might indeed attack Los Angeles, he hired a private security team to protect his children.

While Walt made a conscious effort to treat his daughters equally, he favored Sharon, who was younger, prettier, and adopted. While Diane had angular features, dark hair, and a prominent nose, Sharon had sloe-eyes, a wide white smile, and soft blond locks. Lillian had chosen her over the other candidates for adoption precisely because of her striking good looks. The school she attended, Westlake, was filled with the children of Hollywood's most successful show-business families. It particularly appealed to Disney because, with the exception of one or two "musical Jews," as he referred to them, Westlake was restricted.

One day in 1942, the six-year-old daughter of a well-known Jewish producer was admitted after her father threatened not only to sue the school but to see to it the case received considerable publicity in the press. On his daughter's first day of classes, she was approached by six-year-old Sharon, who, after introducing herself, said proudly, "I heard all about you from my daddy. You're Jewish, right? My daddy says your father made all his money in the last twenty years!"

Neither was old enough to understand what any of that meant, and they quickly became friends. Sharon liked to bring her new classmate home after school for ice-cream sundaes, made at the brand-new soda fountain Walt had installed in the children's den.

In spite of his distaste for her father, Walt was cordial to the little girl, probably because Sharon liked her so much. Years later, the friend recalled that "whenever Walt was around he was like a living Santa Claus, and every so often he would run this big locomotive for us that ran the perimeter of his house. He was like this big kid, so happy his daughter and her little friend liked his toys."

Diane, meanwhile, perhaps jealous of all the attention her half-sister received, announced her intention to convert to Catholicism. Her vow, which Walt took as a disloyal rejection of the family's Fundamentalist heritage, so angered him he reportedly slapped her hard across the face, one of the very few times he ever raised his hand to his children. This Elias-like flash of anger frightened his children and angered Lillian, who warned Walt that if he ever again so much as lifted an eyebrow to either of their daughters, she would take them so far away he would never be able find them. The thought terrified Disney, and he never again raised his voice to either of his girls.

Barely five weeks after his "retirement," in January 1942, the Naval Bureau of Aeronautics offered Walt the chance to make twenty animated training films for a total budget of $80,000. Anxious to get out of the house and back into his studio, Walt instantly accepted the offer.

Walt worked out of an unused building on the studio grounds. By cutting costs and using a skeletal crew of the only acceptable animators available,* he managed to bring the entire series in $8,000 under budget. The initial twenty cartoons proved so popular that Walt was inundated with orders from every government agency for dozens of additional ones, some intended only for military audiences, others as propaganda for public consumption.

The new assignments proved a mixed blessing for Disney. While

---

*The majority of Disney's draft-eligible animators received exemptions by opting for duty in the special services division of the armed forces—the 18th Air Force Base Unit, otherwise known as the FMPU (First Motion Picture Unit). "Fumpoo," as it was called by its troops, was comprised of approximately 150 officers, enlisted men, and civilians, and was located on the grounds of what had been the old Hal Roach Studios in Culver City. The main assignment of the unit was to produce training films.

they did keep him in business, he found it more difficult to deal with those in the military than it was to deal with Rosenberg, the Bank of America, his stockholders, even the most arrogant leaders of the Cartoonists Guild. The army only knew one way of having things done—their way. Disney had to agree to whatever demands the military made regarding the production of their movies.

When Secretary of the Treasury Henry Morgenthau chided him about cost overruns, Disney began to slip back into the same kind of venal anger that had fueled his behavior during the strike. He bitterly complained to Roy and Lessing about how the studio was now being forced to accept "that Jew," as Walt referred to the secretary, as not just an advisor but a full partner who wanted to be in charge of everything. To Walt, the studio now functioned with Morgenthau's message delivered by Disney's messengers—political propaganda films that cashed in on the popularity of that all-American mouse Mickey, his sweetheart Minnie, pal Donald, companion Goofy, and dog Pluto. At one point Disney was said to have referred to his beloved characters as captives, forced to perform like so many little Pinocchios for a Stromboli-like Morgenthau.*

THE THOUGHT that the studio he had fought so hard to create was now, in his mind, being singled out by any and every government agency to use as they saw fit, infuriated him. Time and again he asked Roy why no other studio had to make similar sacrifices.

This was one of Walt's grander misperceptions of the realities of wartime in Hollywood. To begin with, Disney was being paid for his efforts, while nearly every major studio donated the services of its stars without charge for appearances in propaganda films. Many of Hollywood's most durable players, including Clark Gable, James Stewart, and Ronald Reagan, were featured in an endless series of propaganda films that chronicled their "true-life" war experiences. One of the industry's most bankable women, Carole Lombard, lost her life in a plane crash on a war bonds drive.

*The most memorable of Disney's propaganda cartoons was *Der Fuehrer's Face*, in which Donald Duck openly mocked Adolf Hitler. Along with *The New Spirit*, the film that inspired the most animosity between Morgenthau and Walt over budgets and what Disney claimed were unpaid costs and distribution paybacks, *Der Fuehrer's Face* identified Disney as one of the nation's leading celebrity patriots.

Ignoring this, Disney pointed to studios like Republic, whose biggest star, John Wayne, was exempted from military service. Republic received government funding and the free loan of military equipment, personnel, and advisors to produce enormously profitable "war" films. It seemed to him that everyone in Hollywood was cashing in on the war, everyone, that is, except him.

In fact, ever since his subsidized trip to South America during the strike, his studio had been kept in business by the government. And when the war took away his foreign markets, the government quickly provided a new one by ordering animated training films which they allowed him to make for profit. In truth, the Disney studio was heavily subsidized during the war and wound up profiting substantially from it.

Still, Walt continued to feel he had been victimized until, in the winter of 1942, it was announced that he was to be given the prestigious Irving Thalberg Award by the Academy of Motion Pictures Arts and Sciences "for the most consistently high quality of pictures produced." Walt was genuinely moved by what he considered the long-overdue recognition of his work. The award was presented to Disney at that year's Oscar ceremonies by one of Hollywood's most powerful independent film producers, David O. Selznick.

When called to the podium for the presentation, Walt, overcome with gratitude, sobbed uncontrollably throughout his mostly inaudible acceptance speech. Tears steaked down his cheeks while he struggled to get his words out. "I . . . I . . . want to . . . thank everybody . . . here. This . . . is a vote . . . of . . . confidence . . . from the whole industry . . ." He then drifted into a long reverie that mixed humility with self-congratulation.

WHEN IT became clear the Japanese were not going to bomb Los Angeles, the military ended its occupation of the Disney studio eight months after it arrived. No sooner had the last truck rolled off the lot than Disney undertook his first fully commercial production since the outbreak of the war. To reenter "private" filmmaking, he chose a project that *resembled* the many government propaganda films he produced that had proved so popular—*Victory Through Air Power*.

The film, released in 1943, was based on a book written by military aviation expert Major Alexander De Seversky, whose advocacy of wartime aggressiveness particularly appealed to Disney. Like the book, it vigorously defended the war tactics of General Billy Mitchell, who had come under court-martial for his unorthodox military conduct. Although the film proved a financial dud in America, the movie found an audience in, of all places, England, where Disney fare had never been that popular. Winston Churchill personally requested a private screening for himself and Franklin Roosevelt. Both the film and the prime minister's urging helped convince the president to go ahead with the what had been his indecision about the air force's long-range bombing program.

Still, the film's lack of success in America annoyed Disney, who insisted the blame for its failure lay not in the film itself but with those filmmakers he believed had traded their patriotism for profits. He brooded about the film's misfortune (it lost a half-million dollars) until he had expanded the reasons for it into a grand rationale for all that had gone wrong with Hollywood when he announced to the press:

> The motion picture business . . . made truckloads of money during the war. The theaters had little time for our product. We represented the family trade, and theater owners didn't care about that. Our films brought in kids as well as adults, but the kids paid less for their tickets than grown-ups; movie theaters were doing big business with any piece of cheese they booked, so they didn't care whether they attracted the whole family or not.

Then, in May, when the National Conference of Christians and Jews indirectly sought Disney's services to help promote a message of unity in light of the German nightmare, he decided things had gone too far.

The organization had first approached independent Hollywood producer Sol Lesser with an idea for a cartoon they wanted made. As they described it, it would be a "kind of Aesop fable depicting human prejudices." According to their proposal, the organization wanted to show animals in a barnyard setting who decide to hold "a roundtable meeting to stop the use of weasel words of hate against Leghorns and Rhode Island Reds." The moral aphorisms the organization wanted to emphasize were to be highlighted in what it described as "cutesy" dialogue:

Mojacar, Spain. Was this Walt's ancestral homeland?

NIGHT OF THE AMERICAS

LINKED BY NATURE AND WELDED TOGETHER
BY A COMMON WILL TO VICTORY

* * * *

*New Yorkers have an unprecedented opportunity to see and
hear these distinguished artists, leaders and statesmen*

VICENTE
LOMBARDO TOLEDANO

*President of the Confederation of
Latin American Workers*

PABLO
NERUDA

*Great Chilean Poet
Consul General to Mexico*

M A R G O

Chairman of the Evening
DONALD OGDEN STEWART

21029

PROGRAM OF SONG, DANCE AND MUSIC BY CELEBRATED
AMERICAN AND LATIN AMERICAN ARTISTS.

PARTIAL LIST OF
SPONSORS AND GUESTS OF HONOR

FRANCISCO CASTILLO NAJERA
  Mexican Ambassador to the U.S.A.
RODOLFO MICHELS
  Chilean Ambassador to the U.S.A.
LUIS F. GUACHALLA
  Bolivian Ambassador to the U.S.A.
CAPITAN COLON ELOY ALFARO
  Ecuadorian Ambassador to the U.S.A.
RAFAEL de la COLINA
  Mexican Minister Plenipotentiary to the U.S.A.
ADRIAN RECINOS
  Guatemalan Minister to the U.S.A.
LUIS QUINTANILLA
  Mexican Minister to the Soviet Union
J. URIEL GARCIA
  Senator of Peru
LUIS MUNOZ MARIN
  President of the Senate of Puerto Rico
JACQUES ROUMAIN
  Haitian Charge d'Affaires to Mexico
ALFONSO de CASTRO VALLE
  Mexican Charge d'Affaires to China

CARMEN AMAYA
CARMEN CASTILLO
NORMAN CORWIN
XAVIER CUGAT
WALT DISNEY
TITO GUIZAR
JOHN GUNTHER
ELSIE HOUSTON
CARMEN MIRANDA
PAUL ROBESON
BIDU SAYAO
MRS. VINCENT SHEEAN
HERMAN SHUMLIN
GLADYS SWARTHOUT
DEEMS TAYLOR
ORSON WELLES
PAUL MUNI
COL. CARLOS ROMULO
MRS. BORIS G. ORLOVE, Jr.

AND THE COUNCIL FOR PAN AMERICAN DEMOCRACY

ALL SEATS RESERVED $3.30 - $2.20 - $1.65 - $1.10 - 83c.

MARTIN BECK THEATRE · SUN. EVE., FEB. 14
8:30 P.M.

Tickets obtainable at box-office or Council for Pan American Democracy, 112 East 19th St., G R 3-3700

FBI document 21029. The flier for the "Night of the Americas." (Walt
Disney's FBI file)

b.7c

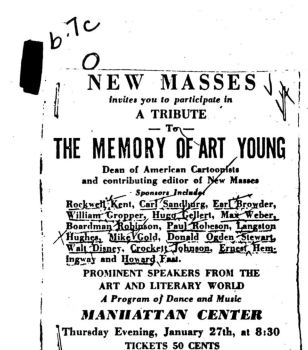

O

NEW MASSES

Invites you to participate in

A TRIBUTE

— To —

THE MEMORY OF ART YOUNG

Dean of American Cartoonists
and contributing editor of New Masses

Sponsors Include:

Rockwell Kent, Carl Sandburg, Earl Browder,
William Gropper, Hugo Gellert, Max Weber,
Boardman Robinson, Paul Robeson, Langston
Hughes, Mike Gold, Donald Ogden Stewart,
Walt Disney, Crockett Johnson, Ernest Hemingway and Howard Fast.

PROMINENT SPEAKERS FROM THE
ART AND LITERARY WORLD

A Program of Dance and Music

MANHATTAN CENTER

Thursday Evening, January 27th, at 8:30

TICKETS 50 CENTS

Get Your Tickets Early at Workers Bookshop, 50 E. 13th St.,
Bookfair, 133 West 44th St., New Masses, 104 East 9th St.

There Will Be No Standing Room

246 505
ALL INFORMATION CONTAINED
HEREIN IS UNCLASSIFIED
DATE 1/15/85 BY SPBB5JUA

This is a clipping from
page ___14___ of the
DAILY WORKER
Date *Jan 13, 1944*
Clipped at the Seat of
Government

INDEXED 61-91-82-A
NOT RECORDED
85 JAN 17 1944

27 JAN 19 1944

b.7c

FBI document 61-91-82-A. The *Daily Worker* ad for the Art Young
Memorial. (Walt Disney's FBI file)

Office Memorandum • UNITED STATES GOVERNMENT

TO : DIrector, FBI Att'n: Training and Inspection **DATE** December 16, 1954
Division

FROM : SAC, Los Angeles (66-new)

SUBJECT: WALT DISNEY
SAC CONTACT
LOS ANGELES FIELD DIVISION

Re SAC Letter 54-54 dated 10/7/54.

Date _/—/2—5 5,_
Approved by Bureau as SAC Contact

POSITION OF CONTACT

Mr. WALT DISNEY is the Vice-President in charge of production and
the founder of Walt Disney Productions, Inc., 2400 West Alameda Street,
Burbank, California. Mr. DISNEY is extremely prominent in the motion picture
industry and his company is the foremost organization in the production of
cartoons.

SERVICES CONTACT CAN PERFORM

b-7d

Mr. DISNEY has recently established
a business association with the American Broadcasting Company - Paramount
Theaters, Inc., for the production of a series of television shows, which
for the most part are scheduled to be filmed at Disneyland, a multimillion
dollar amusement park being established under Mr. DISNEY's direction in
the vicinity of Anaheim, California. Mr. DISNEY has volunteered representatives of this office complete access to the facilities of Disneyland for use
in connection with official matters and for recreational purposes.

PAST RELATIONS WITH LOS ANGELES OFFICE

b-7d

JFM:gmw   RECORDED   DEC 1954

A 1954 FBI memo recommending Disney be promoted to full Special
Agent in Charge (SAC) status. (Walt Disney's FBI file)

RE: WALT DISNEY

BACKGROUND

WALT DISNEY was born in Chicago, Illinois, on December 5, 1901.
He received his elementary and high school education in the schools of that
city and became a commercial artist in 1919. Between 1919 and 1922 he produced a number of cartoons and in 1928 created Mickey Mouse, his most famous
cartoon.

Mr. DISNEY has been associated with his brother, ROY O. DISNEY,
in the management and operation of the Walt Disney Productions since the
establishment of the company by the brothers in the early 1930's. Mr.
DISNEY resides with his wife and family in the Holmby Hills section of
Los Angeles.

DEROGATORY INFORMATION

No derogatory information concerning this individual appears in
the files of this office.

SAC RECOMMENDATION

Because of Mr. DISNEY's position as the foremost producer of
cartoon films in the motion picture industry and his prominence and wide
acquaintanceship in film production matters, it is believed that he can be
of valuable assistance to this office and therefore it is my recommendation that he be approved as an SAC contact.

Extremely rare photo of Walt Disney out for a night on the town with
Dolores Del Rio, who was rumored to have been his lover. (Lester
Nehamkin)

Walt Disney at Mouseketeer Cubby O'Brien's birthday party, on the set of "The Mickey Mouse Club." (Globe, courtesy of Cubby O'Brien)

Disney's hands in the early 1960s, cast in bronze. (Casting and photo by Adrian E. Flatt)

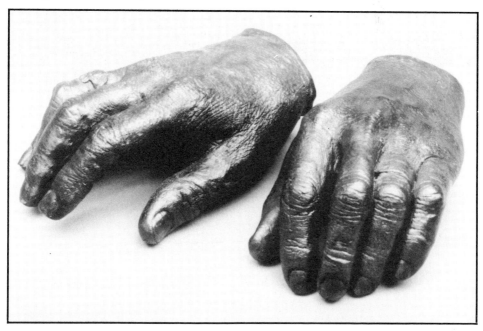

PLAINTEXT

TELEGRAM   URGENT

REC-6- 94-11-4667-60

MRS. WALT DISNEY

CALIFORNIA   67C

INDEED SORRY TO LEARN OF PASSING OF YOUR HUSBAND AND
WANT TO EXTEND MY HEARTFELT SYMPATHY. I KNOW WORDS ARE MOST
INADEQUATE TO EASE YOUR GRIEF, BUT IT IS MY HOPE THAT YOU WILL
DERIVE CONSOLATION FROM KNOWING THAT HIS OUTSTANDING
CONTRIBUTIONS WILL BE A LASTING MEMORIAL TO HIM. HIS DEDICATION
TO THE HIGHEST STANDARDS OF MORAL VALUES AND HIS ACHIEVEMENTS
WILL ALWAYS STAND AS AN INSPIRATION TO THOSE WHO WERE
PRIVILEGED TO KNOW HIM.

            JOHN EDGAR HOOVER

1 - Los Angeles

NOTE: Mr. Disney was on the Special Correspondents' List on a first-name basis
and has been deleted on this notification of his death.

DFC:mel (4)

Telson
DeLoach
Mohr
Wick
Casper
Callahan
Conrad
Felt
Gale
Rosen
Sullivan
Tavel
Trotter
Tele. Room
Holmes
Gandy

MAIL ROOM ☐   TELETYPE UNIT ☐

INITIALED
DIRECTOR'S OFFICE

FEDERAL BUREAU OF INVESTIGATION
U. S. DEPARTMENT OF JUSTICE
COMMUNICATIONS SECTION
DEC 15 1966
WESTERN UNION

J. Edgar Hoover's telegram to Lillian upon the occasion of Walt's
passing. Note the directive to remove Walt's name from the Special
Correspondents' List. (Walt Disney's FBI file)

"Judge every chicken according to her individual merits.

"Make America safe for differences.

"Barnyard defense (against the weasel) demands barnyard unity."

They also asked Lesser to see if he could get Walt to contribute the services of his studio to the project. Walt instantly and angrily rejected Lesser's offer to collaborate, insisting the film was another, thinly disguised attempt to promote communism in America. Who else could a "Rhode Island Red" be, he wanted to know?

Something had to be done, he decided, before Hollywood was consumed by communism. Walt began drawing battle plans to take on those he believed threatened the nation's democratic foundation. Having done that, he began looking for the most able soldiers available for his new army. As far as he was concerned, this war had only now just begun.

By 1943, MANY OF those who had opposed America's entry into the war were convinced the establishment of a second front in Europe and an Allied invasion of France would all but insure a Communist victory in the east. They preferred to have Hitler's army fight a bloody battle to the death with the Soviet Union, the survivor of which could then be easily defeated by the Allies.

With a presidential election less than a year away, the Republican party, led by Thomas E. Dewey, let it be known the central thrust of its campaign for the White House would be that Roosevelt was "soft on communism." The accusation wasn't limited to Roosevelt's war policies but his domestic programs as well.

Numerous political and social organizations supported this platform; among the more prominent were the American Legion, Veterans of Foreign Wars, Daughters of the American Revolution, the Knights of Columbus, and an increasing number of Hollywood's most famous conservatives.

Walt Disney had been among the earliest and most forceful of the film community's anticommunists. From October 1940, he had been a loyal and dedicated domestic spy for the Federal Bureau of Investigation, assigned a Los Angeles–based SAC (Special Agent in Charge) to whom he was to report anything that might be of interest to the FBI. Disney filed dozens of reports on what he believed were "subversive activities," among them the Night of the Americas gala and a meeting of the "New Masses."

The Night of the Americas fund-raising gala, held on February 14, 1943, at the Martin Beck Theater in New York City, was sponsored by the Council for Pan-American Democracy. Walt was invited by the council to attend because of his highly publicized 1941 government sponsored "goodwill" trip to South America. He flew to New York, made an appearance, and, upon his return to Los Angeles, filed a report with his Los Angeles SAC detailing who was there and what was said. The SAC then filed a complete report with the Bureau.

The Council for Pan-American Democracy was an organization concerned with the civil rights of Latin Americans, both in their native countries and in America. The group had been formed in 1939 by several Latin American dignitaries. It sent a series of official delegations to Mexico and Chile to study the development of democracy in those and other South American countries. The council published a bulletin, "The Americas," twice a month and occasional pamphlets and booklets. The Night of the Americas advertised itself as an "unprecedented demonstration of inter-American cultural unity honoring two visiting Latin American leaders, Vincente Lombardo Toledano and Pablo Neruda, designed to promote cultural unity, a program of song, dance and music by celebrated American and Latin American Artists."

Among the many in attendance besides Toledano and Pablo Neruda were the actress Margo; Donald Ogden Stewart; Xavier Cugat; John Gunther; Carmen Miranda; Paul Robeson; Deems Taylor; Orson Welles; and Paul Muni. Shortly after the FBI received its report, the Council for Pan-American Democracy was designated a subversive organization by the attorney general's office.

Several months later Disney agreed to be one of the sponsors of a tribute to Art Young, a liberal activist considered by many to be the dean of American cartoonists. The tribute was hosted by the left-wing magazine *New Masses*. Disney had been a fan of Young's and decided to attend the memorial in person.

The gathering took place on January 27, at New York City's Manhattan Center. Among the evening's sponsors were Ernest Hemingway, Carl Sandburg, Daniel Fitzpatrick, Paul Robeson, and Walt Disney. Speakers included Earl Browder, Rockwell Kent, Langston Hughes, Howard Fast, and Donald Odgen Stewart. Many of those in attendance were already under surveillance by the FBI. Fast, Robeson, and Stewart (who had been at the Night of the Americas gala) had previously been suspected of being Communists by the Bureau. Afterward, Disney filed his report.

Upon his return to Hollywood, Walt decided he needed to do more than merely observe the behavior of "the enemy." To that end, in February of 1944, he became vice-president and one of the founding members of the Motion Picture Alliance for the Preservation of American Ideals. The Motion Picture Alliance (MPA) was an organization founded by Hollywood's most rabid anticommunists. Its principal funding came from the heads of the major studios and William Randolph Hearst. Its first elected president was Sam Wood, a veteran director whose greatest cinematic achievement was to finish the trouble-plagued production of *Gone With The Wind*.

Both Disney and Wood considered the New Deal proof that Roosevelt was a dupe of the grand world Communist conspiracy, and they easily recruited seventy-five of Hollywood's most powerful conservatives into their organization, including actors Adolphe Menjou, Robert Taylor, Gary Cooper, John Wayne, Ward Bond, and Charles Coburn; gossip columnist Hedda Hopper; art director Cedric Gibbons; directors Norman Taurog and Clarence Brown; screenwriters James K. McGuinness, Borden Chase, Bert Kalmar, Fred Niblo, Jr., Casey Robinson, Howard Emmett Rogers, and Morrie Ryskind; Colonel Rupert Hughes (Hearst's Hollywood liaison); and Teamsters leaders Joe Tuohy and Roy Brewer, the latter IATSE's handpicked replacement for the incarcerated Willie Bioff.

In an interview Wood gave the *New York Sun*, he stated that his group of followers "find ourselves in a sharp revolt against a rising tide of Communism, Fascism, and kindred beliefs that seek by subversive means to undermine and change this way of life; groups that have forfeited their right to exist in this country of ours because they seek to achieve their change by means other than the vested procedure of the ballot."

According to the MPA's "Statement of Principles," which Disney helped Wood compose, the purpose of the alliance was to combat the film industry's

> domination by Communists, radicals, and crackpots. . . . We pledge to fight, with every means at our organized command, any effort of any group or individual to divert the loyalty of the screen from the free America that gave it birth. And to dedicate

our own work, in the fullest possible measure, to the presentation of the American scene, its standards and its freedoms, its
beliefs and its ideals, as we know them and believe in them.

Disney was instrumental in pointing the organization in the direction of its first "Communist radical crackpot," Herb Sorrell. This
wasn't the first time Disney had gone after Sorrell. Early in 1942,
after his success with the Cartoonists Guild, Sorrell had founded the
Conference of Studio Unions. The CSU was made up of five member
unions: the Cartoonists Guild, the Screen Office Employees Guild,
the Film Technicians, the Machinists, and the Motion Picture Painters. Sorrell hoped to strengthen the individual unions' power by
having them join forces.

As far as Disney was concerned, the CSU was all part of the same
Communist conspiracy that had struck his studio and continued to
threaten all of Hollywood. As early as October 1941, barely a month
after the studio strike ended, Disney had contacted Jack Tenney,
chairman of the newly formed Joint Fact-Finding Committee on Un-
American Activities of the California Legislature and urged him to go
after the strikers. After turning over all the photos taken during the
walkout, he urged Tenney to launch an investigation of "Reds in
movies." Tenney took his cue from Disney and did just that. The first
witness he called was Herb Sorrell.

Although the Tenney committee was unable to prove a connection
between Sorrell's union activities and the Communist party, the
hearings nevertheless chilled Hollywood's liberal left, who saw the
actions of the Tenney committee as a first dangerous step in the
revival of the government's belief that the entertainment industry
was indeed an enclave of communism.

Only a few years earlier, in 1939, Martin Dies, while serving as
head of the House Un-American Activities Committee, had helped
bring the final curtain down on the Federal Theater Project by
denouncing the government-funded group's so-called progressive
presentations.* The Dies-HUAC investigations, whose methods of

---

*"The Dies Committee (HUAC) spearheaded the attack on the [Federal]
Theater Project, utilizing the sort of demagogic tactics which its successors would
wield even more destructively ten years later. . . . Members of the Hollywood
Left, in alliance with New York artists and intellectuals, responded rapidly to the
attack on the Federal Theater Project." (Ceplair and Englund, *The Inquisition in
Hollywood*, pp. 155–56).

innuendo and intimidation were described by Hollywood's left as blatant red-baiting, left the careers of many of the nation's finest actors seriously threatened, in some instances permanently damaged.

Typical of the kind of intimidation tactics continually used against some of the industry's most outspoken liberals was what happened early in 1942 to James Cagney. Although popular and bankable, he was nevertheless called in for a private meeting with Dies after conducting what amounted to a one-man strike against Warner Bros. over a strictly nonpolitical contract dispute. Nevertheless, the red tint of "striker" now threatened Cagney's professional future, and after assuring Dies there was nothing "Communistic" in his intentions, the actor decided to produce and star in what he predicted would be "the damndest patriotic picture ever." The result was the 1942 jingoist blockbuster, *Yankee Doodle Dandy*.

One of Disney's first official duties as vice-president of the MPA was to send a letter to an arch-conservative U.S. senator, Robert R. Reynolds (D-North Carolina), dated March 7, 1944, urging HUAC to intensify its presence in Hollywood. Walt wanted a full congressional investigation regarding the infiltration of communism into the film community, for the "flagrant manner in which the motion picture industrialists of Hollywood have been coddling Communists and totalitarian-minded groups working in the industry for the dissemination of un-American ideas and beliefs." In a move reminiscent of the tactics of the anonymous antistrike Committee of 21, the only official identification that appeared on the letter was "A group of your friends."

The immediate result of that letter was the arrival in Hollywood, ten days later, of William Wheeler, a HUAC representative, to begin yet another investigation of Sorrell, his Conference of Studio Unions, and their possible link to the Communist party. The studios happily opened their doors to HUAC, and the committee took the opportunity to expand its investigation into every branch of the film industry's working-class population that had sought affiliation with any union or guild during the past decade.

HUAC, with the full support of the FBI, this time subpoenaed everyone suspected of having any subversive, or merely suspicious, affiliations in their background. Virtually no one with any evidence of liberal leanings escaped being summoned before the committee. Ironically, it was many of these same hired hands who had helped produce the movies that celebrated the ordinary American working-man, and in doing so had helped make the studios even wealthier. Still, it was the heads of these studios who remained the most avid supporters of HUAC's Hollywood investigation.

As the House Un-American Committee marched through Hollywood, Disney opened his own second front when he reactivated the struggle to break the monopolistic back of the *the very faction with whom he had sided to rout the industry's Communists*. Although the heads of the studios welcomed him as a powerful ally in their struggle against unionism and communism, Walt felt his contributions were largely unappreciated. In his eyes, he was still being denied access to both the power and the profits of the studio system dominated by Communists and Jews. And he intended to do something about it, even if it meant having to align himself with none other than Sam Goldwyn, whom Disney had once sworn he would never speak to again after the Jewish independent producer had become a partner in United Artists. Goldwyn, Walt believed, had taken an active behind-the-scenes role in forcing him out out UA.

In June 1944, Disney learned that Goldwyn, who, like Disney, was now distributing through RKO, had become embroiled in a major distribution battle with Warner Bros. Goldwyn had just completed production on *Up in Arms*, a $2 million romantic World War II musical comedy. The picture starred Danny Kaye, an actor Goldwyn had once ridiculed in print as having a nose as long as Pinocchio's, a reference at the time Disney had found quite distasteful. However, in spite of his reputation as one of the most powerful independents, Goldwyn faced serious problems getting his new film distributed.

By 1944, most of the nation's theaters were owned outright by "the Big Five"—Paramount, Loews, Warners, Twentieth Century-Fox, and RKO. According to the terms of his distribution deal with RKO, Goldwyn had final approval of every theater, gaining "most-favored" rates whenever his films ran in movie houses RKO owned. However, in territories where RKO had no theaters, Goldwyn had to agree to whatever terms the studio dictated. As a result, a Goldwyn film in a theater owned by another studio usually earned as little as one-eighth as much as it did in a movie house owned by RKO.

When T & D Theaters, a Fox-owned chain based in Reno, Nevada, offered what Goldwyn considered an insulting amount to exhibit *Up in Arms*, Disney advised him that as one of the original members of

SIMPP (Society of Independent Motion Picture Producers) he should challenge T & D's right to dictate terms. With Disney's help, Goldwyn then arranged a screening of *Up in Arms* in Tony's El Patio, a local Reno nightclub, rather than in a traditional movie theater.

The town's commissioners and Reno fire department issued multiple violations for everything from the safety of the carbon-arc projection equipment to the lack of permanently floor-anchored seats. Goldwyn overcame the fire department's objections by announcing his intention to donate the opening-night proceeds to the Reno branch of the Red Cross.

On the evening of August 22, just before the film was scheduled to be screened, Goldwyn stood up before the packed house, filled with more reporters than ordinary filmgoers, and stated his intention to fight "a monopoly which has been able to keep independent producers from showing their films unless the producers are willing to pay prohibitive percentages."

Goldwyn then invited Disney to add his voice to the proceedings. In an impassioned speech that praised Goldwyn for his courage in taking on the "monopolistic forces" of the film industry, Walt concluded by saying:

> I heartily endorse your efforts to carry directly to the people of Reno, and indirectly to the American public, the question whether the motion picture industry as an industry should continue to exist under American competition principles or be throttled by monopolistic restrictions and limitations. Our government has recognized the importance of American films as political and commercial assets in foreign relations for America!

The controversy that surrounded *Up in Arms* catapulted an otherwise quite ordinary film into a major financial success. However, the real victory for Disney and SIMPP lay elsewhere. When Walt returned to Los Angeles he immediately filed a complete report on the proceedings with the FBI. The next day, Hoover put T & D Junior Enterprises under investigation for possible antitrust activities. The following excerpts are from a series of reports from Special Agent in Charge A. Rosen, based on reports by Disney sent directly to the attention of J. Edgar Hoover:

The investigation reflects that Goldwyn and subject company could not agree on the terms under which [this picture] was to be shown by the T. and D. Junior Enterprises, so Goldwyn showed these pictures in the El Patio Ballroom at Reno. Subject company, through the city council, tried to prevent the showing of the picture at the El Patio without success. . . .

25% of subject company's stock is owned by the Fox West Coast Theaters which operates throughout California, Oregon, Washington, Colorado, Wisconsin and Kansas. Subject company operates all theaters at Reno and 45 other theaters in northern California.

Mr. Berge [Assistant United States Attorney General Berge], in a press release concerning this case, has been quoted as saying that there have been several instances in which independent producers have had difficulty in obtaining theaters to show their product because of the "Big Five" chain control and said this was . . . not satisfactory. He also stated, "As long as the independents have to deal with the big five for theaters it seems there will be trouble."

As of October 19, 1944, the investigation of this matter was almost completed. As of that date there were outstanding leads [from] Walt Disney . . . [deletion by FBI] to determine from them any information in their possession concerning monopolistic practices. . . .

The Salt Lake City Field Division, by teletype dated November 10, was instructed to immediately contact the United States Attorney at Reno to determine what further investigation, if any, is desired after which they should conduct an immediate investigation of the additional request received from him.

On December 31, 1946, after an eight-year journey through the federal court system, *The United States of America* v. *Paramount Pictures, Inc.*, *et al.*, SIMPP's challenge of the Majors' monopolistic hold on the three branches of the film industry—production, distribution, and exhibition—was settled in its favor, and the Majors were enjoined "from expanding their present theater holdings in any manner." An immediate appeal was filed by Paramount, with both sides determined to take the case all the way to the U.S. Supreme Court.

As World War II came to a close, Disney, the MPA, HUAC, and IATSE's Roy Brewer united to strengthen their assault upon the "subversives" of Hollywood. The death of President Roosevelt, the spectre of the iron curtain, and the rapid onset of the Cold War were all contributing factors to the groundswell of public support for Disney's team of zealous red-hunters. The next battle front for Walt and his fellow Hollywood warriors was Washington, D.C.

THIRTEEN

Disney, HUAC, and the Blacklist

BY EARLY 1944, with no features scheduled and only a handful of nonmilitary cartoons in various stages of production, the Disney studio faced yet another severe cash-flow crisis. The 1942 release of *Bambi*, which had first gone into production in 1939, proved a disappointment at the box office. As had *Pinocchio* and *Fantasia* before it, *Bambi* failed to make back its costs.

In many ways *Bambi* was the most visually gracious of all of Disney's classic animated features. The purest evocation yet of Disney's vision of a perfect world, not unlike his idealized memories of the Marceline farm, *Bambi* depicted as the only threat to the Lord's gentle creatures the intrusion of His one true beast, the animal Man. In *Bambi*, it is the metaphorical dream world of "good" animals that illustrates the perfect, peaceful human condition, as opposed to the nightmare world in *Pinocchio* and its "bad" boys who literally become animals.

Athough *Bambi* is a film of extravagant surface charm, its forest among the loveliest of Disney's panoramic renderings, the film's emotional power lies in the abstracts of its autobiographical complexities. Made during the period of time when both of Walt's parents died, *Bambi* suggests a melancholic desire on Disney's part to return to his childhood and revisit the animals who first stirred his artistic soul. The climactic fire that destroys Bambi's forest is, in effect, Walt's angry acknowledgment of that impossibility.

The film's failure at the box office left Disney desperate for cash. With nothing looming in his immediate future, he decided to gamble on the past. That summer, he rereleased his only successful animated feature, *Snow White*, betting that six years was enough time for a new generation to discover it. The gamble paid off. *Snow White* proved so successful it lifted the studio's annual net income for 1944 by more than 10 percent from the previous year, to just under half a million dollars, enough of a cash transfusion to move the ailing studio off the critical list. *Snow White* remained in rerelease well into 1945, bolstering that year's net profits as well.

With the successful reissue, Disney realized the financial potential of his back inventory. Unlike live-action features, whose life in the days before television (and video) was almost always limited to a single first run, animated features simply didn't "date." Studios weren't anxious to rerelease features in which their stars would be put in the awkward position of having to compete with younger versions of themselves.

Recalled Jules Engel, a Disney staff artist in the forties: "With the rerelease of *Snow White*, Disney discovered the power of drawing a line rather than taking a photograph. His animated films are the only ones I know of that can come back fifty years later and open in a first-run house. In some ways they are the purest of cinema, timeless, like great paintings."

After *Snow White*, Disney planned reissues of his most successful features in regular seven-year cycles, a policy still in practice at the studio.

It wasn't until January 1945, with the end of the war in sight, that Disney returned to a full schedule of commercial films. Already in preproduction for the new year were a full-length musical that combined live action with animation, tentatively titled "Uncle Remus"; several short features, or "featurettes" (films longer than shorts but like *Dumbo* not quite full-length features), among them *Swing Street*, *Currier and Ives*, and *Cuban Carnival*; and eighteen new cartoons. For 1945 Disney planned a total of one new feature and twenty-two shorts and featurettes, as compared with no features and fifteen shorts in 1944, and two features with ten shorts in 1943.

On February 3, 1945, Walt finally completed postproduction on

The Three Caballeros, the second of the two films (the first: *Saludos Amigos*) he had begun during the 1941 South American trip. The film had suffered several extensive delays due to the shortage of available Technicolor film, most of which had been appropriated by the war department.

Although Walt hoped the feature would restore some of the lost luster to his studio's reputation, and much needed capital, *The Three Caballeros* received universally negative reviews for its weak story, vulgar style, and utter lack of charm. Even with its innovative use of cartoon characters interacting on-screen with live performers, a technique Disney first employed in the early "Alice" series, *The Three Caballeros* angered many who found Donald Duck's lecherous reaction to Spanish women un-Disneylike and totally unacceptable in family entertainment.

Typical of the critical reaction to the film was the *New Yorker's* review, which called *The Three Caballeros*:

> a mixture of atrocious taste, bogus mysticism, and authentic fantasy, guaranteed to baffle any critic not hopelessly enchanted with the word "Disney." . . . In the first place, a somewhat physical romance between a two-foot duck and a full-sized woman, though one happens to be a cartoon and the other pleasantly rounded and certainly mortal, is one of those things that might disconcert less squeamish authorities than the Hays Office. . . . It might even be said that a sequence involving the duck, the young lady, and a long alley of animated cactus plants would probably be considered suggestive in a less innocent medium.

The *Los Angeles Times* in its review warned that

> If Walt Disney does not quickly start a game of "follow the leader" back towards his original standards of poetic beauty and inspiration, the Legion of Decency might well contemplate playing the woodsman by reaching for its axe.

After a brief and financially disastrous initial run, Walt pulled the film from general release. Although he made no public comment about it, in private he expressed to Roy his absolute conviction the unusually harsh criticism was politically rather than artistically motivated, that the liberal media was out to get him for his actions during the strike.

The true feelings of his fans, he believed, were more accurately reflected by the always dependable *Look* magazine, which, just as *The Three Caballeros* was bombing at the box office, released yet another in what seemed an endless series of glowing tributes, this one entitled "Disney—Teacher of Tomorrow," which praised Walt's great and selfless wartime patriotism.

Indeed, it seemed the only achievement for which Walt still received good marks was his patriotism. Shortly after the *Look* article, perhaps the most damning critical piece to date on Disney appeared in the 1945 spring issue of the *Partisan Review*. It was written by Barbara Deming and bore the title "The Artlessness of Walt Disney."

Deming recapped the central plot of the *The Three Caballeros*: Donald Duck opens three birthday packages from his Latin American friends (holdover characters from the first South American feature, *Saludos Amigos*), each of which transports him to a different locale. The critic concluded:

> [Disney] finally surrenders to his material and lets it have its own way with him—much as Donald Duck, after he has pulled at the ribbons tying the third package, lets himself get sucked into the kaleidoscopic vortex they promptly form. . . . We have a nightmare view. From this point on [the film] is monstrous . . . lewd, psychopathically chaotic, [and] very hard on the eyes. The film mounts in hysteria.

In truth the film's images were as disturbing as anything Disney had yet brought to the screen. However, the basis of the pathology of *The Three Caballeros* wasn't limited to its surface images. Rather, they were the most vivid representation yet of Disney's raging unconscious.

During the three years it took to complete the film, Hoover was feeding Walt a continuous stream of information regarding the possibility of his Spanish heritage. At the same time the true facts of his birth were being investigated, Disney "gave birth" to Donald Duck, in many ways Walt's "second-born" and Mickey Mouse's antithetical "sibling." Donald Duck made his official debut in 1935, the same year the Disneys began the process that led to Sharon's adoption, in a cartoon short entitled *The Orphans' Benefit*.

The short was greeted with the kind of media attention usually accorded a royal birth. Helen G. Thompson, in a 1935 issue of *Stage* magazine, wrote:

> . . . at the opening of *The Orphan's Benefit* [sic], he [Donald] brought down the house, along with bricks, potted palms and other available impedimenta . . . the bad penny de luxe . . . the greatest pest since . . . chain letters . . . no one has been as beguilingly cross-eyed since Ben Turpin. No one has been flattened out with such finality since the steam roller ran over little Fido.

However, more revealing was the third-person description Disney himself gave for Donald in a studio press release, as if the animated character not only had a life of his own, but one that resembled Walt's a little too closely:

> Donald Duck came into being in 1934 to fit a voice which had interested me a couple of years before. . . . He was a character we simply couldn't keep down. . . . IIis towering rages, his impotence in the face of obstacles, his protests in the face of injustice, as he sees it. . . .

At the same time, an "anonymous" Disney writer, probably Disney himself—a method Disney had often used in the past to express himself without signature—revealed even more about Donald, particularly his relationship to Mickey:

> Mickey is limited today because public idealization has turned him into a boy scout. Every time we put him into a trick, a temper, a joke, thousands of people would belabor us with nasty letters. That's what made Donald Duck so easy. He was our outlet. We could use all the ideas for him we couldn't use on Mickey.

Clearly, Disney regarded Mickey and Donald as more than just animated characters. They were, in many ways, his most important progeny, over which he maintained absolute creative control in projecting his own, conflicted personality: Mickey as superego—humble, chaste, cerebral, asexual, always in control, universally adored; Donald as id—darker, volatile, emotional, sexual, always out of control, not quite as popular and angry because of it.

Disney had produced *The Three Caballeros* during the war years, a time during which Walt had temporarily retired Mickey from the screen, claiming, as he had once before (prior to "The Sorcerer's Apprentice") his favorite star had gone a little stale. However, the real reason probably had less to do with movies than emotions. Mickey's absence may have signaled the breakdown of Walt's fragile emotional balance, externalized in the emergence of an unleashed Donald, the sexually provocative, libidinous duck, who thumped with desire for all make and manner of *unattainable Spanish women*.

The extraordinary image of an animated duck in hot pursuit of a real-life woman was no casual mixed-media metaphor, but a full-scale merging of Disney's psychic lifeblood with his animated ink-world: Donald the externalization of Disney's inner emotions, the Spanish women the objects of a complex brew of repressed sexual desires. The merging of "real life" and animation on film signaled in its way a further breakdown of Walt's always tenuous ability to distinguish fully the character of his soul from the souls of his characters.

Before its opening, Disney had confidently predicted *The Three Caballeros* would recapture the glory of the studio's animated "golden era." Privately, however, Disney had already begun his withdrawal from actively participating in the production of movies and decided *The Three Caballeros* would be his final creative venture into animation.

Nearly a year before its release Disney had begun preparing his studio for the shift to more profitable, if less creative, live action. In the summer of 1944, construction work was started to accommodate the studio's soundstages for live-action production, and he approved the "Uncle Remus" final shooting script only when it complied with his mandate of 80 percent "live" action, 20 percent animation.

As production began on the film, Disney announced in the trades "Uncle Remus" would be an "epochal event in screen history." Following the announcement, a newly formed Hollywood organization, the Interracial Film and Radio Guild, expressed concern that the film might portray blacks in a degrading fashion. The guild's board included such prominent blacks as George H. Schuyler and Adam Clayton Powell, Jr. and, according to their charter, "other Chinese, Mexicans, Jews, and Negroes." Disney responded by changing the name of the film to *Song of the South*, a title he considered less offensive. He declared the film would be "a monument to the Negro race" with as much historical impact as *Gone With the Wind.*

The guild's reaction had angered Walt. After making that announcement, his enthusiasm for the film evaporated, and he put the production entirely in the hands of his staff. That same week a file was opened by the FBI on the activities of the guild and its board of directors.

In January 1945, following his loss of interest in *Song of the South*, Walt continued his withdrawal from moviemaking when he shocked everyone by suddenly and without warning resigning as president of Walt Disney Productions. He appointed Roy the new president and hired John F. Reeder, an advertising executive fresh out of Young and Rubicam as the studio's new vice-president. Although Walt retained his chairmanship of the board of directors, a position filled thick with bureaucratic responsibilities, he gave as his reason for resigning the need to relieve himself from the overload of administrative work.

A few weeks later *New York Times* film critic Bosley Crowther visited the Disney studio and was startled to find that Walt seemed "totally disinterested in movies and wholly, almost weirdly concerned with the building of a miniature railroad engine and a string of cars in the workshops of his studios."

Disney now preferred to spend almost all of his time at the studio sequestered in his private inner office, passing countless hours playing with his trains, supervising by intercom the building of more miniature engines in the studio's prop shop. At home, Walt concentrated on the construction of a one-eighth-scale working steam locomotive, the "Carolwood Pacific," named for the street where his house was located, Carolwood Drive. The engine car was big enough for him to actually sit on while he "conducted." He loved to ride his train around the perimeter of his Holmby Hills home and down a half-mile track along the canyon side of his property.

Walt put as much effort into the building of his home railroad as he used to in his movies. He painstakingly designed each car so that it had a personality of its own. In the caboose he installed a working potbellied stove. He had replicas of nineteenth-century newspapers reproduced for the passenger car. He even had power lines removed and buried underground so they would not obstruct the view or impinge on the fantasy.

In an attempt to assuage his wife, he named his engine "Lilly Belle." Lillian was not amused. She had no idea why her husband had stopped going to work, missed meetings, skipped meals, and sometimes didn't bother to come to bed just so he could keep riding his "choochoo."

It wasn't until late in 1945 that a jolt of reality pulled Walt back into the real world when one of the leaders of the 1941 strike, Arthur Babbitt, was discharged from the marines. Upon returning to Hollywood, Babbitt immediately applied to get his job back at the studio. Walt personally refused to rehire him, even after a directive from the NLRB ordered him to do so.

Babbitt recalled, "He did everything to make a case for legitimately firing me, and he didn't stop at anything. He sent a notice around that I was to be given the 'silent treatment.' Anyone caught talking to me was to be summarily fired. When Disney and Lessing would come walking down the hallway, Walt would always get coughing fits when we passed [each other], so he could cover his face and not have to look at me.

"Besides constant anonymous threats of physical violence, they'd sometimes put pretty girls in my room, where I worked, to distract me, to try to catch me in some kind of compromising position. But I was one tough sonofabitch and wouldn't fall for it.

"The final decision came from the Supreme Court, which found in my favor. Disney was ordered to rehire me and make a large settlement. In addition, he had to post public notices for six weeks that I'd been right and the studio had been wrong. They had to take me back at my former position and my former rate of highest pay.

"Still, after I won every appeal and received my settlement, in January of '46, I knew it was time to leave, to pursue a sane career, which I did, voluntarily, first at UPA, and then at several commercial houses."

Babbitt suffered a nervous breakdown after the Supreme Court decision which required several months of hospitalization. He never fully regained his artistic status within the industry nor the forward momentum of his career.

Once Babbitt left, Disney ordered the animator's name permanently removed from the credits of all films he had worked on and any and all related periodicals, books, bios, and public-relations documents. Ironically, doing political battle with his former animator seemed somehow to stimulate Disney's artistic juices. He felt creatively reinvigorated and began to look for new properties to make into animated features.

Having finally acquired the rights to *Alice's Adventures in Wonderland*, Disney commissioned Aldous Huxley to turn it into a screenplay. His relationship with Huxley began cordially enough and remained that way until Walt learned Huxley's twenty-three-year-old son Matthew, a script reader at Warner Bros., had joined Herb Sorrell on the latest picket line of the Conference of Studio Unions (CSU).

The postwar shift in the country's political sentiments was reflected in the new administration in Washington. Less of a liberal than Roosevelt had been, Truman was nowhere near as enthusiastic in his support of the nation's unions. Shortly after the war ended, the Hollywood branch of IATSE, with the full support of the heads of the studios, sought to have the concessions made to the film industry's unions during Roosevelt's presidency rescinded.

The CSU chose to defend the hard-won contracts of its combined membership, which, by 1945, had swelled to 10,000 in contrast to IATSE's 16,000. When IATSE refused to recognize the defection of one of its member unions, the Society of Motion Picture Interior Decorators, to the CSU, the resulting deadlock sparked Sorrell to call the entire CSU membership out on strike.

The CSU focused its attention on Warner Bros., primarily because the three Warner brothers, Jack, Harry, and Al, continued to operate one of the strongest antilabor studios in the industry. In retaliation, the studio, ably assisted by IATSE, hired scabs, backed them with thugs, and used tear gas and water hoses to disrupt the picket lines and break the strike. Matthew Huxley was among a handful of picketers who were beaten bloody in one of IATSE's goon-squad attacks. Until then Aldous Huxley had remained politically neutral. Now he publicly decried IATSE's actions as nothing more than bully tactics. Angered by the actions of the son and the criticisms of the father, Disney abruptly ended his association with the famed novelist.

The strike dragged on for eight months and broke the spirit and the bankbooks of the strikers. Many wound up deserting the CSU for IATSE's awaiting arms and jobs. Disney followed the strike closely and, when it appeared that Sorrell had suffered a major defeat, decided the time was right to go after the Cartoonists Guild, which had just concluded a successful negotiation with his studio for higher wages.

A week after the negotiations ended, Disney announced his intention to lay off more than four hundred employees, out of approximately one thousand. He told the *Los Angeles Times* he was doing so because "of economic conditions reflecting increased wage demands by union crafts, as well as other inflated costs." The next day the studio's new president, John Reeder, amplified Disney's position in an inter-studio memorandum:

Last week we acceded to the demands of the Screen Cartoonists' Guild for a 25 percent increase in base minimum wages. This was imposed on us as a condition for the continuance of negotiations on other clauses in the contract, all of which have an important bearing on our production costs.

This increase, in addition to similar increases granted numerous other union crafts employed by the studio, many which were retroactive to Jan. 1, makes it imperative to sharply curtail our operating expenses at once and to completely revise our plans for future pictures.

As employees you should know that during our contract negotiations with the guild we repeatedly pointed out, with complete frankness, that the granting of such a large increase at this time would necessitate a sharp reduction in our staff. The wage boosts would add a million dollars annually to our current four million dollar payroll. We cannot afford it.

That same day production on all studio projects was suspended with the exception of *Song of the South, Fun and Fancy Free, So Dear to My Heart*, and *Melody Time*, all predominantly live-action features requiring little or no animation. Specifically highlighted for indefinite suspension was the all-animated *Alice in Wonderland,* which wouldn't be completed for another six years and was finally released in 1951. Although thirteen writers eventually received credit for the screenplay, which included parts of Huxley's original script, his name, at Disney's insistence, was omitted from the credits.

As promised, three days later Disney laid off 450 workers, declaring the studio was "through with caviar; from now on it's mashed potato and gravy." The Cartoonists Guild lost no time in accusing him of forcing an illegal lockout and threatened an immediate retaliatory strike.

This time Walt was hopeful the Guild would do just that. Privately, Roy Brewer, who had replaced Willie Bioff as the head of the Hollywood branch of IATSE, told Disney a new strike would give IATSE the opportunity to play hero by regaining the cartoonists' lost jobs, and along with them their loyalty.*

The first night after the layoffs, Disney met with representatives of the Guild and found them more amenable than he had expected or hoped. Sorrell, who believed Disney was trying to pull the Guild into another strike, was determined to reach a settlement. Sorrell settled for the rehiring of only 94 of the laid-off cartooonists and two weeks' severance for the other 215. The remaining clerical and maintenance workers received nothing. Disney viewed these concessions as a total victory.

Without losing a single day of production, Disney had won a significant reduction of his staff and payroll and severely weakened the Cartoonists Guild's ability to dictate studio policy. Walt then promised Brewer complete cooperation in helping to rid the industry permanently of Sorrell and his fellow insurgents.

That opportunity came in November 1947, with the commencement of HUAC's next series of investigations into the entertainment industry. Now under the chairmanship of J. Parnell Thomas, a noto-

---

*According to Dan Moldea, in *Dark Victory*, pp. 65–69, 332: "Instead of trying to rid the union of its gangster image and all remnants of mob control, Brewer was obsessed with eliminating the 'Communist Influence' within the union and the movie industry in general. 'When Browne [and Bioff] went to jail,' Brewer insisted, 'that ended any connection with the mob in the IATSE . . . the truth is, [the Communists] had this town in the palm of their hands, and they were calling the shots.' Brewer was appointed by President Reagan in 1984 as chairman of the Federal Service Impasse Panel, which arbitrated disputes between federal agencies and the unions representing federal workers."

riously antilabor congressman, HUAC received the warm endorsement of IATSE, the American Legion, and the Catholic church and the full cooperation of Hollywood's studios. A group of left-wing writers, which came to be known as the "Hollywood Ten," symbolized the relentlessly persecutory actions of Thomas's investigation. The Ten were deemed "unfriendly" witnesses after each cited his right under the First Amendment to refuse to respond to the most famous question of the era: Are you now or have you ever been member of the Communist party?* All ten were immediately blacklisted, their careers shattered, and their lives disrupted by jail sentences for contempt.

Brewer became the guardian of the industry's notorious and feared blacklist. During HUAC's investigation, the head of the Hollywood branch of IATSE sent letters to every major industry figure, on-screen talent and off-, warning that if they didn't now declare their open support for IATSE, they would be considered enemies of the Hollywood establishment. He warned failure to support IATSE would make them subject not only to industry boycott, that is, inclusion on the blacklist, but investigation by Thomas's HUAC.

Brewer operated with the full support and encouragement of Eric Johnson. A successful businessman from Seattle, during the war Johnson had served as the vice-president of the United States Chamber of Commerce. He was also a member of the Economic Policy Subcommittee of the State Department's Advisory Committee on Postwar Foreign Policy, and an outspoken foe of the Soviet Union. In September 1945, he was appointed the new president of the Motion Picture Association of America (MPAA), replacing the far more liberal Will Hays.

Johnson urged the studios to band together and refuse to hire anyone who was blacklisted. The time had come, he warned, for Hollywood to "fish or cut bait" on fighting communism. On November 24 and 25, 1947, Hollywood's most powerful executives and producers—members of the Association of Motion Picture Producers, the MPAA, and Walt Disney's SIMPP—and Roy Brewer and

*The Hollywood Ten were screenwriters Alvah Bessie; Herbert Biberman; Lester Cole; Edward Dmytryk; Ring Lardner, Jr.; John Howard Lawson; Albert Maltz; Samuel Ornitz; Adrian Scott; and Dalton Trumbo. All served time in jail for contempt of court.

Eric Johnson convened for a two-day conference held at the Waldorf-Astoria in New York. The purpose of the conference was to decide whether the industry would endorse the looming fate of the Hollywood Ten.

The result of the conference was a jointly issued proclamation which came to be known as the "Waldorf Statement." It said, in part:

> We will forthwith discharge or suspend without compensation those in our employ and we will not re-employ any of the Ten until such times as he is acquitted or has purged himself of contempt and declares under oath that he is not a Communist. . . .
>
> On the broader issues of alleged subversive and disloyal elements in Hollywood, our members are likewise prepared to take positive action. . . .
>
> We invite the Hollywood talent guilds to work with us to eliminate any subversives. . . .

Although the Waldorf Statement was intended as a statement of unity, there were many in Hollywood who were concerned about granting so much power to HUAC. To them, the real issue was the film industry's right to free expression. Many older members of the Academy in particular, liberals and conservatives alike, remembered what had happened the last time the government had tried to regulate the content of motion pictures. They feared a return of the type of hysteria that ran through the industry during the 1920s when Congress had attempted to use the issue of morality as the springboard to create a federal board of censorship.

Even some members of Disney's Motion Picture Alliance expressed their concern that an endorsement of HUAC and the blacklist might lead to permanent government regulation and censorship of motion pictures. However, no one wanted to risk his own career by protesting HUAC's hearings or the legitimacy of Brewer's blacklist. Merely to question HUAC was enough to raise suspicions of political allegiance. The situation had turned nightmarish.

One of the biggest battles that took place following the Waldorf Statement was the decision to invite the industry's guilds to join the fight against communism. The intent was, obviously, to force the guilds either to come out against subversion or risk being accused of it themselves. As a result, no effective coalition of opposition emerged to protest HUAC, and shortly after the Waldorf Statement, the powerful blacklist was born.

By May 1947, the mere receipt of a HUAC subpoena implied Communist affiliation, and investigation by the FBI's "Compic" (Communist pictures) team of Hollywood-based informers, in which Walt was by now an active participant. Among the first to capitulate to the specter of HUAC and Brewer's blacklist were the leaders of the Screen Actors Guild, onetime liberal Roosevelt supporter Ronald Reagan and song-and-dance-man George Murphy, who hastily convinced their membership to reject Sorrell and the CSU in favor of IATSE.

That same month, Parnell Thomas met with a group which, in direct contrast to the Hollywood Ten, became known as the "Friendly Witnesses."* On September 20, HUAC subpoenaed forty-three prominent Hollywood actors, directors, writers, and producers to testify on Communist influence in the motion picture industry. Walt Disney appeared before the committee on the afternoon of Friday, October 24, following a morning session with Gary Cooper and Roy Brewer.

After providing a brief history of his career in Hollywood, including his military films, Disney was then asked by HUAC Counsel H. A. Smith about the presence of communism at his studio:

Smith: Do you have any people in your studio at the present time that you believe are Communist or Fascist, employed there?

Disney: No. At the present time I feel that everybody in my studio is 100 percent American.

Smith: Have you had at any time, in your opinion, in the past, had any Communists employed at your studio?

Disney: Yes. In the past I had some people that I definitely feel were Communists.

Smith: As a matter of fact, Mr. Disney, you experienced a strike at your studio, did you not?

Disney: Yes.

*Robert Taylor; Richard Arlen; Adolphe Menjou; Leo McCarey; Howard Emmett Rogers; James Kevin McGuinness; Rupert Hughes; and Lela Rogers, mother of movie star Ginger Rogers.

Smith: And is it your opinion that that strike was instituted by members of the Communist Party to serve their purposes?

Disney: Well, it proved itself so with time, and I definitely feel it was a Communist group trying to take over my artists and they did take them over.

Chairman Thomas: Did you say they did take them over?

Disney: They did take them over.

Smith: Will you explain that to the committee, please?

Disney: It came to my attention when a delegation of my boys, my artists, came to me and told me that Mr. Herbert Sorrell—

Smith: Is that Herbert K. Sorrell?

Disney: Herbert K. Sorrell was trying to take them over. I explained to them that it was none of my concern, that I had been cautioned to not even talk with any of my boys on labor. They said it was not a matter of labor, it was just a matter of them not wanting to go with Sorrell, and they had heard that I was going to sign with Sorrell, and they said that they wanted an election to prove that Sorrell didn't have the majority, and I said that I had a right to demand an election. So when Sorrell came I demanded an election.

Sorrell wanted me to sign on a bunch of cards that he had there that he claimed were the majority, but the other side had claimed the same thing. I told Mr. Sorrell that there is only one way for me to go and that was an election and that is what the law had set up, the National Labor Relations Board was for that purpose. He laughed at me and he said that he would use the Labor Board as it suited his purposes and that he had been sucker enough to go for that Labor Board ballot and he had lost some election—I can't remember the name of the place—by one vote. He said it took him two years to get it back. He said he would strike, that that was his weapon. He said, "I have all of the tools of the trade sharpened," that I couldn't stand the ridicule or the smear of a strike. I told him that it was a matter of principle with me, that I couldn't go on working with my boys feeling that I had sold them down the river to him on his say-so, and he laughed at me and told me I was naive and foolish. He said, you can't stand this strike, I will smear you, and I will make a dust bowl out of your plant.

Thomas: What was that?

Disney: He said he would make a dust bowl out of my plant if he chose to.

According to one eyewitness, it was actually Gunther Lessing, not Sorrell, who warned Disney prior to the strike that the Cartoonists Guild would turn the studio into a dust bowl.

Disney's testimony continued with his recollection of the meeting with Sorrell:

> I told him I would have to go that way, sorry, that he might be able to do all that but I would have to stand on that. The result was that he struck.
>
> I believed at that time that Mr. Sorrell was a Communist because of all the things that I had heard and having seen his name appearing on a number of Commie front things. When he pulled the strike the first people to smear me and put me on the unfair list were all of the Commie front organizations. I can't remember them all, they change so often, but one that is clear in my mind is the League of Women Voters, the *People's World*, the *Daily Worker*, and the *PM* magazine [sic] in New York. They smeared me. Nobody came near to find out what the true facts of the thing were. And I even went through the same smear in South America, through some Commie periodicals in South America, and generally throughout the world all of the Commie groups began smear campaigns against me and my pictures.

At this point Chairman Thomas interceded, for the sake of an emphatic clarification. Disney took the opportunity to point out what he claimed was his unswerving allegiance to the National Labor Relations Board:

> Thomas: Excuse me just a minute. I would like to ask a question. In other words, Mr. Disney, Communists out there smeared you because you wouldn't knuckle under?
>
> Disney: I wouldn't go along with their way of operating. I insisted on going through the National Labor Relations Board.
>
> Smith: At the time of this strike you didn't have any grievances or labor troubles whatsoever in your plant?
>
> Disney: No. The only real grievance was between Sorrell and the boys within my plant, they demanding an election, and they never got it.
>
> Smith: Do you recall having had any conversations with Mr. Sorrell relative to Communism?

Disney: Yes I do.

Having taken care of Sorrell, Disney next accused Hilberman of being a Communist:

Smith: Can you name any other individuals that were active at the time of the strike that you believe in your opinion are Communists?

Disney: Well, I feel that there is one artist in my plant, that came in there, he came in about 1938, and he sort of stayed in the background, he wasn't too active, but he was the real brains of this, and I believe he is a Communist. His name is Dave Hilberman.

Smith: How is it spelled?

Disney: H-I-L-B-E-R-M-A-N, I believe. I looked into his record and I found that, no. 1, that he had no religion and that no. 2, that he had spent considerable time at the Moscow Art Theater studying art direction, or something.

Finally, Disney was given ample time to express his opinion of the Communist party:

Disney: Well, I don't believe it is a political party. I believe it is an un-American thing. The thing that I resent the most is that they are able to get into these unions, take them over and represent to the world that a group of people that are in my plant, that I know are good, 100 percent Americans, are trapped by this group, and they are represented to the world as supporting all of those ideologies, and it is not so, and I feel that they really ought to be smoked out and shown up for what they are, so that all of the good, free causes in this country, all the liberalisms that really are American, can go out without the taint of Communism. That is my sincere feeling on it.

Just before he concluded, Disney took the opportunity to distinguish his support of unionism from his suspicion of union corruption:

Disney: . . . I know that I have been handicapped out there in fighting it, because they [Communists] have been hiding behind this labor setup, they get themselves closely tied up in the labor thing, so that if you try to get rid of them they make a labor case out of it. We must keep the American labor unions clean. We have got to fight for them.

Disney's testimony helped destroy Herb Sorrell's Congress of Studio Unions, already weakened by the 1945 strike. The decline of the CSU signaled the end of Sorrell's career as a fighting voice for Hollywood labor. Even before this round of hearings came to an end, he was fired as head of the CSU. Shortly after, his organization disbanded, leaving IATSE unchallenged as Hollywood's most powerful closed-shop union. A relatively young man in his mid-forties, Sorrell died later that year of a heart attack.

As for Dave Hilberman, he had indeed attended the prestigious Leningrad Art Theater for six months in 1922. Along with hundreds of other politically nonaligned foreign students, he had traveled to the Soviet Union solely to study art. Nevertheless, as a result of Walt's testimony Hilberman was marked as a Communist, blacklisted, and put under surveillance by the FBI for the next fifteen years. He eventually joined Tempo Productions, a New York–based animated-commercial house, as a partner and was promptly listed in *Red Channels*, a periodical that specialized in identifying, without the burden of proof or the bother of explanation, those people its publishers believed were Communists. After appearing in *Red Channels*, Tempo Productions went out of business.

During his testimony, Walt had also singled out the League of Women Voters as a "Commie front organization" which had attempted to smear his studio. That night, Lillian, quite annoyed, informed Walt he had confused that organization with another, the League of Women *Shoppers*, an organization Gunther Lessing had originally brought to Walt's attention.

The League of Women Shoppers was a nonpolitical consumers' organization. According to its constitution, the league was "founded on the principles that working conditions are important considerations in the purchase of goods." The organization had notified Disney in writing during the cartoonists' strike that it supported the Guild and would not patronize any theaters where Disney movies were being shown until his dispute with labor was settled.

After wide coverage of his attack on the League of Women Voters in the national press, this telegram was read into the record of the hearings, at the request of Walt Disney:

Some confusion has arisen over my testimony regarding the
League of Women Voters. My testimony referred to the year
1941, at which time several women represented themselves as
being from the League of Women Voters. I want you to know
that I had no intention of criticizing the League of Women
Voters as of now.

Dissatisfied with what it considered a very limp correction, the
League of Women Voters urged women to boycott all Disney's
movies until finally, a month later, on November 3, 1947, Walt sent
the following telegram to J. Parnell Thomas and HUAC:

Gentlemen: I am taking the liberty of referring you to my
testimony before your committee in Washington, D.C., on
October 24, 1947, in the course of which, and in answer to a
question by your chairman, I stated substantially that when Mr.
Sorrell "pulled the strike," the first people to smear me and put
me on the unfair list were certain organizations among which
was the League of Women Voters.

Since returning to my office in Burbank, Calif., I have had an
opportunity to carefully review my files pertaining to this matter. I can now definitely state that while testifying as above I was
confused by a similarity of names between two women's organizations. I regret that I named the League of Women Voters
when I intended to name the League of Women Shoppers.

Therefore I trust your committee will find it consistent to
make requisite amendment to the record with respect to my
testimony so as to erase any implication that the League of
Women Voters had at any time intervened or taken any action
with regard to the matters about which I was being interro-
gated. . . .

Disney's testimony helped strengthen Brewer's industry-wide
blacklist. The mere whisper of a name was enough to eliminate
someone from consideration for a job. Because no proof was required,
nor any defense short of confession acceptable, the assumption of
guilt until proven innocent replaced the constitutional rights of everyone accused, and plunged America into one of its darkest political
periods.

Of those most directly affected by the blacklist, some, like the

Hollywood Ten, served time in federal prison on contempt charges. Others, including actor John Garfield, died prematurely. Like Sorrell, Garfield suffered a fatal heart attack while still in his late thirties. Still others, like veteran actor Philip Loeb, grew despondent and, their professional lives shattered, committed suicide.

And still others, like Charlie Chaplin, were literally exiled. Long a thorn in the side of conservative Hollywood, Chaplin had been immune to the powers of the industry because he himself was one. After amassing a fortune for his work in silent films and his participation in forming United Artists, he began his own studio.

Throughout the thirties, up to and including *The Great Dictator*, he made highly entertaining movies infused with populism. His active campaign for a second front against the Axis powers during World War II and his pleas for the curtailment of anticommunist propaganda angered Disney, who had once so idolized Chaplin.

Chaplin's actions also angered HUAC. After three postponements of his subpoenaed testimony, he sent HUAC a telegram in which he stated that "I am not a Communist; neither have I ever joined any political party or organization in my life." Although HUAC was apparently satisfied by his response and wrote back that his appearance was no longer necessary, the matter was far from closed. Chaplin, who was British, had never applied for U.S. citizenship. In 1952, at the height of the blacklist era, while Chaplin was on a six-month tour of England and Europe, the Immigration and Naturalization Service barred his return to the United States under a code denying an alien entry on grounds of morals or Communist affiliation. Chaplin vowed never to set foot in America again and blocked stateside showings of most of his feature films.

Thus ended the Hollywood career of perhaps the greatest single talent the world of film had ever produced. Although Walt declined to comment publicly on the matter of Chaplin's exile, in private he told one of his "Nine Old Men" studio loyalists that the country was better off without "the little Commie."

The blacklist remained unchallenged until 1959, when Kirk Douglas insisted that Dalton Trumbo receive on-screen credit for writing *Spartacus*, a movie with obvious allegorical reference to the madness that had infected Hollywood. Still, it would take several more years for many of those denied the chance to earn a living wage to regain their right to a decent life.

FOURTEEN

New Directions

IT WASN'T UNTIL 1947, nearly two years after the end of the war, that the Disney studio turned its first profit in nearly seven years ($265,000 net for the first half-year, as opposed to a net loss of $23,000 in 1946). Disney's initial postwar features, *Make Mine Music* and *Song of the South*, both released in 1946, were only marginally successful. However, because they made even a little money, Roy believed the financial difficulties the studio had endured for most of the decade might actually be coming to an end.

As 1948 began, Walt turned to his financial liaison at the Bank of America, Joseph Rosenberg, for an immediate infusion of capital to finance the return to a full schedule of production. However, Rosenberg and the bank read the bottom lines of Disney's books a little differently than Walt did. On the basis of six straight years of loss with only one modest gain, the bank was reluctant to increase its investment in the studio. The studio's debt had risen to over $4 million. Instead, Rosenberg met with Walt and urged him to accept an offer by his distributor RKO and its new owner, Howard Hughes, who wanted to buy the 16-millimeter nontheatrical, nonbroadcast rights of the Disney studio's entire back inventory for classroom and community-organization rentals.

The tall, eccentric Texas billionaire had enjoyed moderate success as a producer of several features before abandoning Hollywood in the thirties to concentrate on aircraft production. In 1948, Hughes decided to reenter the motion picture business by purchasing a controlling interest in the RKO studio. Shortly thereafter, at Rosenberg's suggestion, Hughes offered to help Disney out with a million-dollar interest-free loan in exchange for the studio's nontheatrical rights, repayable from the earnings of new films in foreign countries.

The initial meeting between Hughes and Disney was quite friendly. The two had known each other casually for many years, and while never close they shared a kinship based on their many similarities. Both were approximately the same age; both were Middle Americans, Disney raised in Kansas, Hughes in Texas; and both headed large, complex businesses. Both suffered from a variety of facial tics including, most noticeably, rapid eye-twitching; both chain-smoked; and both were arch right-wingers who had taken active roles in the crusade against communism.

Disney found Hughes's offer irresistible, and with the new influx of cash expanded the studio's 1948 production schedule to eighteen two-reel subjects, including four new animated features—*The Adventures of Ichabod and Mr. Toad, Cinderella, Alice in Wonderland,* and *Peter Pan.* "As you walk down Dopey Drive and turn left on Mickey Mouse Avenue to the studio gate," Disney told the press the day after closing the deal, "the sunshine seems a little brighter." With this new influx of cash, Disney hoped to redirect his studio toward live-action features.

It had becoming increasingly clear to everyone, including Walt, that where once the Disney studio had been the undisputed leader in its field, the cartoons of one of its competitors were now being hailed as the best in the business. The smart-aleck cynicism of Warner Bros.'s "Looney Tunes" not only borrowed Disney's original concept of "Silly Symphonies" but modernized it. While the style of Disney's cartoons remained fixed in the chilly clasp of their prewar Fundamentalist vernacular, Warners's offered the kind of warm, streetwise *Yiddish* humor postwar America lovingly embraced. "Looney Tunes" were clever social satires generously overlaid with sexual innuendo, its characters always winking knowingly at the audience rather than innocently batting their eyes.

Bugs Bunny, Warners' number-one animated star, was a rabbit in the heat of his pubescence. Mickey's fundamental roundness—eyes, ears, face, body—recalled maternal security in the comfort of their breastlike shape. In contrast, Bugs's ears were phallic attitudinizers that never failed to rise to the occasion. In the years immediately following the war, "Looney Tunes," created by several former Disney staffers, most notably Friz Freleng, far more accurately reflected the mood of the country than "Silly Symphonies," and as such became the most popular American theatrical cartoon shorts.

However, the success of "Looney Tunes" didn't seem to matter very much to Walt. In truth, he had lost interest in animation and its two-dimensional mice, ducks, dogs, and puppets. The engine of Walt's imagination now ran down a different track, and while he was not opposed to the studio's return to animated features, he had not not yet pinpointed the next stop on his own creative map.

He enjoyed starting each day alone in his office poring over the trades' daily accounts of the latest HUAC hearings, dining while he did so on his breakfast of choice: fresh doughnuts dunked in scotch. With the war over, the HUAC hearings had captivated the nation, as the congressional red-hunters continued to make villains out of victims and heroes out of themselves.

He often planned his working day around lunch, dining usually two or three times a week with Hedda Hopper at one of his favorite restaurants, usually the Brown Derby. To his delight, Hopper, Louella Parsons, Ed Sullivan, and others continued to praise his strong anticommunist stance, hailing him as Hollywood's bravest, most loyal American.

This uncritical acclaim inevitably spilled onto his work. The re-release of *Bambi*, a film cited by Disney in several promotional pieces as his personal favorite, was hailed in the press. *Liberty* magazine, one cheering voice among many, praised Disney's "revolutionary" achievements in sound and color and described him as "Hollywood's Rembrandt."

On the days he didn't bother to go to the studio at all, he would arise early in the morning, usually before seven, put on a pair of striped overalls and engineer's cap, and slip behind the controls of his beloved "Carolwood Pacific" to steam around the perimeter of his home.

One particular morning in the spring of 1948, as he rode around his yard, he tried to pull into focus an idea that had been on his mind one way or another for so long now, certainly since his 1930 visit to the

Statue of Liberty, and probably before that.* What if he could actually *re-create* the *physical* world of his idealized past? Now, he told himself, that would be one hell of an amusement park.

After he had circled the house half a dozen times, lost in preoccupation, the "Carolwood Pacific" suddenly jumped track, slammed into the side of a ninety-foot S-shaped "tunnel" he had recently installed—which Lillian approved only after Walt convinced her it was really a disguised fallout shelter—and crashed through the living-room wall of the house before finally coming to a halt.

Although Disney tried to blame the accident on the tunnel's poor sight lines, Lillian feared the real cause was Walt's increasing dependence on sleeping pills. She knew he sometimes used them in place of tranquilizers and washed them down with alcohol. His drinking now started first thing in the morning and continued steadily throughout the day. She could always tell when he added the pills to his liquid diet because they visibly affected his speech, temperament, and motor skills.

The accident threw Walt's creative nurturing process offtrack, out of which a fresh round of increasingly bitter arguments developed between Walt and Lillian. Not only did she refuse to believe his story about the tunnel's sight lines, but the train had wrecked most of the room's furnishings. Lillian, an obsessive redecorator, had recently replaced the entire contents of the west wing, the side of the house where the wreck had occurred. The tension spilled over to the children, Diane, now fifteen, and Sharon, twelve, whom Disney, despite Lillian's warning him not to, once again began to angrily admonish over the slightest provocation, deserved or not.

Things were no better at the studio. The main topic of conversation among the staff was Walt's bizarre behavior. He had resumed his habit of locking himself behind the closed doors of his private office. He emerged only for a late-afternoon stroll through the studio's subterranean maze of plumbing, cooling, and heating pipes, where he would chat with the maintenance engineers he now considered his only trusted employees.

---

*According to Charles Solomon, in his *History of Animation*: ". . . Rudy Ising recalled that as early as 1920 he and Walt used to go out to an electric park; it was one of the best amusement parks in Kansas City then. One time Walt said to me, 'One of these days I'm going to build an amusement park—and it's going to be clean!' "

Even when Roy wanted to talk to his brother, he had to make an appointment with Walt's secretary. The two brothers would then get into angry confrontations over what appeared to be the most minor of operational details. Walt often refused to meet with Roy, sometimes for weeks. During these periods, on the rare occasions they passed each other in the halls, neither uttered a single word nor acknowledged the other's presence.

Lillian, meanwhile, fearing Walt was going to drink himself to death or overdose on pills, pleaded with Roy to overlook his personal animosities and try to pressure Walt into seeing a doctor. Reluctantly, that June, Walt paid a visit to the family physician and upon returning home announced he had decided to follow the doctor's advice and take a summer vacation. And, he added, without Lillian. Although neither wanted to admit it publicly, it was, after twenty-three years of a marriage more formal than intimate, a trial separation.

In the weeks before his scheduled departure, Walt, for the first time in his life, allowed himself to be photographed in a social setting with a woman other than his wife. Dolores Del Rio, a comely actress of Spanish descent, became a frequent dinner, dancing, and drinking companion. Rumors of an affair between them circulated throughout Hollywood, although not a word found its way into the gossip columns.

That June, Walt took the adolescent Sharon with him to Alaska, to scout locations for a new series of real-life documentaries with naturalist photographers Alfred and Emma Milotte. In reality, however, Walt spent as little time as possible with the Milottes, preferring to be alone with Sharon.

He delighted in being both mother and father to his adopted daughter on the trip, roles he assumed with a degree of enthusiasm nestled in the thin border that separated his fantasies from his obsessions. He took special delight in bathing Sharon every night, combing her hair, washing her underwear, carefully dressing her from head to toe before taking her out to restaurants, even following her around as she sleepwalked, a strange habit of hers which, rather than concerning Walt, openly fascinated, entertained, and apparently inspired him. Sleepwalking soon became a running gag in Goofy cartoons, one of the few personal "Disney" touches added to his late-1940s cartoons.

Walt was having such a good time being alone with Sharon that late in August, shortly before his scheduled return, he decided to extend their vacation a few extra days and flew to the Arctic Circle to see

Mount McKinley. Moments before they were to board the plane for the return flight, Disney's personal tour guide and pilot, Russell Havenstrite, received the news he had become a grandfather for the first time. The pilot decided to celebrate by sharing a bottle of scotch with Walt.

Once airborne, the inebriated Havenstrite lost his sense of direction and on the first leg of the trip, from Nome to Candle, barely missed crashing into the side of a mountain and almost ran out of fuel trying to find the airport. The story is told that Walt kissed the ground upon their safe landing. What actually happened was that he stepped off the plane and fainted.

The near-fatal experience, Walt's second in three months—the crash of the "Carolwood Pacific" the first—rather than unnerving him seemed to instill a newfound sense of invulnerability. The two events also did something else: There had been an undeniable thrill to it all, not unlike the thrill of, say, a parachute jump, or a ride on a roller coaster . . . or standing at the top of the Statue of Liberty.

At the end of the summer, when Walt finally arrived home, he greeted Lillian warmly. She immediately noticed the change in Walt. He looked healthier. His weight was up but he carried it well, the color that alcohol and pills had drained from him had returned to his cheeks, and his eyes sparkled with restored clarity. In his absence, Lillian had redecorated the house and was eager to show him all she had done. There was no further talk between them of separating. They even began appearing together in public at Chasen's, Romanoff's, Trader Vic's, and Musso and Frank, all restaurants whose maître d's were far more familiar with Walt than with Lillian.

During the day Disney liked to go to the Hollywood Stars baseball games and the Santa Anita racetrack in season. Lillian hated sports and almost never accompanied him. She preferred staying home and gradually stopped going out with Walt for fancy dinners, preferring her simple home-cooked menu of steamed fresh vegetables and whole-grain breads.

She did, however, insist their adopted daughter attend boarding school in Switzerland.

ON HIS FIRST DAY back at the studio Walt greeted his brother with a hug and eagerly began production of the "True-Life Adventure" series of live-action shorts, the first of which, *Seal Island*, he felt could be put together from the footage the Milottes had shot in Alaska.

The practical advantages to the series seemed obvious to Disney. He quickly pointed out to his brother that it was much less expensive to simply film creatures than to animate them. Roy remained skeptical about the ability of nature films to attract a wide audience. At the same time Walt approved production of a live-action version of *Treasure Island*, to be shot on location in England, starring fourteen-year-old Bobby Driscoll, Disney's favorite "live-action" child star, in the starring role. Walt often referred to Driscoll with great affection as the living embodiment of his own youth and believed the role in *Treasure Island* would make the boy a star.

Still, the motivation for the project was primarily financial, a way to utilize the postwar "frozen" pounds neither he, Hughes, nor any other American studio had thus far been able to extract from Great Britain. Hughes, hoping to renew RKO's distribution deal with Disney, generously allowed the money to be used, with the proviso the film require no additional funding.

As Roy had predicted, *Seal Island* proved a tough sell, even to RKO. Howard Hughes remained baffled by it and after several private screenings was reluctant to distribute it. Walt became furious when Roy, who had so often complained about the cost of animation and had pushed for more live-action movies, openly sided with Hughes. Later, in private, Roy calmly explained that to him "live action" meant films with actors, not animals.

To prove both Hughes and Roy wrong, Walt rented one theater in Los Angeles for a week late in December to "sneak" *Seal Island*, a move which happened to qualify it for Academy Award consideration. Walt's vindication came early in 1949 when, after having won a limited release based on the film's positive audience reaction, *Seal Island* won the Oscar as 1948's Best Short Subject. The morning after the ceremonies, Walt, in his moment of triumph, burst into Roy's office and threw the statuette at his head, missing his brother by inches as Roy dove behind his desk.

Seal Island's success at the March 1949 Oscar ceremonies came just as the studio's net profits had taken yet another perilous dip. The figures from the last quarter of 1948 revealed a profit of just $68,000, about a quarter of what they had been for the same time period a year before. The award-winning short thus had an additional value as one of the studio's most profitable films when it came to dealing with

Joseph Rosenberg and the Bank of America for the following year's financing.

Disney received unexpected help in March of 1949, when the Soviet Union, reacting to his aggressive anticommunism, offically "purged" his films, accusing Walt of having attempted to "infiltrate" Russia with his propagandistic animation.* In direct response the Los Angeles Chamber of Commerce awarded Disney their annual "Bronze Plaque" for outstanding contributions to world trade. The award received a great deal of press and, in an odd variation of the effects of the pervasive power of the blacklist, made even the thought of withholding additional financing from Disney by the Bank of America not merely bad business but dangerously close to appearing unpatriotic. Shortly after receiving the Bronze Plaque, Disney was notified by the Bank of America it intended to extend his credit for the rest of the year.

Walt continued to concentrate on consolidation and the maximizing of profits, his first priority continuing the studio's shift from making movies to making money. He used the much-publicized sale of the five millionth Mickey Mouse watch to announce the re-signing of Kay Kamen to a long-term merchandising deal. Even as Kamen's financial success and company loyalty were being publicly lauded by Disney, Walt had decided to limit Kamen's future earnings. He informed Kamen he would be allowed to continue to sell licenses only within the boundaries of the United States; the remainder of the world's markets, where the bulk of merchandising profits originated, would remain in-house, under Roy's personal supervision.

Days of increasingly private, often acrimonious negotiations followed, during which Kamen felt he was being cut out of the very markets he had spent nearly twenty years developing, the profits he produced often the difference between the studio surviving or going under. Within weeks, all merchandising, domestic and foreign, came under the exclusive control of the Disney studio.

At the same time Disney quietly made inquiries into the availability of eleven acres of vacant land directly across from his studio on Riverside Drive. When he discoverd the land belonged to the city of

---

*During the war Disney's government-funded cartoons had been shown to Soviet troops.

Burbank, he requested it be assessed for purchase. That July, Burbank's Board of Equalization placed a value of $170,000 on the land, a figure Walt felt was too high and immediately appealed, on the basis that it was entirely undeveloped. When his request for a 10 percent reduction was denied, Walt had the studio purchase the property. He justified the purchase to the bank as part of a necessary expansion needed to increase production.

The Bank of America frowned on the acquisition. To approve it, Rosenberg insisted Disney provide a detailed schedule for the repayment of all outstanding notes to the bank. In response Disney promised in writing to reduce his payroll an additional 34 percent. That figure happened to correspond exactly to the number of employees still with the studio who had participated in the strike. Disney also committed his studio to a strict adherence to all production schedules, a nonbreakable commitment to initial budgets under penalty of individual project cancellation at the bank's discretion, and more detailed preproduction outlines to prevent costly revisions and reshoots.

In truth, Disney would have promised the bank anything to acquire the property. When Roy, who had heard nothing about plans for expansion before the purchase, asked what was really going on, Walt shrugged and said it was something he thought they needed. Although he had plans for the property, studio expansion was not exactly what he had in mind. For the moment, however, he decided to keep his ideas to himself.

By December 1949, when *Look* magazine's "End of the Forties" issue honored Disney for "Distinguished Achievement Making the Most Original Films in the World," the grim fact was that the studio's fame far outweighed its fortune. Despite the cost-cutting procedures Disney had promised the bank and to which he studiously adhered, the studio showed a net loss of nearly $40,000. Beyond whatever specific reasons may have accounted for this failure, including the number of releases and the gross receipts of each against its costs, one overriding fact existed that pertained to the entire film industry: People no longer went to the movies as often as they had the first two years after the war.

The primary reason was the mushrooming popularity of television. In the three years since commercial broadcasting had been introduced in 1946, people preferred to stay home and watch television, which had become a major threat to the movie industry.

So desperate were the four eastern-based networks for programming to fill airtime between commercials, they turned to Hollywood in the hopes of acquiring old movies that had presumably run their theatrical course and could be leased for less than the cost of producing original shows. The universal acceptability of Disney's family-oriented films, and the timelessness of his animated classics and cartoon shorts, made his movies the most sought after. NBC made the first official offer, followed quickly by ABC and the Dumont network, all of which Disney flatly rejected.

Unlike every other Hollywood studio head, Walt had objections to television that had less to do with its competitive threat than its inherent technical limitations. Almost all Disney films after *Steamboat Willie* were in color, and television was, at this stage of its development, exclusively black and white. This meant all his films would have to be "decolored," a process Disney felt was artistically detrimental.

EVEN THOUGH he continued to resist the new medium, television had, in a way, helped Disney survive his studio's latest economic crisis. When Stanley Myers, one of the creators and executive producer of "Dragnet," found himself in a financial bind, his banker, who happened to be Joseph Rosenberg, sent Myers to see Walt, believing he might be able to help. "Dragnet" was being shot at Republic, where, early in 1949, Myers found himself avoiding Herbert Yates, the head of the studio, because he (Myers) had been caught in a cash crunch and was having trouble paying the rent. Rosenberg suggested to Myers he might be able to rent studio space from Disney for less than what Yates charged.

According to Myers:

"Walt was very amenable to our proposal, his only stipulation being that no one was to know we were shooting our show on his lot, because "Dragnet" didn't exactly fit the Disney image. The cover story was to be, if anyone wondered, that we were on the lot as advisors, there to show Disney how to improve his live-action filming techniques.

"I remember meeting Walt, and I didn't like him. For one thing, he insisted I call him that—Walt—rather than Mr. Disney. I told him, I see L. B. Mayer and I say Mr. Mayer. I see Darryl Zanuck and I say hello Mr. Zanuck. I never say hello L.B., or Darryl. And Disney just smiled and said, 'Well, Stanley, I have a policy here. I let everybody call me Walt instead of giving them a $5 raise.' That was supposed to be funny."

Myers believed Disney's desire to keep their association secret had do at least in part with the fact that Myers was a Jew. He said, "I knew Joe Rosenberg should have been on the Disney board of directors. After all, he'd attended every board meeting since the late thirties, sitting right alongside Walt, advising him on long-range financial planning, and more than once bailing him out of sticky situations. It was Joe who brought me to Walt in the first place. So why wasn't he a member of the studio's board? For the same reason Disney didn't want it known he was doing business with me. Because his name was Rosenberg, simple as that. Being in business with a Rosenberg and a Myers didn't sit very well with a Disney."

Walt's deal with Myers provided enough capital to justify additional funding from the Bank of America. In July 1949, Disney was able to announce a full schedule of new films and the completion of the long-awaited *Cinderella*, the studio's first fully animated feature in seven years.

The public eagerly awaited the film's February 1950 release. Although it received mediocre reviews and was hurt by comparisons to *Snow White*—a comparison initially encouraged by Disney, who, although his personal involvement in the making of the film was limited, now insisted all its ads include the tag line: "Not since *Snow White and the Seven Dwarfs* has there been a picture like this"—*Cinderella* was the studio's first legitimate box-office smash in nearly a dozen years. Audiences the world over cheered what they perceived as Disney's return to form.

Indeed, the film was the first from the studio since *Bambi* to approach any of the familiar Disney thematic flourishes. Once again, Walt's vision of a world based on the sanctity of family held together by unshakable moral conviction, threatened by stepparents and vicious siblings, and redeemed by a fairy godmother, was trotted out for dramatic display.

Cinderella cost $3 million to make and grossed more than $5 million domestically, prompting *Variety* to compare the studio's good fortune to that of its heroine: "Disney's Own *Cinderella* Yarn." The film's premiere coincided with the postwar reopening of several world markets, which helped push its eventual gross to more than $20 million worldwide. Based on *Cinderella's* financial success, Howard Hughes offered to finance *The Story of Robin Hood,* to be shot in England, and sweetened the deal with an additional guarantee of full funding for thirty-six new cartoon shorts.

Disney's financial rebound was all that more remarkable when compared to the rest of Hollywood's declining fortunes. Not only had television severely cut into every major studio's profits, but the industry itself suffered a further, potentially fatal blow as the result of the Supreme Court's February 1952 decision in the *SIMPP* v. *Paramount Pictures* case.

When the Court finally decided in favor of the independents, the Majors' forty-year monopolistic domination of the three primary branches of the American film industry—production, distribution, and exhibition—came to an inglorious end. As a result of the Court's decision, the Majors were now forced to relinquish control of any one of those branches. They chose to surrender the least profitable, exhibition, and sold their theater chains. Not long after, dozens of newly formed independent distribution networks emerged. For the first time independent movie producers could compete with the Majors in an open, competitive market for theaters, without having terms dictated to them on a take-it-or-leave-it basis.

Weeks after the Supreme Court decision, Disney made a deal with Columbia Pictures in which he reacquired all fifty cartoons they still controlled from their original 1930 distribution deal. This gave Walt, for the first time, sole ownership of all Disney studio productions and characters. As he explained in an interview he gave the *Motion Picture Herald* that summer, his intention was to protect his films from ever being sold to television without his permission.

In the interview he stated unequivocally that, in spite of his participation in a Coca-Cola–sponsored Christmas special for CBS, "No television deal can equal what we do on theater reissues." He also denied that the studio's newest wholly owned subsidiary, Hurrell Productions, a television commercial house, was in any way involved in producing original Disney movies for broadcast. Walt insisted Hurrell's only function was to produce in-house television commercials for Disney's theatrical features.

That same day Disney flew to New York to meet in secret with broadcast executives at CBS. Afterward, he attended a closed-circuit screening of several of his cartoons over the network's still-experimental color equipment. He was disappointed in the results and refused discussions of the possibility of releasing his films to CBS.

Roy confronted Walt when he returned from New York over his continuing lack of personal involvement with the studio's new films, on which they were spending lavish amounts of money. *Alice in Wonderland*, Roy pointed out, had cost more than $3 million to produce and, he insisted, because of Walt's inattention to its production had proved a failure at the box office. Walt told Roy to mind his own business.

Besides Walt's indifference to finances, the brothers fought over the overall direction of the studio, live action or animation. Roy insisted that in spite of *Seal Island*, the nature series held little commercial potential. And in spite of his public denials, Walt was eager to broaden the studio's involvement in television, while Roy remained vehemently opposed to any such move.

In December 1952, as they had in the past when neither would budge from a position, they simply stopped talking to each other. Instead, they continued their argument indirectly, through a series of conflicting public statements. Early in March 1953, Walt announced that, despite his earlier statements, Hurrell Productions was now exploring the possibility of "producing serialized dramatic and comedy shows on film for television." Walt quickly added that Disney Productions still had no intentions of selling any of its back library of features and shorts to television.

In March 1953, Roy held a press conference to quash the persistent rumors, fueled by Walt's statement, that the studio was about to make a deal with one of the networks. Roy assured everyone no future existed in television for the Disney studio. He described the hundreds of thousands of dollars in potential television profits as "piddling" in comparison to the millions such films as *Snow White* earned with each theatrical rerelease.

That same month, in recognition of his "contribution to truth and knowledge" through his films, the French government awarded Disney its highest cultural honor, the title and decoration of *Officer d'Academie*. Shortly thereafter, Walt announced a $20-million, three-year commitment to the production of new theatrical movies. The new films included all-animated versions of *Peter Pan, Lady and the Tramp*, and *Sleeping Beauty*, and live-action feature productions of *When Knighthood Was in Flower* and *20,000 Leagues Under the Sea.*

The Bank of America approved Disney's projected 1953 operating budget on the strength of the studio's newest deal with RKO, which gave Walt a 70–30 split in his favor on the profits of all new product. Although RKO's 30 percent cut was among the lowest in the business, it still bothered Walt that, in light of the Supreme Court decision, he was still dependent on an outside, "Major" distributor at all.

Anxious to start his own independent distribution network, Walt held a secret meeting with "Dragnet" executive producer, Stanley Myers. Disney knew that Myers had connections in the industry which gave him access to otherwise unavailable facts and figures. Calling in a marker, Walt summoned Myers to the studio for a late-night meeting.

Myers recalled: "Walt sat across his desk with a bottle of Cutty Sark and a pack of Lucky Strike cigarettes and proceeded to pick my brain. One thing that became clear to me was his tremendous dislike for Sam Goldwyn, in spite of his having supported him several years earlier during the *Up in Arms* controversy.

"One of the things that stuck in his craw was how little Sam Goldwyn was rumored to be paying to his distributors. I happened to know all the facts and figures because I'd worked for Charlie Skouras, the head of Twentieth Century-Fox, during the *Up in Arms* lawsuit, which involved Fox-controlled theaters. And Disney knew it.

"Now he wanted to know what Goldwyn's current distribution deal with [Fox] was. I was reluctant to reveal the figures, but finally I told him. Goldwyn's swing [payout] was between 15 and 18 percent, depending upon the specifics of each deal. Disney didn't say a word. He just reached for that bottle of Cutty and, without a glass, lifted it to his lips.

"I then went on to explain to him that it didn't necessarily have to cost even that much, that the distributor naturally had a profit built-in for himself. You can distribute for about 12 percent by eliminating all the fat. At that point I looked at him. He was staring out his window at a vacant building across the way. I said to him, 'Why don't you create your own distribution wing and call it Buena Vista?' He asked me where I got the name from, and I told him that was the street sign just in front of the main entrance to the studio. Walt thanked me, we had a final drink, and that was that."

It would take a year to pull Buena Vista together. During that time, Walt planned to offer RKO a deal that would, in effect, reverse their present relationship, making RKO a distribution subsidiary of Buena Vista, with the possibility of jointly producing movies later on. The offer, however, was never made. Late in the fall of 1953, Disney and Hughes had a falling out over the release of Walt's first full-length live-action "True-Life Adventure" film, *The Living Desert*, made by the same team that had produced the award-winning *Seal Island*.

Hughes still hated the idea of nature films, considered the personal habits of animals too unhygienic for audiences, and, although he had reluctantly agreed to distribute the nature shorts, wanted no part of features. Cleanliness, however, wasn't Hughes's only consideration. He had grown disenchanted with Disney after suffering heavy losses from the string of features that followed *Cinderella*, including *Treasure Island*, *Alice in Wonderland*, *The Story of Robin Hood*, *Peter Pan*, and *The Sword and the Stone*. While *Alice* and *Peter Pan* were the most financially successful of the group, neither had approached *Cinderella*'s profits.

Walt considered Hughes's refusal to distribute *The Living Desert* a breach of contract. After five years of Hughes's inept management, RKO had fallen into such disarray that the increasingly reclusive billionaire agreed to simply let Walt out of his contract. Having grown weary of the film business in general, Hughes then surprised Disney by offering first to sell him RKO outright, and when Walt declined, to give it to him for free, along with an active $10-million credit line.

Walt wanted to take Hughes's offer immediately. Roy, however, became suspicious and insisted on first auditing RKO's books. The audit revealed that even with the added $10 million, the studio's liabilities still far outweighed its assets. Walt personally met with Hughes to reject the offer. The meeting remained friendly, and with a handshake, a drink—a scotch for Walt, plain soda for Hughes—a cigarette, and eyes blinking up a storm, the seventeen-year relationship between the Disney studio and RKO came to an end.

Not long after, Walt announced the formation of his new in-house distribution wing, Buena Vista, and its debut feature, *The Living Desert*, scheduled for release that fall.

Despite extraordinary visuals that Disney claimed captured the natural behavior of the desert's creatures, critics attacked the film for what appeared to be the staging of a rooster cocking his head to the sound track's syncopation and the mating of two scorpions in what looked like nothing so much as a carefully choreographed square dance.

Nevertheless, *The Living Desert* became Disney's second box-office smash of the fifties (*Cinderella* was the first). *The Living Desert* went on to win the 1953 Academy Award for Best Documentary Feature. That Oscar pleased Walt a great deal, but not as much as the fact that he didn't have to split his profits with an outside distributor.

The Living Desert couldn't have come at a better time. The film's financial numbers increased the value of Disney's inventory, just as he was about to enter secret negotiations with the American Broadcasting Company for the broadcast rights to his studio's films.

Walt was now looking for a way to finance the building of an amusement park on the studio's newly acquired adjoining acreage, and he believed television could provide it. He was so excited about the idea he effected another reconciliation with his brother, just so he could tell him his new plan.

As far as Roy was concerned, Walt's description of "Disneylandia," which he was calling his project, was the clearest evidence yet he had finally and completely gone out of his mind.

FIFTEEN

King of the New Frontier

To MAINTAIN absolute control over Disneylandia, Walt created a separate, privately held corporation, Walt Disney, Inc., in January 1953, of which only Disney, his two daughters, and brother-in-law Bill Cottrell were principals. Lillian refused to have anything to do with the new company, and Walt excluded Roy because of his skepticism regarding television and Disneylandia.

Shortly after its inception, to avoid confusion and a threatened lawsuit from the stockholders of the film company over the un-licensed use of the name "Walt Disney," he changed the name of his private corporation to WED Enterprises—taken from his initials, Walter Elias Disney. One of the first things WED did was to to represent Walt in his negotiations for a new seven-year contract with Walt Disney Productions' only executive producer, himself. The new contract called for an increased salary from $2,000 to $3,000 a week, with renewals at his option for the next forty years. It also gave WED the right to purchase, at any time, up to 25 percent of stock in Walt Disney Productions.

Walt also formed Retlaw Enterprises (Walter spelled backwards) as a subdivision of WED, which Disney also owned. Retlaw had two primary functions: the acquisition and administration of rights to all future merchandising of the name "Walt Disney" (specifically for use in the name of his theme park and on any future television shows, along with 5 percent of all studio merchandising that used it), and the right to invest up to 15 percent in any and every Disney studio project, film, product merchandising, publishing, etc. Because the name "Walt Disney" appeared on everything, from merchandising to every film the studio made, Retlaw generated instant and enormous profits.

Retlaw "hired" Walt at a guaranteed annual salary of $50,000, plus annual bonuses of $30,000, in addition to his pair of $3,000 weekly salaries from WED and Walt Disney Productions.

The whole idea of a separate arrangement surprised and angered Roy, who was convinced that Walt was now attempting to dissolve their partnership. In fact, Walt's reasons for creating a separate corporation were threefold: He wanted to guarantee lifetime financial security for his children. He no longer wished to battle Roy, the bank, and the stockholders over the future direction of the studio. Finally, he believed WED could, on its own, generate all the funding necessary to allow him to build his dream park. At least on one count, Walt figured correctly. Within months, the formation of WED had made him a millionaire.

The sudden influx of money changed little about his daily habits. At the age of fifty-two, he still ate the same oatmeal breakfast at the same Burbank diner he passed every day he went into the studio. He sat on the same counter stool and ordered from the same waitress, whom he would always leave a 10-cent tip—a gratuity which had become the talk of the restaurant, the studio, and the town for years.

He had always hated wearing ties and decided that now he no longer had to. With the exception of public appearances and the television shows, he almost never wore one, preferring a kerchief. He allowed himself a completely new wardrobe every two years at Bullock's department store on Wilshire, replacing his light gray business suits with the same models, regardless of changing fashions.

What did change was his pursuit of Disneylandia, beginning with his search for fresh seed money. While Disney had considered several offers from CBS over the past two years, which, because of the network's lack of color-transmission development he had turned down, he now actively pursued a deal with the American Broadcasting Company. In 1953, ABC was a struggling network with no hit shows, no stars, and no prospects. It was deeply in debt and had only fourteen affiliate stations, as compared to CBS, which had seventy-four, and NBC, which had seventy-one. Earlier that year, the network merged with United Paramount Theaters, Paramount Pictures's former in-house chain it was forced to sell after the Supreme Court decision. Walt chose ABC over its rival NBC, because ABC's newly appointed president, Leonard Goldenson, happened to be close to two of Walt's Hollywood friends: Ronald Reagan, fellow "Commie" hunter, and David Wallerstein, now a major theater-chain owner.

Wallerstein had managed Warner Bros.'s B&K circuit of theaters before purchasing it outright. Walt was familiar with B&K because it had hosted the world premieres of both *Fantasia* and *Cinderella*. Wallerstein secretly continued (illegally, in direct violation of the terms of the 1952 Supreme Court decision Disney had championed) to lend Walt "emergency" bridge money against future rental fees, sometimes up to $300,000 in cash.

Goldenson, a sharp, wiry, prematurely gray man in his early forties with excellent survival instincts, believed the Disney name and inventory of films could make the network an equal competitor with CBS and NBC. Disney met with Goldenson in New York the first week in July and said a deal could be made if the network would agree to finance Disneylandia.

After several days of marathon sessions, the two seemed on the verge of working out a financial arrangement when Disney was hit with a major lawsuit that led to the suspension of negotiations. In July 1953, Clement J. Melancon, an accountant with five hundred shares of Walt Disney Productions stock, sued Walt Disney and WED. Melancon believed Walt had created the new corporation to siphon profits illegally from Walt Disney Productions. What prompted the lawsuit was the studio's 1953 annual statement to its stockholders, which revealed that for the last half of fiscal 1953 (January-June 1953), Walt Disney Productions' net profit was $142,723, a slight increase from the year before. During the same period, the studio's total income had dropped by more than a million dollars.

Walt's annual letter to the stockholders explained the improved profits-to-gross-income ratio as the result of the studio's successful film productions, but failed to explain how the value of a share of Disney stock could rise 22 cents in one year and not be accompanied by stockholder dividends. The real reason was Roy's creative book-keeping. By taking the grosses from films in release and applying them against the budgets of those in production, he was able to postpone reconciliation indefinitely and create a paper profit.

According to Clement Melancon's suit, common stockholders had not received a dividend since 1947 because of the "excessive and unreasonable" salaries paid by Walt Disney, Inc., and WED to Walt Disney. Melancon wanted the courts to void all Walt Disney Productions—WED contracts until stockholders received a dividend.

While Roy publicly supported his brother, the lawsuit only increased the personal animosity between the two, as each accused the other of serious corporate misconduct. Their relationship soon reached another breaking point, and all communication between them broke down. They even refused to take calls from one other, communicating only when absolutely necessary, via missives routed through Roy's son, Roy E.

Walt's response to Melancon's charges was public silence and private outrage. What, he wondered, would Melancon and all the other stockholders have if he, Walt, hadn't worked so hard the past quarter century? As always during times of crisis, his temper grew short, and he became increasingly confrontational, both at home and at the studio. Around the house, he complained the new chairs Lillian had picked out for the living room were too uncomfortable and the bedroom wallpaper too loud.

Moreover, his chronic shoulder arthritis flared up. It fell to Hazel George, his private in-studio nurse, to apply daily hot water bottles and limited traction to Walt in the special anteroom he had built as an extension to his office. George also offered a sympathetic ear for Walt to confess his most private inner doubts and fears.

It quickly became apparent to her that Walt might not be that concerned about the lawsuit, or even his battles with Roy. Lawsuits could be settled and family relationships could be mended. Walt had done both before, many times. What was really bothering him, she believed, was the one problem which grew with each passing day.

Disney's worsening arthritis had triggered an obsessional preoccupation with death. Nearing fifty-three, the inevitable signs of physical aging were starting to show. His hair had begun to to thin on top and turn gray at the sides. His eyelids had grown thick and droopy. His cheeks had sunk into low jowly sacs, and a belt of fat around his middle had slowly begun to spread.

As a defense Walt retreated once more into memories of the past. Each day he spent part of his physical therapy recalling to the matronly nurse vivid details of his childhood on the Marceline farm.

Sometimes he complained to her about the pressures of being the "benevolent monarch" for so many employees. He would philosophize about religion, confessing his belief that smoking and drinking were his worst sins. When Hazel George gently suggested to him that cutting down his consumption of fats might help reduce his weight, which had ballooned to 210 pounds, he took her warning as further proof his health was rapidly failing.

His preoccupation with death was further intensified by the passing of his ninety-one-year-old uncle Robert. For several days Walt wept openly in front of Nurse George while he recalled the details of how Uncle Robert had given him a place to stay when he first came to Hollywood and how his crucial $500 loan had made everything that followed possible.

At times during these sessions his melancholia turned to rage, as it did when he focused on yet another lawsuit, this one by Vincent I. Whitman, an inventor who lived in New York City. Whitman contended that the multiplane animation process patented by the Disney studio was a lift of Whitman's 1937 patent for essentially the same device. This wasn't the first time the origin of the multiplane had been challenged in court. This lawsuit, however, coming as it did while Melancon's was still being contested, enraged Disney, who insisted there was a conspiracy to steal everything it had taken him a lifetime to earn.*

To TRY TO ELEVATE his mood and ease his physical and emotional tension, Lillian convinced Walt to take her on a long European vacation. Although intended as a rest, Walt spent much of his time visiting amusement parks, to study their layout, attractions, and rides. He also received regular communiqués from his staff, several of whom urged Walt to allow them to film in the newly patented widescreen process developed by Twentieth Century-Fox. Disney, always excited by new technology, approved several features to be shot in "CinemaScope," as the process was called. Among the films were the animated *Lady and the Tramp*, the live-action *20,000 Leagues Under The Sea*, several "True-Life Adventures," and one cartoon short, a

---

*The case was settled out of court. Several others, through the years, including one by the Fleischers, had also challenged Disney's multiplane patent.

pet project of one of the "Nine Old Men," animator Ward Kimball's *Toot, Whistle, Plunk, and Boom.*

To acquire the rights to the new wide-screen process, Disney had to agree to allow *Toot* to open Fox's big-budget biblical Scope epic, *The Robe.* Because of time constraints, Disney gave the go-ahead for the cartoon while still in Europe.

Toot, Whistle, Plunk, and Boom proved a radical departure from the Disney studio's style, both in the look of its animation and the nature of its story. Kimball, an amateur musician who led his own Dixieland jazz band, the Firehouse Five Plus Two, envisioned *Toot* as a light entertainment that would teach the four families of musical instruments.

When Walt returned from Europe and screened the film, he was appalled at its unrepresentative, non-Disney visual style and lack of formal narrative. Walt and Kimball argued vehemently over the film. Frustrated by what he took to be Kimball's obstinance, Disney at one point considered his animator, and would have done so if *Toot* hadn't won the Academy Award for Best Short Subject (Cartoon) of 1953. Nevertheless, Walt explicitly banned all further stylistic experimentation by any animator and limited Kimball's participation on future film productions.

While the Melancon lawsuit dragged on, Disney found himself in still another battle, this time with the city of Los Angeles and the Burbank City Council over the proposed future site of Disneylandia. The Los Angeles City Council refused to agree to build a train that would link Disneylandia (or "Mickey Mouse Park," as Walt also considered calling it) to nearby Griffith Park, a condition Walt considered crucial if he were to attract large crowds of children. Burbank's council cited longstanding zoning restrictions, thus deciding the raw acreage could not be commercially developed. Walt challenged the initial verdict, and an additional hearing was held.

The mood during the hearing was inhospitable, as one council member after another declared their unwavering opposition to having an amusement park built in their community. "We don't want the carny atmosphere in Burbank," one councilman declared. Added another, "We don't want people falling in the river or merry-go-rounds squawking all day long." After hearing this last statement, Walt stood up and walked out of the meeting without saying a word.

While he continued to battle Burbank with a battery of lawyers, he

secretly commissioned the Stanford Research Institute to find an
alternate site for Disneylandia. Although he was never able to prove
it, he remained convinced the rest of his life that his Burbank
neighbor, Universal Pictures, located about three miles to the north-
west, had pressured the community board to "outlaw" his park. Years
later, his suspicions seemed confirmed when, in 1964, Universal
opened an amusement park–style attraction of its own in Burbank.

Several months passed before Disney found a new site. His first
choice was the old railroad terminal in downtown Los Angeles. When
that proved unattainable, Walt settled on his second choice, a 160-
acre orange grove in Anaheim. The acquisition of the much larger site
was made possible by its lower cost per acre.

Anaheim was twenty-seven miles from the city of Los Angeles but
less than one mile from a new freeway, the Harbor, on which
construction was about to begin. Stanford estimated the cost of
purchasing the land and developing the park at $11 million. Builders
escalated that figure to $17 million. At this point Walt decided to
renew his stalled deal with ABC, hoping to get the network to pay for
the building of his park as part of the deal. In July 1954, Disney
petitioned in federal court for the dismissal of Melancon's lawsuit.

Before a decision was handed down, Melancon withdrew his case,
after refusing to post an additional $10,500 cost bond. Although the
litigation wasn't officially terminated until nearly a year later, in
January 1955, Melancon's lack of compliance cleared the way for
Disney and Goldenson to work out an arrangement.

Disney then put together a secret team, from those he considered
his most talented art directors, that included Richard Irvine, Harper
Goff, Bill Martin, Bud Washo, Herb Ryman, and Marvin A. Davis.
They set up operation in an abandoned warehouse in Glendale,
which Walt believed no outsider could penetrate. There they worked
with Walt on the design of the park's layout. As his general director
for the project, Disney recruited C. V. Wood, the former head of the
Stanford Research Institute. To pay for an intricate scale model of the
park, Walt borrowed against his life insurance. When it was completed, he took the highly detailed five-foot-square model, complete
with street signs and working doors and windows on the buildings, to
New York.

Disney met with Goldenson at ABC's midtown corporate offices.
However, negotiations collapsed when Goldenson claimed he hadn't

been able to convince the board of directors to undertake the financing of Disneylandia. Walt then lugged his scale model four blocks south to Rockefeller Center where he met with NBC's General David Sarnoff. Sarnoff had become the acknowledged leader in color-television development. Only a year ago he had been in hot pursuit of Disney. In the interim NBC's president had decided the network's interests lay in public affairs. "Television," he told Walt, "will never be a medium of entertainment," and turned him down cold.

Disney did no better at CBS, where William Paley equivocated for weeks, unable to make a commitment. Walt finally met with Goldenson one last time to attempt to make a deal. Disney's primary condition remained unchanged. Any agreement for his films would have to include funding for Disneylandia. While both CBS and NBC wanted his films, they had no use for an amusement park. Goldenson finally offered Walt the opportunity to argue his case directly before the network's board.

At that meeting Walt presented what he claimed was a new offer. Rather than having to make Disneylandia a part of the deal, the network could simply pay him $15 million plus one minute of free network advertising a week to promote his latest theatrical release. In return the network would be given complete and exclusive access to his entire backlog of films. The board rejected his proposal.

Goldenson, desperate to get Disney's films, refused to give up, believing a deal was still possible. He made one last attempt to see if he could help Walt raise enough outside money to improve his chances of convincing the board of the feasibility of the park. Disney's own bank had already passed on Disneylandia. After being rejected by every major financial institution, Goldenson, as a last resort, approached Sid Markley, his Harvard Law School roommate now in charge of ABC's recently acquired southern circuit of movie theaters, to see if there was anything he could do.*

Markley suggested Goldenson get in touch with Karl Hoblitzelle, owner of the Interstate Theaters chain as well as the chairman of the Republic Bank of Dallas. Goldenson persuaded Hoblitzelle to have his bank put up $5 million, enough to convince several New York banks to approve additional funding.

---

*The Supreme Court decision did not prevent television networks from owning movie theaters.

This infusion was still inadequate, so Goldenson returned to ABC's board and, based on these commitments, got it to agree to advance $500,000 in cash to Disney and guarantee all WED bank loans in exchange for 35 percent ownership of Disneylandia. ABC also received 100 percent of the profits from the park's food concessions for a period of ten years, and an eight-year programming commitment with the Disney studio for the use of its back inventory. The films would be shown in a one-hour original television program with an annual budget of $5 million, to be hosted by Walt.

Walt Disney Productions then purchased a third of WED's outstanding stock, and Western Printing and Lithographing, the publisher of Disney comic books, bought 13.8 percent of the remaining shares. Walt retained all remaining WED stock. The deal, completed in the spring of 1954, was the largest and most expensive outside programming package in the new medium's young history. Not only did it provide the initial financing for Disneylandia, it made ABC fully competitive with NBC and CBS.

Disney was thrilled by the arrangement, almost as much as he was by another event which occurred a month later. On May 9, 1954, Diane married six-foot-five, two-hundred-pound Ron Miller, star tight end of the University of Southern California football team. They had met in 1953, while both were students at USC. A far better athlete than scholar, Miller left school at the end of his junior year after signing a contract to play for the Los Angeles Rams.

They had been dating for three months when Miller asked Diane to marry him. She agreed and dropped out of school to prepare for her wedding. Walt promised his new son-in-law a prominent place in the family business. Although Miller interpreted this to mean an executive appointment, Walt assigned him to the Disneylandia construction crew in Anaheim, under the direct supervision of the project's general director, C.V. Wood.

Lillian was less thrilled with Diane's selection of a husband, feeling she could have done much better. The wedding left Lillian with a feeling of emptiness and loss. To cheer her up, Walt presented his wife with a solid gold bracelet decorated with twenty-nine miniature Oscars, one for each award the studio had received. Precious metals always seemed to do it for Lillian, and these pieces of jewelry proved no exception. The bracelet returned the smile to her face. As if to thank her husband, Lillian made a rare "appearance," of sorts, by "writing" an article for *McCall's* magazine entitled "I Live With a Genius," probably ghosted by journalist Pete Martin, who later did the same for Diane's "memoir" of her father.

It was a curious article, in which Lillian gushed about the domestic bliss in the Disney household. Perhaps her most interesting revelation was the unqualified approval of and support for Walt's home railroad. "When he decided to build a new house," she reported, "Walt began making plans to run the track for his miniature train all through the grounds. Now I approve of that train. It is a wonderful hobby for him. He has built much of it himself, and it has been a fine diversion and safety valve for his nervous energy."

The "Disneyland" television show premiered on October 27, 1954, with an episode entitled "The Disneyland Story," an obvious promotion with film clips from upcoming shows and a report on the progress of the amusement park. Although Walt appeared to host the program from behind the desk in his studio office, his scenes were actually shot on a soundstage replica of his office, the same one now on permanent display at Anaheim's Disneyland. The program's originally intended name, Disneylandia, was rejected by ABC for sounding too exotic. They pointed out that *Fantasia*, which Walt had in mind when he came up with the original name for his park, had not been a hit with the public. At their suggestion Walt agreed to change the name of his park to the more accessible Disneyland.

According to *Time* magazine, the show was "a bang that blew Wednesday night to kingdom come for the [other] two major networks." The Nielsen ratings for the first week were a phenomenal 41, more than twice the number that generally defined a hit. Approximately 30.8 million viewers out of 75 million Americans who watched television that night were tuned in to Disney. Bob Kintner, an ABC executive, said the show established Walt as the new king of television, "cutting [Arthur] Godfrey [Disney's competition on CBS], the best in the business, down to size."

The success of "Disneyland," which would go on to become one of the longest-running prime-time network TV series, literally changed the face of both the television and movie industries. That same year Warner Bros. followed Disney's lead and became the first of the Majors to produce an original network television series, again on ABC, in return for the right to plug one of its films at the end of each episode, a precedent established by Walt. Before the year came to an end, every major studio had made a programming deal with one of the networks.

All of which pleased Walt greatly. He envisioned himself both prophet and pioneer in this new media frontier. Unlike his late entrance into films, this time around he had the satisfaction of watching others follow in his footsteps.

So IT WAS that on the last evening of 1954, Disney found himself alone at his desk in his office at the studio, a bottle of scotch his only companion to greet the new year. New Year's Eve was as good a time as any to look back. Before him was a report that detailed the numbers of the payout from his original $500 gamble thirty-one New Year's Eves ago. Since 1923, more than a billion people, one-third of the world's population, had paid money at the box office to see at least one of the 657 films the studio had produced, in any one of fourteen different languages. Thirty million 10-cent copies of Walt Disney comic books had been sold in thirty-six countries, plus 100 million more expensive editions, from 25 cents to $2.95; $250,000 in sheet music and records graced family pianos and phonographs; $750 million in merchandising revenues supported 740 separate companies that turned out 2,928 different souvenir items twenty-four hours a day, seven days a week—everything from Mickey Mouse watches to Donald Duck toilet seats. And, thanks to televison, the face in the morning mirror was now as familiar to America as Mickey's. Everwhere he went, people stopped him in the street and treated him with the kind of disbelieving reverence usually reserved for movie stars.

Next to that report was a letter he had received from J. Edgar Hoover, the contents of which meant as much to him as the financial report. In his letter Hoover informed Walt he had been officially promoted to the position of Special Agent in Charge contact.

Here is the confidential 1954 FBI inter-office memo that describes the promotion:

Mr. Walt Disney is the Vice-President in charge of production and the founder of Walt Disney Productions, Inc., 2400 West Alameda Street, Burbank, California. Mr. Disney is extremely prominent in the motion picture industry and his company is the foremost organization in the production of cartoons.

Mr. Disney has recently established a business association with the American Broadcasting Company . . . for the production of a series of television shows, which for the most part are scheduled to be filmed at Disneyland, a multimillion dollar amusement park being established under Mr. Disney's direction in the vicinity of Anaheim, California. Mr. Disney has volunteered representatives of this office complete access to the facilities of Disneyland for use in connection with official matters and for recreational purposes. . . .

Because of Mr. Disney's position as the foremost producer of cartoon films in the motion picture industry and his prominence and wide acquaintanceship in film production matters, it is believed that he can be of valuable assistance to this office and therefore it is my recommendation that he be approved as a Special Agent in Charge (SAC) contact.

Being made an official SAC contact pleased Walt greatly, because it meant that in addition to continuing to supply his data to the bureau, other informants could now supply reports to him. It was Hoover's Christmas present to Walt, the timing of which was no accident. Hoover, as he implied in his directive, wanted to capitalize on Disney's involvement with network television. The FBI had thus far been unable to penetrate the middle echelon of the new medium's power loop. What the Bureau wanted was someone it could trust on the inside. As far as J. Edgar Hoover was concerned, the man most qualified for that assignment was the Bureau's proven Hollywood veteran, the man everyone, including the head of the FBI, called "Uncle Walt."

WALT WORKED around the clock to meet Disneyland's much publicized July 1955 opening. He expanded his secret team of builders to include former employee Richard Irvine, lured away from Twentieth Century-Fox where he had landed after teaming with Disney on *Victory Through Air Power*. He also called on veteran storyman Ken Anderson, who was working on *Sleeping Beauty*, which Disney hoped would mark the studio's return to its more traditionally gothic style of animation. (Several animators, hoping for the opportunity to produce more contemporary work, were already referring to the movie as "Sleeping Duty"). To the original team he added staff artists Claude Coats and Marc Davis. Walt, never at a loss for nicknames and labels, called this group his "Imagineers."

Disney now envisioned his park as a series of individual three-dimensional "movies" which a visitor could actually enter into and wander about, with "Main Street, USA," the aisle that led to each individual fantasy. Main Street, USA, happened to be an exact replica of Main Street, Marceline.

Walt insisted Disneyland's Main Street, down to "every brick and shingle and gas lamp," be built five-eighths normal size. Further, he insisted that every exterior's level be larger than the one above it, to create a sense of depth that both shortened and stretched one's perception at the same time. The intended effect was to recall the main street of every adult's distanced youth, as well as his own, with the remembered perspective of a child's eye.

From Main Street, one should be able literally to step into any one of a number of imaginary lands—the primitive West in Frontierland, the forest in Adventureland, every child's Fantasyland, and the science-fictional future of Tomorrowland. Within each, rides, designated by letter—A being the simplest, E the most exciting—were accessible with tickets from a book purchased at the park's front gate.

Finally, Walt wanted a full-scale old-style steam train to ring the entire park. Rather than buying or building one, he sought to borrow the one from Ward Kimball, who had built a full-size replica that ran on a track around his San Gabriel home. Walt decided that Kimball's, modeled after the one-eighth–scale "Carolwood Pacific," would be perfect for Disneyland.

"He'd call all hours of the day and night," Kimball remembered. "He'd say, 'Kimball, this is Walt,' and I'd say, 'Walt who,' and he'd say, 'Disney, for crissakes!' Then he'd tell me how much the park needed a train like mine, life-size, and he'd ask if he could borrow mine for the park. The deal was, on the day the park was closed, Mondays, I could come down and ride it to my heart's content. I said no, I didn't think that was a good idea. I had changed the mechanism of my train to burn wood and told Walt it wouldn't be practical. He told me to think about it anyway."

Realizing he wasn't going to get Kimball's, Walt bought a restored train for the park.

As the opening deadline approached, new problems arose. Mechanical equipment failed to work. "Rivers" drained themselves into the dry desert soil faster than they could be filled. Buildings built to scale threatened to topple due to miscalculated centers of gravity. Then, in late spring, the local Orange County plumbers and asphalt workers went on strike. Just as his animators had fifteen years earlier, a new generation of union men threatened to turn Walt's dream into an endless nightmare.

Disney tried desperately to keep the strike from the press. He had learned his lessons well from the 1941 confrontation with the Cartoonists Guild. He knew now the quickest way to settle a dispute was to do exactly that, settle it, without a public monitoring of the process.

When negotiations began to drag, Walt was advised by his management team to postpone the opening of the park until September, which he considered an unthinkable alternative. Instead, Walt ended the walkout by agreeing to pay the plumbers retroactively whatever amount was finally settled upon through negotiation.

The asphalt workers proved harder to deal with, and after trying several times, Disney risked a general shutdown by purchasing truckloads of hot asphalt from San Diego, about fifty miles south, and hiring outside workers to lay it down. The gamble paid off, and to his great relief, general construction continued without any further serious delays.

While Walt continued to supervise the building of Disneyland, back in Burbank the studio had experienced two of its biggest successes, the theatrical run of the live-action feature *20,000 Leagues Under the Sea*, starring Kirk Douglas, and what had become a television sensation, the three-part saga of Davy Crockett.

Walt had assigned Richard Fleischer to direct *20,000 Leagues Under the Sea*. Fleischer, the son of former competitor Max Fleischer, along with art director John Meehan and cinematographer Franz Planer, had produced an outstanding version of the Jules Verne science-fiction classic. Besides Douglas, the film featured excellent performances by James Mason, Peter Lorre, and Paul Lukas, and at least one unforgettable sequence, the famous battle with the giant squid. Upon viewing rushes, Disney insisted on personally reshooting the squid's scenes, to capture the visual excitement he thought Fleischer's version lacked.

Disney had dedicated an entire episode of his television show to the making of *Leagues*, "Operation Undersea," which aired the week of the film's 1954 opening. The show emphasized the squid sequence and the *Nautilus* submarine. The show proved a ratings smash, went on to win an Emmy, and set the stage for the feature's record-breaking run. *Leagues* became the most successful (cost versus profit) live-action dramatic film the studio had yet made, grossing $6.8 million in its initial release (and an additional $2.2 million in its 1963 rerelease).

After the film proved a hit at the box office, Walt quietly transferred its specially constructed *Nautilus* submarine to Disneyland and placed it on permanent exhibition. This transfer was followed by another one, when the cost of building the sub was removed from the budget of the picture and paper-transferred to Disneyland, to keep the film's negative cost attractively low to the bank and stockholders, one of the reasons *Leagues* was so "profitable." The move also helped fill the financially pinched Disneyland with "free" attractions.

The film's opening was followed only weeks later by the even more successful three-part "Davy Crockett." Fess Parker, until then an unknown actor, became a star and a sensation as the result of his portrayal of the buckskin frontiersman who became a maverick congressman and one of the heroic defenders of the Alamo. Moreover, "The Ballad of Davy Crockett" shot to the top of the pop-music charts, where it stayed at number one for thirteen weeks.

Walt did not spend a lot of time on *20,000 Leagues Under the Sea*. The story apparently didn't interest him except for its submarine and squid sequences. However, he paid great attention to the Crockett series. He took time away from the construction on Disneyland to pore over the details of the story, personally visiting the set during shooting, constantly making script revisions, calling camera angles, and even giving the actors, particularly Parker, specific line readings.

For reasons perhaps inspired less by creative impulse than financial necessity, Walt looked to his personal angels and demons to produce a remarkable work of entertainment. No doubt, to Disney, Crockett's appeal lay in his single-minded Fundamentalist commitment to American virtue, at least in Walt's version, where the life of the frontiersman/politician/patriot was sanitized and idealized. Disney's Crockett was ever the stoic, whose most often-repeated line in the series, "Be sure you're right, then go ahead," became yet another of Walt's externalized alter egos. Whether he was wrestling bears or battling congressmen on the floor of the House and Mexicans at the Alamo, Crockett's courage and ideals in the face of enormous odds clearly symbolized Walt's struggle during his battles against the established powers that had dominated the Majors and against the Communist "invasion" of Hollywood.

No one anticipated the kind of commercial success the series would enjoy—least of all, it would seem, Walt himself, who went so far as to issue the following statement when the show proved so popular:

"We had no idea what was going to happen to 'Crockett.' Why, by the time the first show finally got on the air, we were already shooting the third one and calmly killing Davy off at the Alamo. It became one of the biggest overnight sensations in television history, and there we were with just three films and a dead hero."

Despite Walt's self-deprecating words, he probably knew very well what he had in the can. Even before the first episode had aired, he quietly purchased thousands of raw raccoon tail skins for 5 cents apiece from a manufacturer after a government embargo prevented him from selling them to mainland China. The day the first episode premiered, Walt launched a fully prepared merchandising campaign that resulted in the sale of more than ten million hastily sewn "Davy Crockett coonskin caps." Not long after, retailers gleefully proclaimed that "Davy Crockett is bigger even than Mickey Mouse!"

Further, because the series ran over the course of several weeks, it would have been easy for Walt to change the last scene of the last episode and have Davy live. More likely, it was Walt's obsession with his own aging and death that dictated his glorifying depiction of alter-ego Crockett's premature passage through the heavenly gates.

With Disneyland's debut edging ever closer, the success of *20,000 Leagues Under the Sea* and the "Davy Crockett" series strengthened Walt's confidence. He couldn't wait now for the opening day of what he believed was destined to be his E-ticket to immortality.

SIXTEEN

Disneyland:
Forward to the Past

ON JULY 13, 1955, FOUR DAYS before Disneyland's scheduled opening, Walt and Lillian celebrated their thirtieth wedding anniversary
by inviting three hundred friends, mostly studio employees and their
wives, to a private "Tempus Fugit Celebration" at the park. Disney
planned a "cruise down the Mississippi" for guests on the *Mark
Twain* riverboat. By the time the group was served dinner at one of
Frontierland's restaurants, Walt was too drunk to make a proper toast
to his wife. He wound up blowing noisemakers into the microphone
and was finally pulled away by an embarrassed Lillian, who at that
point considered the party over.

DISNEYLAND'S official July 17 opening was televised live on ABC in
an unprecedented broadcast hosted by three of Walt's old-guard
conservative Hollywood allies: Robert Cummings, Art Linkletter,
and Ronald Reagan. In spite of Walt's best efforts, the "happy place,"
as the plaque over the front gate described Disneyland, was not quite
completed in time. Because of broadcast obligations, Disney had to
open, no matter how much of the park was still under construction.

Of the one hundred sixty total acres, the approximately two that
Tomorrowland occupied were in the worst shape. Walt directed C.

V. Wood, the park's general director, to smother the entire area with balloons and peanuts, in the hopes no one would notice. Tomorrowland turned out to be the least of Walt's problems. By all accounts, the day was a total disaster, referred to forever after by those employees who participated in it as "Black Sunday."

Among the more memorable moments captured by the cameras were actress Irene Dunne's inability to break a christening bottle across the bow of Frontierland's *Mark Twain* riverboat, Fess Parker's horse panicking at the sound of gunshots and trampling a row of newly planted pine trees, Parker and "Davy Crockett" costar Buddy Ebsen being doused by sprinklers as their horses brought them to their televised interviews, and Walt Disney's unscheduled broadcast of a barrage of four-letter words during a tirade at a Disneyland crew while he mistakenly believed his microphone was turned off.

According to C. V. Wood:

> The worst thing that happened during the live television show was when the program first came on, it showed everybody coming underneath the railroad track and into Main Street. But no one realized the asphalt on the street was still hot. The high-heeled shoes that the women wore literally sank into the pavement.
>
> It was a madhouse. We printed fifteen thousand [special admissions, by invitation only], but people were counterfeiting the damn things. We even found a guy who had built a ladder and flopped it over the barbed wire fence back where the stables were. You could just walk up and over real easy. He was letting people in for five damn bucks a head.

Fifteen thousand guests, mostly employees, their families, and friends, had been invited to the opening. More than thirty-three thousand showed up. More than half were gate-crashers.

There were several major mechanical mishaps that somehow missed the eyes of the fifteen television cameras strategically placed around the park, including a gas leak which caused Fantasyland to be shut down; leaking "rivers"; power failures; a total breakdown at the "Mr. Toad" ride; and, on this particularly sweltering summer day, a notable lack of water fountains. There were, however, plenty of Pepsi stands, which angered many who thought Disney had purposely failed to provide free water in order to sell a lot of soda. According to Disney, the reason for the lack of fountains had to do with the plumbers' strike. Because of lost construction time during the walk-out, he claimed he was forced to choose between installing toilets or drinking fountains. Not wanting, as he later put it, to see kids "peeing on the sidewalks of Main Street," he chose the former.

Jack Kinney, one of Disney's animators involved with the park's design, remembered:

> My group [of studio employees, whose presence at the opening was mandatory] had been assigned to the *Mark Twain* river-boat. We gaily tripped up the plank and wandered around. It was still hot, and the passengers were all sweating on the crowded boat. There was no bar, fountain, no water aboard, and no way to jump ship after you were on because some so-and-so had removed the gangplank. . . . Later, we traded stories with other employees and found that some were locked in cattle cars on the Disneyland railroad, marooned on Tom Sawyer's Island, restricted to the crowded theater, and jammed into rocket rides and other "fun" places.

Although the television special scored impressively high ratings, several members of the press emphasized in their reviews the high cost of admission for the general public ($15—though admission included a book of alphabetically listed free-ride tickets), the lack of conventional amusement park rides, and, of course, those missing water fountains.

The last week in July, Disney called a press conference and yelled at a reporter from United Press International who questioned the high price of admission. "We have to charge what we do because this park cost a lot to build and maintain. I have no government subsidy. The public is my subsidy. I mortgaged everything I own and put it in jeopardy for this park."

The day after the press conference, Walt called upon his always-reliable coterie of available columnists and requested they write pieces that praised his park. Predictably, a blitz of articles by Hedda Hopper, Ed Sullivan, Walter Winchell, and dozens of others appeared, dutifully raving about the wonders of Disneyland. Louella Parsons called Disney a "genius," her favorite description of him, and marveled at how well he had realized his great "vision" in the new park. During the first seven weeks, more than a million people visited Disneyland.

No doubt, more than one FBI agent was among them, for reasons both social and professional. According to a confidential FBI memo, written in January 1955, for its own reasons, the Bureau was not only delighted with Walt's new venture but kept a complete dossier on its financial structure:

> Mr. Disney has recently established a business association with the American Broadcasting Company–Paramount Theatres Inc. for the production of a series of televsion shows, which for the most part are scheduld to be filmed at Disneyland, a multi-million dollar amusement park being established under Mr. Disney's direction in the vicinity of Anaheim, Calif (SIC). Mr. Disney has volunteered representatives of this office complete access to the facilities of Disneyland for use in connection with official matters and for recreational purposes.

For the next six months Walt spent all his days and nights at Disneyland, making sure everything operated the way it was supposed to. During this period he was often accompanied by Lillian, who, although reluctant to be out among so many people, agreed to do so until a guard at the entrance to the Monsanto exhibit, which had not as yet opened, refused to let them in until they could establish their identities. When Walt explained who he was, the guard said he could enter, but, inexplicably, not Lillian. Walt had him immediately fired, and thereafter called a meeting of the entire staff, reminding them that every courtesy was most important in making sure the public was properly accommodated. Walt declared anyone who paid money to come to Disneyland was to be treated as if he or she were guests at Disney's home.

Lillian refused to return to Disneyland. Walt, on the other hand, had trouble leaving it and moved into a private apartment directly above the fire station adjacent to Main Street's city hall. At times he loved to walk along Main Street, talk with the visitors, and tousle the hair of the children. However, he passed most days locked inside the apartment, where he would stand by the window with tears streaming down his face as people walked along the boulevard of his dreams.

After a while, the apartment became the source of unfounded rumors among the employees of the park, which later spread back to Burbank, that it was Walt's new love nest for endless assignations with certain lady friends. The apartment's decor, personally chosen by Disney, didn't help. The lavender, red, and pink flocked wallpaper, offset by thick red rugs and Victorian furniture, gave the impression of nothing so much as the anteroom of a New Orleans whorehouse.

That wasn't, however, what Walt had had in mind. The faux gas lamps, thick upholstery, heavy drapes, china trinkets, windup phonograph and working fireplace were all exact duplicates, as he remembered them, of the living room of the Disney family farmhouse in Marceline. From within this most private retreat, sitting alone on his overstuffed sofa, a fifty-four-year old Disney joyfully ruled the kingdom of his past: the eternal land of his imagination east of Once-Upon-a-Time and down a ways from Never-Never-Land.

THAT FALL, the television show began its second season, still the nation's top-rated prime-time network program. When Goldenson began pressuring Disney for another series, Walt decided to launch the "Mickey Mouse Club." With the network's enthusiastic nod, Walt plunged into its development, supervising every aspect. He personally designed the show's multifunctional television soundstage. He came up with the idea for the Mickey Mouse March; the Roll Call; M-I-C-K-E-Y M-O-U-S-E; and the songs and segments for "Do What the Good Book Says" and "Meesa-Mooska-Mouska-Teers, Mouse Cartoon Time Now Is Here."

He personally selected the club's hosts, B-movie-musical player Jimmy Dodd and veteran Disney animator Roy Williams, and the original dozen "Mouseketeers," signing each to six-month contracts with options of up to seven years at a salary ceiling of $500 a week. To his surprise and delight, he found it easier to treat these children as if they were little adults than he ever had the adults on his staff, who he tended to treat as if they were big children. While his animators had always resented what they considered Walt's consescending paternalism, the children reveled in it.

The Mouseketeers were instructed by Dodd to address Disney as "Uncle Walt," which added to the sense of extended family. Disney always made sure there was a big cake on a Mouseketeer's birthday and that all production stopped so that everyone could enjoy a big birthday party.

Cubby O'Brien, an original Mouseketeer, recalled Disney's obsessive protectiveness: "Walt used to talk to us all the time and ask us how it was going. We found out later there were memos that went out everywhere, warning about using bad language anywhere near the lot. Anyone caught cursing was fired immediately, even so much as a 'damn' or 'hell,' no matter who they were or how important they were to the show."

Sheri Alveroney, a second-season replacement Mouseketeer, also thought of Walt as a father figure and remembered that "Walt was warm, nice, grandfatherly. I remember being told years later by a casting director that 'Walt raised you kids right.'"

The "Mickey Mouse Club" premiered the first week in October 1955. Broadcast every weekday afternoon at the previously dead five o'clock hour, it proved an immediate sensation. The show's theme became a national anthem for America's children. "Mouse ears" became even more popular than coonskin caps and sold, the first year they were available, at a rate of twenty five thousand sets a day.

And yet, while the show made a fortune for the network, it was never a money-maker for Walt, due to the outsize expense involved with producing five filmed hours a week. Disney worked within a budget set by ABC that was well below what each episode actually cost. Nevertheless, the show lasted for seven years. Walt was willing to have WED subsidize it out of the profits from Disneyland and the prime-time television series. It was a privilege both WED and Walt could by now easily afford.

Walt's growing fortune nourished his insatiable appetite for its fraternal twin, fame. As 1955 drew to a close, Disney thought nothing of packing his bags and flying off to anywhere in the world to personally receive yet another award, often staying in a city for days and sometimes weeks before and after the ceremony. More often than not, he did so without Lillian.

Prestigious organizations continued to fall over one another to acknowledge his lifetime of accomplishments. At times accolades came from the most unusual places. In December he received what he considered his most cherished trophy, one he believed ended the persistent and long-standing rumors of his anti-Semitism. At a fancy ceremony the Beverly Hills chapter of the B'nai B'rith proudly cited Walt Disney as their choice for its 1955 "Man of the Year."

Because of his chronic neck pain and, more recently, frequent and persistent sore throats, in January of 1956, Disney was forced to cut back his travels and public appearances. For the first time in his life he spent weeks at Holmby Hills enjoying something other than riding his cherished "Carolwood Pacific." The reason was Walt's newest grandchild, Christopher Disney Miller, whom he utterly adored.

Lillian was not used to Walt's presence around the house. Holmby Hills was her domain. Frustrated by this invasion of her privacy, she decided to remodel the entire house. Walt's taste in decor, perhaps best described as early Roy Rogers—heavy paneling, western-style furniture, rocking chairs, giant wooden wagon wheels, miniature train models, plaid sofas, and artificial flowers—gave her headaches, especially with a lit cigarette constantly clouding up the air.

One change called for the removal of the front living-room wall, to be replaced with a picture window to better keep an eye on Christopher and make sure he didn't accidentally fall into the new Olympic-sized swimming pool Walt had installed (and almost never used), and drown.

Although money was no longer a problem, Walt insisted Lillian use a crew of technicians and builders from the studio, delighting in the idea of not having to pay them anything extra, seemingly oblivious to the fact that this was the very action of studio moguls that had, in the late 1920s, precipitated the film industry's great union movement.

That June, reflecting perhaps Hollywood's changing times, the Guild of Variety Artists, once an avowed enemy of Walt, awarded him a lifetime membership for his "increasing efforts to discover new ways to keep the greatest number of people in the field of show business gainfully employed."

In July, Disney returned to Marceline for "Walt Disney Day" and dedicated a public swimming pool on the site, as Disney recalled tearfully in his speech, "where we swam in a cow pond, after we chased the cows out." The pool was the centerpiece of a ten-acre park named in his honor, which he had helped finance.

A week later he was sued by Kirk Douglas. The Douglas lawsuit was an odd one. It was unusual for "talent" to sue a studio or executive because, win or lose, the actor or actress was almost always tagged a troublemaker and often suffered some form of de facto blacklisting.

Disney had, for the first time, approved the hiring of expensive stars to help insure the success of a film, in this case, *20,000 Leagues Under the Sea*. Had Disney been more involved with production it's almost certain Douglas, one of Hollywood's most outspoken liberals, would never have been hired.

Early in 1956, Walt had used home movie footage of the Douglas family taken at the Holmby Hills home on an episode of the weekly television show. Douglas then sued Disney for $200,000 actual and $200,000 punitive damages. According to Douglas:

> "Uncle Walt" . . . invited [my sons] Michael and Joel and me to his house. We spent one Saturday afternoon riding around [on his train]. A few weeks later I was surprised to see film of my two kids and me on Walt Disney's television show . . . film of "Kirk Douglas and his sons Michael and Joel riding toy trains all round my home." I was shocked at Disney's audacity in exploiting my children. Two months later he broadcast the shots again. I was furious. I talked to my lawyer and he advised me to sue.

Douglas could never understand the reason for the invitation in the first place and suspected he had been asked to come specifically for the purpose of being filmed for television.

Walt angrily responded to the lawsuit, claiming rather cryptically that Douglas had been at the Disney family home "voluntarily and without any invitation. The entire appearance of Mr. Douglas on television was for 26 seconds and it is inconceivable that a man who has appeared so extensively in motion pictures, magazine and television could be damaged on a television screen in that amount of time."

The next day Douglas responded by issuing the following statement:

> I like Walt Disney. I enjoyed working with him during the production of the film *20,000 Leagues Under the Sea*, and I hope that sometime in the future we will again work together. But as a professional actor I am quite concerned with any action that may hurt my craft.

Early in December, depositions were taken by both sides, after which Superior Judge Leon T. David refused to dismiss the lawsuit and ordered Disney to answer it within twenty days. Walt's response came in the form of a defense of the "freedom of the press." That argument was also thrown out. Then, just days before the trial was scheduled to begin, Douglas unexpectedly dropped his suit.

I thought, what am I doing? There are some people in our profession—Bob Hope, Walt Disney—who can do no wrong. Most people think that Walt did things for children out of the goodness of his heart, that he wasn't making millions of dollars. Over [my laywer's] objections, I decided to drop the suit. You can't sue God.

More likely, Douglas's sudden turnabout occurred when he became painfully, if somewhat belatedly, aware of the extent of Disney's power and influence. With plans to begin his own independent production company, Douglas may have been warned, either by friendly advisors or operatives of a more official capacity, not to risk his investment or his future.*

THAT SAME YEAR, 1956, Disney's relationship with the FBI took an unexpected turn. It was a bizarre episode that demonstrated the spreading infection of political paranoia. The FBI had begun to question the allegiance, patriotism, and loyalty of one of its own, most revered, and presumably immune operatives.

The trouble began early in the year, in January, when Disney sent producer Jerry Sims to Washington to finalize plans with the Bureau for a two-minute "Mickey Mouse Club" newsreel of a group of children touring the Bureau's D.C. headquarters.

Sims submitted a preliminary script to an FBI agent identified only as Kemper, who dutifully passed it on to Lou Nichols, the Bureau's head of public relations. Nichols reviewed the material and initially

---

*The blacklist was finally broken in the late fifties by the independent production company Kirk Douglas formed, which insisted screenwriter Dalton Trumbo receive on-screen credit for one of its biggest films, *Spartacus*, based on a novel by Howard Fast, a writer who had spent several months in jail in the 1940s for his association with the Communist party.

approved the venture. However, a week later he apparently changed his mind when he returned Kemper's report with a message scrawled in ink across the bottom that read "I don't think we should." Kemper than called Sims and told him the Bureau would be unable to assist on the project.

When Walt received news of the FBI's turndown he phoned Hoover to find out why. Hoover told Disney he would personally look into the situation and asked his close friend Clyde Tolson, the Bureau's assistant director and second in command, to investigate the matter. Tolson ordered a complete review of what had now become known in FBI headquarters as the "Disney situation," after which he reaffirmed Nichols's decision not to cooperate with Disney.

Two months later, a disgruntled Walt personally resubmitted a revised and expanded outline directly to the head of the Bureau. It detailed the "Mickey Mouse Club" newsreel spot and, perhaps as a way of stroking Hoover's ego, a new outline regarding a possible FBI exhibit for Disneyland. On March 7, Tolson received a confidential memo from Hoover, from which the following is excerpted:

. . . On February 27, 1956, SAC Malone of Los Angeles was visiting with SAC Contact Disney . . . [Disney] mentioned that his company is currently producing a television series known as the "Mickey Mouse Club.". . .Walt Disney has been quite friendly with the FBI. He is an approved SAC Contact. His television programs have been very popular and educational and have been conducted on a high plane. . . . Disney's two proposals at this stage seem rather vague, and it might be desirable to have him furnish more facts so that each can be considered.

A week later, SAC Malone received the following memo from Tolson:

The Bureau has considered very carefully your contacts with Walt Disney and his desire to include the FBI in his Disneyland Amusement Park and also [in his] television series the Mickey Mouse Club [broadcast] over the American Broadcasting Company.

Please advise Mr. Disney that at the present time our commitments are extremely heavy and that it is not possible to cooperate in this regard.

Disney pressed Hoover to explain why the Bureau had become so uncooperative. Hoover told Disney to be patient and let the matter rest.

Why had the FBI apparently turned its back on Disney? The answer lay in a confidential internal Bureau memo, dated March 21, 1956:

March 21, 1956

WALTER E. DISNEY—Summary
(Walt Disney)
Born: December 5, 1901
Chicago, Illinois

No investigation has been conducted by the FBI concerning the captioned individual. However, this Bureau's files reflect the receipt of a flier issued by the Council for Pan-American Democracy advertising the "Night of the Americas" to be held at the Martin Beck Theater on February 14, 1943, in New York City. The flier carried a partial list of sponsors and guests of honor which included the name of "Walt Disney."

The Council for Pan-American Democracy has been designated [to be a subversive organization] by the Attorney General of the United States pursuant to Executive Order 10450.

The "People's Voice," issue of January 15, 1944, contained an article captioned "New Masses Sponsors Tribute to Art Young." The article set forth that "New Masses" was sponsoring a mass meeting to pay tribute to Art Young, Dean of American Cartoonists, who died recently. It was indicated that the meeting would be held on January 27, 1944, at Manhattan Center, 34th and 8th Avenue in New York City. Among the individual sponsors of the meeting was listed the name "Walt Disney."

According to the Special Committee on Un-American Activites in its report dated March 29, 1944, "New Masses" is a nationally circulated weekly journal of the Communist Party.

The foregoing information is furnished to you as a result of your request for an FBI file check and is not to be construed as a clearance or a nonclearance of the individual involved. This information is furnished for your use and should not be disseminated outside your agency.

The unsigned memo was probably requested by Hoover. Incredibly, some mid-level bureaucrat, unaware of Disney's status within the FBI, had turned up what he believed was information that linked Walt Disney to subversive Communist organizations and activities in the early forties. Even more astonishing, of the two "incidents" cited, the first, the "Council for Pan-American Democracy" had been attended by Disney as an undercover spy for the FBI, either by his own initiative or at the Bureau's directive, after which he supplied a detailed report to his Los Angeles SAC. As for the "tribute" to Art Young, Disney had never made a secret of his admiration for the renowned artist's work, and upon Young's untimely death in an automobile accident, Walt attended a public memorial, made a small donation to a memorial fund for Young's family, and filed a complete report about who else attended the tribute to his SAC.

Somehow, the FBI had construed from these two incidents that Walt's political loyalties were questionable. They did so in spite of his official SAC status and long history of informing, his anticommunist activities, his government contracts, his involvement with the Hollywood Alliance, his friendly testimony before HUAC (which he had been instrumental in bringing to Hollywood), and his active support of the blacklist.

When Hoover finally read the memo, he was aghast and immediately approved the "Mickey Mouse Club" segment.

That November, Disney was named the recipient of the Screen Producers Guild's very prestigious Milestone award for a lifetime of great professional achievement. When Hoover was made aware of the selection (he was told about it before Walt was, since Samuel G. Engel, a former president of the Screen Producers Guild, was also an SAC contact), he took the opportunity to write Disney the following letter:

November 9, 1956

Mr. Walt Disney
2400 Alameda Avenue
Burbank, California

Dear Mr. Disney:

Mr. John F. Malone, Special Agent in charge of our Los
Angeles Office, has advised me of the annual Milestone Award
of the Screen Producers Guild which is to be presented to you
on February 3, 1957.

You must derive great satisfaction from this recognition, and I
want to be among the many persons in this country who will
extend congratulations to you on this occasion. Your work in the
past has been a credit not only to the motion picture industry
but to the entire Nation [sic], and I want to assure you of my
every good wish for continuing success.

Sincerely yours,
J. Edgar Hoover

In a blind note attached to the bottom, Hoover added the following, to insure no further Bureau slipups involving Disney:

NOTE: The Bureau has had cordial relations with Disney
who is an SAC contact of the Los Angeles Office. There is no
derogatory data in [the files] on the Screen Producers Guild.
Samuel G. Engel, a producer at 20th Century Fox and an SAC
contact of the Los Angeles Office was president [sic] of the Guild
in 1955.

Disney replied to Hoover's letter with one of his own:

November 26, 1956

Dear Mr. Hoover—

It was good of you to take time from your busy day to send me
your very complimentary letter of November 9th.

To say that I am pleased about the forthcoming Milestone

award is definitely an understatement and my only hope is that I will always be able to live up to it and be deserving of this great tribute. Your congratulations in this connection are deeply appreciated.

Warmest regards and many thanks.

Sincerely,
Walt Disney

With the exchange of letters, Disney believed his problems with the Bureau had come to an end.

Four ten-minute "Mickey Mouse Club" newsreel segments were filmed in 1957, all of which starred Dirk Metzger as the principal child tourist. Metzger was the son of Col. Louis Metzger, United States Marine Corps. The cinematographer for the piece, Hugo Johnson, was an "approved" veteran cameraman who had done many "newsreel jobs" for the Bureau, according to an FBI clearance report filed on him in connection with filmed spots. The Bureau requested more than twenty-one changes in the five-minute script before it would give its final approval. Disney had to agree to every change in order to complete the episode.

In 1961, Disney approved a comedy feature entitled *Moon Pilot* (released the following year), which intentionally spoofed, among other things, the general incompetence of the FBI.

From a confidential FBI memo regarding the script of *Moon Pilot:*

> The FBI is brought into the story when the Air Force Officer is thought to be kidnapped. The writer apparently had read little concerning rockets or the FBI. Most references to the FBI are handled inaccurately and some are ludicrous. The Air Force officer, for example, is continually outwitting surveilling Agents who are following him for his protection, and at one point when a note is unaccountably slipped into a room, the Agent in Charge of the detail immediately arrests all kitchen and dining room help to have them interrogated. . . .
>
> The story has references to telephones being tapped by the FBI and the Agents are generally pictured as bumbling, heavy-footed incompetents . . . the attached should be sent to Los Angeles instructing the SAC to contact Mr. Walt Disney and tactfully advise him of our objections. . . . Walt Disney is on the Special Correspondents List.

The Bureau also complained to Disney about the negative treatment of agents in *That Darn Cat* (1965), in which a couple of FBI men are depicted as inept buffoons. After Hoover personally intervened, Walt changed the script of the movie so that the FBI agent originally portrayed in what the Bureau considered "an uncomplimentary manner" was made a generic government security agent instead. As for *That Darn Cat*, in spite of continual pressure from the Bureau, Walt refused to make any changes in the film's shooting script.

From the time of the flap over the 1957 "Mickey Mouse Club" newsreel segments, Disney never filed another SAC report with the FBI. In the years that followed, he seized every opportunity to ridicule the Bureau's personnel and tactics in his films.

In March 1959, President Eisenhower sent a "Personal and Confidential" memo to J. Edgar Hoover which requested the following:

Dear Mr. Hoover:

Will you please run rush name checks on the individuals listed below who are being considered for appointment to the Advisory Committee on the Arts, National Cultural Center? Biographical information is enclosed.

The names in question included Katharine Cornell, Peggy Wood, Carl Sandburg, and Walt Disney. Hoover sent a letter back to Eisenhower noting that of the above-named, three, Katharine Cornell, Carl Sandburg, and Walt Disney, all had files. The White House was then informed of the two "incidents" in Disney's file—the "Night of the Americas" and the memorial for Art Young.

Disney was not appointed to the advisory committee.

IN FEBRUARY 1957, Disney was formally presented with the Milestone award at a ceremonial banquet held in the main ballroom of the Beverly Hilton Hotel. After cocktails and hors d'oeuvres were served in the outer hallway, the invited guests were seated in the ballroom, where a dais of Disney "characters" in tuxedoes awaited them. A very formal Mickey Mouse sat in Disney's seat of honor. Eddie Fisher began the ceremonies by singing the National Anthem, after which

Lowell Thomas read congratulatory messages from several prominent figures, including *Fantasia* collaborator Leopold Stokowski.

Norman Vincent Peale stepped to the podium and informed the gathering: "In our nation of one hundred seventy million people, one-third are seventeen or under. Walt Disney thus deserves every good thing said about him for his wonderful influence on our beloved country."

Washington's most successful hostess, Perle Mesta, was the next in line to praise Disney for having the "gentle spirit to create a character like Mickey Mouse. Walt Disney is the greatest ambassador of good-will today. It is because he expresses so much love. And we know that love is the greatest thing in the world."

Comedian Ed Wynn spoke of Walt's contributions to humor. General Omar Bradley acknowledged Disney's war and peacetime service to the armed forces.

Thomas than read a telegram from President Eisenhower:

Your genius as a creator of folklore has long been recognized by leaders in every field of human endeavor, including that most discerning body of critics, the children of this land and all lands.

As an artist your work has helped reveal our country to the world, and the world to all of us. As a man your sympathetic attitude toward life has helped our children develop a clean and cheerful view of humanity, with all its frailties and possibilities for good.

The presentation of the plaque was made by Yul Brynner, standing in for the previous year's winner, Cecil B. DeMille, unable to attend the ceremonies because of prior filming commitments.

Disney, openly moved, fought back tears when it was his turn to speak. After acknowledging the "magic power" at every producer's disposal, he congratulated DeMille and fellow independent producer Samuel Goldwyn and thanked Joseph Rosenberg, recently retired from the Bank of America, whom he referred to as his "personal fairy godfather."

Walt began a long, rambling reminiscence of his professional life, from the earliest days at the Kansas City ad agency to the fabulous success of Disneyland. He then paused, wiped away a tear, and stood silently before the hushed room. He resumed speaking in a voice choked with emotion: "In any career it helps to have some kind of genius. I've got it—but it happens to be in the person of my brother. Roy runs the company, the whole works, at home and abroad. . . . He has a talent for self-effacement which isn't going to do him a bit of good right at this moment."

The long years of bitter feuding came to an end as Walt called Roy to the podium and hugged him in the shared spotlight. Then, as Gene Kelly and Pat Boone joined together to sing "When You Wish Upon a Star," with a final wave and smile, Walt disappeared through the ballroom's heavy drapes into the hard, cold darkness beyond the bright span of fame's fancy hot lights.

SEVENTEEN

Final Destinations

HAVING GRADUATED from a Swiss boarding school in the spring of 1957, twenty-one-year-old Sharon Disney returned to Holmby Hills with the desire to become an actress. Walt immediately arranged for her to play a small role in the studio's feature adaptation of the Revolutionary War novel *Johnny Tremain.*

Not long after the picture opened, Sharon lost her interest in performing and announced her engagement to an architect, Robert Borgfeldt Brown, whom she had met on a blind date. Brown, soft-spoken, intense, and something of a stoic, was born in Kansas City to Fundamentalist parents, and both physically and in his personality resembled a tall, thin, younger version of Walt.

Unlike the joy he felt when Diane married Ron Miller, Disney was not happy with Sharon's decision to wed, and especially not to Robert Brown. Whoever her choice would have been, Walt probably would have found something wrong with the man. Disney believed his adopted daughter could have anyone she wanted and therefore could not understand why she would settle on a man Walt described to one friend as seeming "rather dull, don't you think?"

At his fifty-seventh birthday dinner, in December 1958, attended by Lillian, Sharon, and Brown, Walt threw what amounted to a temper tantrum, scooping handfuls of whipped cream off the top of his dessert and hurling it into everyone's face, including Brown's.

IN THE SPRING OF 1959, Sharon and Brown were married in a formal Presbyterian ceremony. "Well," Walt joked to the bridegroom just before the ceremony, "she's your problem now." He then broke down and wept when the groom placed a ring on Sharon's finger.

Sharon's marriage caused Walt to sink into another depression. The "loss" of his last child, as he once described the circumstance of Sharon's marriage to a friend, was the clearest reflection yet of his own impending mortality. Once again he was consumed by a growing obsession with death. When a reporter from the *Los Angeles Times* asked Disney "What now?" he seemed caught off guard by the question. His mood darkened as he recapped old films. Pressed to comment about his future, Walt spoke only of building more Disneylands.

He felt increasingly removed from filmmaking. New "Disney" films he had little or nothing to do with became hits, which only deepened his growing sense of alienation. Even the outsize success of such films as *Old Yeller*, the Disney live-action 1957 Christmas picture which proved to be one of the studio's biggest box-office hits in years, seemed to Walt little more than a vivid reminder of how far afield his studio had gotten from the classic animated style that had helped make *Snow White* and *Pinocchio* classic additions to the American cinema.

By now production of theatrical cartoon shorts had come to a complete halt. Disney had been thinking about reviving the "Silly Symphonies," an idea he abandoned after *Sleeping Beauty*'s 1959 release. The film earned $5.3 million, half of what *Old Yeller* did at twice the cost.

Still the combined profits from the success of the nature series, Disneyland, and television had allowed the studio for the first time since *Snow White*'s original release to pay off all its outstanding debt to the Bank of America. By 1960, Walt Disney Productions held $80 million in available assets, making it one of the wealthiest movie studios in the world.

However, Walt seemed less concerned with profits than with his desire that his classic cartoons continue to be seen, and in color. To insure this, Disney decided to move to NBC, the undisputed leader in color broadcasting. In December 1960, the final year of Disney's original contract with ABC (which still broadcast exclusively in black and white), Walt and Roy traveled to New York to meet personally with Leonard Goldenson, the head of the network, to inform him that NBC had made a highly competitive offer.

A month earlier, Walt had secretly made contact with General Sarnoff, the head of NBC, in direct violation of his contract which forbade talks with either of the two other networks. After seeing Goldenson, Disney met with Sarnoff, who, unlike the last time they had met, was now eager to strike a deal.

That was all Walt needed. He then leaked the ostensible cause of his dissatisfaction with what he referred to as the "Mickey Mouse Club" situation to his reliable network of columnists and reporters. What had made Disney so angry was that ABC had canceled the show, in spite of its continual high ratings.

Disney's agreement with ABC required him to deliver finished shows at a predetermined price per episode. Many factors added to the show's expense: the superior technical quality Disney demanded for each filmed program; several self-contained miniseries embedded in its overall format (*The Hardy Boys, Spin and Marty, Corky, The White Shadow*); an unusually large cast of child performers which by law required double-casting to prevent them from being overworked; and the establishment of a complete on-site school. Even the additional profits from related merchandising was not enough to offset the several hundred thousand dollar deficit WED had assumed for each episode. As far as Walt was concerned, the "Mickey Mouse Club" had been a bargain for the network.

When ABC canceled it, Walt publicly accused Goldenson of loading the show with too many commercials, which had caused children to lose interest in it. Goldenson then canceled "Zorro," another hit series from Disney.

However, there was another reason ABC canceled both Disney shows. The network had recently decided to air only programs produced in-house and therefore wholly owned. Further, before he could complete his new arrangement at NBC, Walt was notified he was barred by contract from selling either show to any other network. Walt then sued to have all rights to his programs revert to him. ABC used this opportunity to rid themselves entirely of Disney. The network quickly settled out of court, relinquishing the rights to "Zorro," the "Mickey Mouse Club," and "Walt Disney Presents" (the name of the TV show "Disneyland" was changed to "Walt Disney Presents" in 1958 by ABC).

In spite of its success, the show no longer fit the ABC board's new in-house policy. Because of the intricacies of its original deal with Disney, it would have been more difficult to drop "Walt Disney Presents" than the other two shows. Instead, the network goaded Disney into the lawsuit as a way for them to shed ABC of his unwanted prime-time program.

The only association ABC still had with Walt was its one-third interest in his Disneyland park. The network then insisted Disney buy it back for a nonnegotiable figure of $17 million. Walt, while eager to make the deal, nevertheless balked at the price, complaining to Roy that ABC had really done nothing to help build Disneyland except guarantee a few loans, none of which it actually had to pay off, and therefore should not profit from the sale of its shares.

As far as Goldenson was concerned, Disney was being remarkably ungrateful. Goldenson knew that without the network's initial investment Disneyland might have never been built. He recalled:

I thought it was time we reevaluated our whole relationship with Disney. The only reason we'd taken a position in Disneyland was to get [Disney] into television, but the Disneys turned out to be terrible business partners. Disneyland had become enormously successful, but Disney kept plowing his profits back into park expansion. We made a $17,000,000 deal to sell back our share of Disneyland, and we parted company.

By the fall of 1961, Disney and WED, free of all remaining ties to ABC, moved to NBC where "Walt Disney Presents" became "Walt Disney's Wonderful World of Color." The new version of the show premiered September 24, 1961, on a new night, Sunday, at a new time, 7:30 P.M., so as not to dislodge the enormously popular "Wagon Train" series NBC had put up against Disney's ABC Wednesday night broadcast.

Once the move was completed, Walt thought about closing his office at Burbank and moving WED and his family to Anaheim. He probably would have done so except that Lillian was vehemently opposed to the idea. Always the recluse, Holmby Hills was more than her home, it was, to a great extent, her world. She had lived there for more than twenty years and raised her children there.

It was all Walt could do to get Lillian to drive with him to their new house, the Smoke Tree Ranch, near Palm Springs a few days every month. Walt had built the desert home so he could go bowling, his latest athletic passion, or play golf with Bob Hope and Ed Sullivan, whenever either happened to be in town. Disney, who always loved the desert, would have spent a lot more time in Palm Springs if Lillian had been willing to do so. She hated everything about it, from its arid climate to its lack of what she considered the real warmth generated from within the privacy and security of Holmby Hills.

To Walt, however, Holmby Hills never seemed quite like home. For many years the children had proved an unbearable distraction from his creative preoccupations. His train-riding hobby had been a constant source of tension between Lillian and himself. Since childhood he had loved pets. Yet he had acquiesced to Lillian's refusal to allow "creatures," even the family dog, inside the house. The closest he came to having pets were the mechanical toys and stuffed animals he collected, as well as dozens of cuckoo clocks from all over the world. Among his most prized objects was a cage that housed a mechanical bird whose intricate movements and lifelike sounds fascinated him. He passed many evenings transfixed as he watched the bird "move about" in its cage, open its mouth, chirp, and flap its wings.

HE TURNED SIXTY in December 1961, a milestone which intensified the lingering depression brought about by Sharon's marriage. "No man can go on forever" became his answer to anyone who asked him how he was feeling. His obsession with mortality increased. He began making plans to insure that upon his death, which he feared was imminent, his family would maintain control of the studio. At Walt's insistence, Ron Miller, having completed two years of military service and a season with the Los Angeles Rams, during which he was knocked unconscious during one game, decided he would devote all his energies to learning the motion picture business.

Miller might not have been Walt's first choice if there had been a second one. It hadn't occurred to Disney that either of his daughters might be capable of running the studio. Up to his death, Walt never wavered from his conviction that women simply did not have the ability to manage in big business. Indeed, in his lifetime, no female studio employee ever reached the executive level at either the Disney studio or WED.

Walt made Ron the director of the television segments of "Walt Disney Presents." On more than one occasion they argued heatedly over filming. Walt constantly "directed from the set," correcting camera angles, revising the script, even altering lighting while he was supposed to be "performing."

One time, Ron expressed his disagreement over a change, and Walt dressed him down in front of the rest of the crew. Ron then calmly reminded Walt that he was neither producer nor director of the segment and should follow orders from the person who was, or didn't Walt understand how the film business worked? Walt nodded in silence and never again criticized Ron in public. Everyone present was amazed Walt didn't fire him on the spot.

In spite of Disney's encouragement, Miller developed a reputation around the studio as being singularly possessed of an alarming lack of ability. After line-producing several forgettable Disney features, one studio executive recalled the general consensus: "As a producer Ron was one hell of a football player." Nevertheless, Walt continued to push him up the company's gilded ladder.

Although disapproving of Miller, Roy remained silent, unwilling to risk his newly reconciled relationship with Walt. Roy believed if Miller took over the studio he would prove incapable of running it, and eventually Roy's son, Roy E., would rise to the occasion and save the kingdom by assuming the throne.

Roy E. seemed to think so too and quietly dedicated himself to learning all aspects of the business. He had joined the studio in 1953 at the age of twenty-six as an apprentice film editor on "Dragnet". Roy E. benefited from his father's personal tutelage and, unlike Miller, rose smoothly through the ranks to the level of assistant producer on several episodes of the television show. While doing so, he also managed to serve as comptroller on half a dozen of the studio's features, thereby gaining valuable creative and administrative experience. Many staff members frowned on what appeared to be a sibling rivalry between the two brothers that had manifested itself in the promotion of their chosen heirs apparent. Most considered Roy E. not much better than Miller. Both were considered weak and ineffective, with little demonstrated artistic talent or leadership ability. Around the lot Roy E. was often referred to as "the idiot nephew."

In 1961, Walt seized the opportunity of the birth of his fifth grandchild to confront Diane and Ron over what he considered to be a long-standing oversight. Disney's message was quite clear. Their future depended on how they treated him during his few remaining days. He was upset that they had not found it in their hearts to name any of their children after him. On November 14, the Millers christened their fifth child Walter Elias Disney Miller.

As a reward Walt offered Ron an opportunity to produce a film called "Khrushchev in Disneyland," loosely based on the Soviet leader's celebrated nonvisit to the park. In 1960, Nikita Khrushchev had gone on a prolonged tour of the United States and expressed a desire to see Disneyland. After he visited the Hollywood soundstage where *Can-Can* was being filmed, the American government abruptly canceled his scheduled trip to Walt's park on the grounds that sufficient security couldn't be guaranteed. The decision outraged the Soviet premier and made headlines around the world.

Everyone had something to say about the incident which, improbable as it seemed, threatened to raise the temperature of the Cold War several degrees. At an appearance in Alaska, Bob Hope told his audience: "Here we are in America's forty-ninth state, Alaska. That's halfway between Khrushchev and Disneyland!"

Herman Wouk couldn't resist taunting both Khrushchev and Disney when he wrote: "I don't really blame Khrushchev for jumping up and down in a rage over missing Disneyland. There are few things more worth seeing in the United States or anywhere in the world."

As the world turned toward California, Disney decided to personally tweak the nose of the leader of the Communist world. He now told Bill Walsh, one of Disney's most favored line producers, to sign Peter Ustinov to play Khrushchev. Ustinov, however, had an intense dislike of Disney and refused to even consider the offer. As a result the project remained stalled for six years. Ustinov, in late 1965, changed his mind and agreed to do it. By then Disney's interest had faded, and it became his turn to say no.

Walsh was one of Disney's few close friends during this period of Walt's life. In addition to producing many of the studio's live-action features, Walsh had become Disney's newest favorite traveling companion. A middle-aged, soft-spoken man afflicted with diabetes, Walsh had, in addition to his feature work, played a vital role as producer of the "Davy Crockett" television miniseries. Disney rewarded him by making him the producer of the "Mickey Mouse Club" television program.

In 1961, after the show's cancellation, Disney found himself left with little to do at the studio. He occupied much of his time writing letters, mostly, as it turned out, condolences to employees when their parents passed away or responses to former friends and acquaintances. He tried to answer personally as much fan mail as he could. He contributed to several charities and made regular donations to St. Joseph's Hospital, directly across from the studio.

With summer's approach, Walt and Lillian embarked on a European trip to seek out the new and unusual in amusement parks around the world. He planned a visit to Switzerland to learn about a wave-making machine for possible use in his *Nautilus* exhibit. In Milan he studied the large-scale processing of espresso to see if it couldn't improve the quality of the output of Disneyland's concessions. A trip to Germany satisfied Walt's desire to ride top speed along the autobahn. Cuba gave him the chance to study the site of a volcano, which somehow found its way into the newly planned "Pirates of the Caribbean" exhibit. In Puerto Rico Walt picked up several new mechanical birds. In Paris he brought Lillian to one of his favorite sites, the Eiffel Tower, after which he took her on a nostalgic drive along the routes he had traveled as a Red Cross volunteer in World War I.

Walt and Lillian never traveled alone. Invariably included in Disney's entourage was one specially chosen staff member and his wife. The employee always had to be married. Animators Ward Kimball and Marc Davis and storyman Joe Grant had been invited in past years. Now it was Bill Walsh's turn. The two men spent many hours together discussing future projects, leaving their wives to get along by themselves.

Lillian, hardly a great sharer or socializer, resented the Walshes' presence, as she did most "outsiders" Walt invited to travel with them. She especially didn't like Walsh's much younger wife Nolie, a former dancer half her husband's age. Nolie, in turn, had no love for Lillian and was far less enamored with Walt than Bill was.

Indeed, to Walt, Walsh seemed an excellent candidate to be Miller's second in command. Disney was convinced that the team of Miller and Walsh would one day keep the studio operating at its maximum creative potential.

UPON HIS RETURN to Los Angeles, Walt resumed his search for suitable projects for Ron. At the same time, through WED, Disney began to develop several exhibits for the 1964 New York World's Fair. Projects he worked on included those for General Electric, Pepsi-Cola, Ford, and the state of Illinois. Disney's involvement prompted Robert Moses, the legendary "architect" of twentieth-century New York and president of the fair, to visit Disney in Anaheim for a personally guided tour of Disneyland. There, Walt "introduced" Moses to one of Illinois's most famous citizens, Abraham Lincoln.

Disney took great pride in having the "live" president right there in his park. The lifelike, fleshy robot was in fact the rather morbid result of a technique developed by Marc Davis at WED called "audio-animatronics." With it, Disney hoped to push "animation" one step beyond even the three-dimensional cartoon characters and backgrounds that peopled his park. "Lincoln" would be the closest thing yet to the *restoration of life*. And, if successful, only the beginning. *Why not an audio-animatronic Disney seated atop the highest vantage point of Disneyland, from where he could rule his domain forever?*

Disney's growing preoccupation with his own mortality also led him to explore the science of cryogenics, the freezing of an aging or ill person until such time as the human body can be revived and restored to health. Disney often mused to Roy about the notion of perhaps having himself frozen, an idea which received the same kind of indulgent nods from his brother as did the suggestion of creating an artificial King Disney.

Approaching his mid-sixties, Walt played host to a new cluster of aches and pains culled from a lifetime of late nights, chronic insomnia, sports injuries, poor diet, excessive drinking, and dozens of cigarettes a day. To fight off his vulnerabilities and the grim inevitability of the future, Disney, in 1963, looked for one, final celebratory hurrah—a last and lasting reminder intended for all who had been there during his glory years and a primer for those too young to remember.

He had been moved to action by the release of two films, one recent and one old. The studio's 1961 animated hit *One Hundred and One Dalmatians* had received high praise from the critics, many of whom hailed it as the studio's best release since *Snow White* and the closest to a real "Disney" film in many years. Walt, however, had liked it less than they did. While the story contained elements of "classic" Disney—an evil, hellish, witchlike villainess, Cruelle de Vil, who wanted to kill the litter of adopted dalmatians in order to sell their skins—he believed that it failed stylistically. Disney considered it little more than an exercise in sketchpad pen-and-inking, cleverly augmented by the innovative mechanics of Ub Iwerks, whose adaptation of the Xerox duplicating system had made it possible to duplicate great numbers of dalmatians at a fraction of what the cost would otherwise have been. Missing were the trademark Gothic stylistics, complex plotting, righteous morality, and shadowed characters that had marked his greatest and most personal films.

A year and a half after *One Hundred and One Dalmatians*, Disney successfully rereleased of one of his biggest commercial failures, *Fantasia*. The film's revival was boosted by a Bosley Crowther review in the *New York Times* which said, in part, that:

> . . . The public is clamoring to knock down the doors of the Tower East [theater] and practically every other theater in the country in which [*Fantasia*] is being revived. The response to it was disappointing—dismally so—when it was originally released. There were numerous explanations: the war in Europe, the change in Disney's cartoon style, the belief that art was too short for long-hairs and too long for the rest. . . .
>
> Despite the obvious public interest in this picture and in cartoons generally, the knell is tolling for the big cartoon film. Indeed, it has tolled already for the little cartoon film, unless the latter is put together at a minimum of production and cost.
>
> Mr. Disney is no longer making his erstwhile programs of famous cartoon shorts—the Mickey Mouses, Donald Ducks, Plutos, Goofys, and such enjoyable specialities as *Toot, Whistle, Plunk, and Boom*, which is being shown as a prelude to *Fantasia*. And he is making only one big feature every two or three years. . . .
>
> Evidently whatever future the animated cartoon film has . . . will be along lines much simpler than those of *Fantasia*. It will be along the lines of simplicity developed in the films of UPA, which brought a delightful new vigor to the field with the adventures of Mr. Magoo and Gerald McBoing Boing.

The review galvanized Disney to act, not so much for what he considered the long-overdue praise for *Fantasia*. Rather he was motivated by Crowther's excessive and, for the most part, ignorant praise of UPA's "progressive" style of animation.

Staggering and wobbly-kneed like an aging prizefighter, Disney felt compelled to step back into the magic ring one last time. For his grand farewell, Walt peered once more into the prism of his soul to produce what would be his summary work of grand reconciliation. In the film, shot in the bright colors of sunny comedy, darkened by the shadows of its emotional interior, and liberated by its physical rapture, Disney had at last fully illuminated his vision of the ultimate fairy godmother, personified by a sweet little British nanny known as Mary Poppins.

Disney had been aware of the original P. L. Travers novel for many years. *Mary Poppins*, the story of a magical nanny who restores the missing element of paternal love to the children of a wealthy but stodgy banker, had occupied the place of honor on Diane's night table her entire childhood. Often, at bedtime, Lillian would read a chapter aloud until her daughter fell asleep. On several occasions Lillian and Diane came separately to Walt to ask if he could make the book into a movie.

Disney first approached the Australian-born author during World War II. Travers had moved to America to avoid the bombing of London, where she had lived for most of her adult life. Learning that Travers was in New York, Walt dispatched Roy to visit and make an offer for the rights to her novel.

Travers turned Roy down, as she already had with every other studio. The matronly and stubborn Mrs. Travers thoroughly disapproved of what she considered the "vulgar art" of the movies, particularly those made in Hollywood.*

In the years that followed, Walt tried and failed several more times to acquire the rights to *Mary Poppins*. Finally, in 1960, he traveled to London and met personally with Travers, who found *this* Disney, unlike his brother, clever, charming, and quite persuasive. He soon convinced her he was the only one who could properly film her book. To finalize the deal, Walt agreed to the two conditions Travers insisted were nonnegotiable: first, that he not turn the book into an animated cartoon, and second, that she have final script approval.

---

*There was a production of *Mary Poppins* on live television on "Studio One" on December 19, 1949, starring Mary Wickes.

Excepting the war department's dictates during World War II, the latter demand was unprecedented in the history of the Disney studio and would remain that way. Having secured the rights, Disney completely ignored all of Travers's suggestions. After viewing a rough cut of the film, she demanded extensive reediting. Disney then explained to her that script approval only applied to the script, not the film.

After rejecting a long list of possible stars for the crucial title role, Walt went to see Julie Andrews in the Broadway production of the musical *Camelot*. He was so taken with her grace and beauty he offered her the part the next day. She politely but firmly turned him down. The trauma of having been rejected by Jack Warner to re-create her award-winning stage portrayal of Eliza Doolittle in the upcoming film version of *My Fair Lady* had left Andrews convinced she had no future in American movies. Ironically, Warner had dismissed her because he felt she lacked the sexual "heat" necessary to play the street urchin who captivates Higgins, which was precisely the reason Walt wanted her. Once again Walt used his powers of persuasion, and Andrews accepted the role.

Returning to Hollywood, Walt appointed Bill Walsh the film's line producer and prevailed upon Iwerks to develop new special visual effects that would allow the film to look contemporary while feeling classic, the Disney signature style.

When production began, Walt became obsessed with *Mary Poppins* the way he hadn't been with any film, animated or live-action, since *The Three Caballeros*. He worked on *Poppins* day and night for months, moving into his office at the studio as he had so often done in the old days. He demanded everything to the smallest detail be executed exactly as he wanted, no matter how much time or money it consumed, until he was satisfied.

This relentless, obsessive involvement showed on-screen. *Mary Poppins*'s perfect blend of live-action and animation transformed the novel's series of loosely connected anecdotes into a unified depiction of the nature of childhood fantasy. In *Mary Poppins*, Walt created a world where identity, happiness, expression, and satisfaction were determined solely by the joys of physical freedom. A world, as Mary informs the decidedly unphysical Mr. Banks, where nothing ever need be explained.

The film's family of characters were further "related" by Disney in an autobiographical jigsaw puzzle of emotions that seemed to fill in the missing pieces of his body of work. The two Banks children, Jane and Michael, evoke images of Walt and Roy in their youth: the obedient, reserved, traumatized offspring of a humorless disciplinarian father and loving, if ineffective mother. Mr. Banks's emotional and physical makeup connects Walt to Elias (complete with pencil mustache) as the benevolent, if unloving head of a household.

Mary Poppins, on the other hand, is "unreal," a literal fairy, while somehow managing to retain the essence of a perfect living "mum." She can be firm, adoring, magical, and, when necessary, authoritative without being abusive in her determination to "rescue" the Banks children and "humanize" their parents. She also reflects an image of Disney, who was, in his way, the ultimate nanny in the service of eternal childhood.

Bert, the chimney-sweep/one man band, entertains a crowd in the park with a vaudevillian turn reminiscent of yet another side of Disney—the early stage career of young Walt who would grow up to become the "one-man-band" head of his own studio. Bert also possesses the talent to draw, and his sidewalk sketches, laid out in sequences like so many animation storyboards, become the passageway to a world of magic and merriment. Thus are we introduced to the film's masterful visual motif, the redemptive journey, by means of "magic pictures," from the restrictive world of adult reality to the liberating one of childhood fantasy.

In *Mary Poppins*, freedom is defined as the release from the constraints of time, a liberation, finally, of the soul. When, at the film's climax, Mr. Banks undergoes his transformation and is "humanized" along with the crotchety banker Mr. Dawes, Sr., the feeling is again one of great release. Rather than the film's childlike characters and children having attained a new sense of maturity, the adults are redeemed by the freeing of the eternal child within. *Mary Poppins* is Disney's greatest depiction of the eternal triumph of hope over cynicism, of youth over old age, of life over death. It is his grand monument to immortality.

The film premiered in Hollywood at Grauman's Chinese Theater on August 27, 1964, to rave reviews and great commercial success. *Mary Poppins* grossed a phenomenal $45 million in its initial release, which made it at the time the sixth highest-grossing film ever produced.

The movie was nominated for thirteen Academy Awards and won five—Film Editing, Original Score, Song ("Chim-Chim-Cheree"), Special Effects, and Best Actress. Julie Andrews, the sentimental favorite for the snubbing she took over the *My Fair Lady* casting flap, won out over Audrey Hepburn, nominated for her performance as Eliza Doolittle. Even Jack Warner admitted he had voted for Andrews.

More important to Walt than all the awards, however, was what he considered *Mary Poppins*'s most important accomplishment, the restoration of his reputation as one of Hollywood's most enduring filmmakers.

STILL, his great achievement was darkened by what had become for him the requisite clouds of despair. Even before the film's initial run had ended, he had slipped back into a deep depression. Ironically, the enormous success of *Mary Poppins* was what triggered it. What had, for however brief a time, given him a sense of personal and professional redemption, followed now by the lifeless dismay of knowing he would never be able to top it.

Seeking a fresh outlet for his creative energies, he decided he would teach all that he had learned about making movies to a new generation of artists. And, he believed, with a few key improvements, he had the perfect place to do it.

Disney had been involved with training artists from the time he first met Nelbert Chouinard. In 1955, she named him to Chouinard's board of directors. This appointment was taken by several other members as a brilliant move to boost the school's lagging fund-raising efforts. Not long after, Disney granted the school two full two-year scholarships for deserving artists, to be supervised through the newly formed Walt Disney Foundation. Walt then suggested to Nelbert that the appointment of a new school administration might help solve the school's financial stagnation. At Disney's recommendation, she appointed Mitchell Wilder to be the school's new executive director. Upon his arrival Wilder immediately instituted a series of unpopular program cuts and faculty firings. He became known around campus as Disney's "hatchet man."

By 1960, Chouinard's had come totally under Disney's financial control. According to Wilder, "My appointment was entirely the responsibility of Walt Disney, and since Walt was calling the shots for the board of trustees, they naturally went along with [his] decisions."

By 1963, the institute's now mandatory academic courses outnumbered art classes, a situation that angered the student body, which erupted into an ongoing series of campus protests. A year later, in April 1964, Walt received the nation's highest civilian honor, the Medal of Freedom, presented to him by President Lyndon Johnson at the White House for a lifetime of achievement. Disney, a staunch Republican, had no love for the president. He believed the protest problems on America's campuses, Chouinard's included, was a product of the very liberalism which Johnson and his "Great Society" championed. At the ceremony Disney wore a "Goldwater" button prominently displayed on his lapel.

Returning to Los Angeles, Walt made plans to merge Chouinard's with the California Institute of the Arts (Cal-Arts), to be patterned after the California Institute of Technology, (Cal-Tech). The merger proceded without incident until Chouinard's newly acquired academic accreditation was suddenly threatened by an obscenity "scandal," the result of an exhibition of several works of protest by the school's "lib-rad art" students angered by what they felt was Disney's destruction of their art school for his own academic glorification. To offset the damage, Disney announced his intention to donate all profits from the fabulously successful *Mary Poppins* to the new complex. As a further gesture, Walt included in his gift thirty-eight acres of the Golden Oaks Ranch, a 778-acre property north of Los Angeles that belonged to the studio, for the site of the institute's new campus. The merger of Chouinard's and Cal-Arts took place without any further challenge or delay in December 1965.

The new Cal-Arts board of trustees included such Hollywood luminaries as Disney animator Marc Davis, Edith Head, Chuck Jones, Henry Mancini, Marty Paich, Nelson Riddle, and Gale Storm, all of whom had been personally recommended by Walt himself. Cal-Arts quickly became known as "the House That Walt Built." The new campus provided him with great personal satisfaction. He told Roy he intended to spend his remaining years teaching there: *Dr. Disney, Professor of Story Techniques for Film.*

At the same time, serious talk circulated in Paris, where Disney was revered by the film intelligentsia, about the possibility of his being nominated for a Nobel. When Walt heard about the burgeon-ing movement, he helped plan a major publicity blitz, calling on his always dependable coterie of colunnists for their assistance. In spite of his best efforts, he failed to win the prize.

REINVIGORATED by the merger with Cal-Arts—what one Chouinard's veteran referred to rather bitterly as Disney's academic amusement park—Walt began to formulate plans for the next Disney-land, to be located in Orlando, Florida. Late in 1964, Disney had bought 27,500 acres of Orlando swampland. One of the most grievous errors he believed he had committed with Disneyland was the size of the property he had secured. The original 160 acres, all that he could afford, eventually proved too small. Moreover, opportunistic builders had bought the surrounding property and filled it with everything from motels to fast-food restaurants and at least one competing amusement park. In real dollars, for every one that Disneyland took in, the "parasitic" businesses that surrounded it took in two. As insurance against such a disaster happening again, Walt bought every available square foot of Orlando acreage, a site specifically chosen for its cheap price and relative remoteness from any other commercial ventures.

While Disneyland had been dominated by Walt's obsession with the past, with Disney World—the name later changed at Roy's directive to Walt Disney World—he seemed to fixate on the future. He wanted to call the new park EPCOT—"Experimental Prototype Community of Tomorrow." EPCOT's center was to be an amusement park not unlike the original Disneyland, surrounded by a totally enclosed Utopian city of the future, where everything from the weather to housing employees would be controlled by EPCOT for maximum enjoyment and productivity.

Even as he witnessed EPCOT's 1965's groundbreaking, Walt re-searched his "Mineral King" project, a year-round outdoor recre-ational facility surrounding yet another Disneyland-type amusement park. It would be located in the heart of northern California's ski country. To begin building this park, Walt personally put up a $15-million bond with the county to guarantee the integrity of the area's natural resources.

That summer, Walt chartered a yacht for Lillian, Diane, Ron, and their children for an inland channel trip north of Vancouver. He brought two books along with him that consumed most of his time. One was a work on city planning, the other discussed how to structure a university. He told his wife and daughter that in the coming years he intended to concentrate on teaching and building amusement parks.

However, early in 1966, at the age of sixty-five, before he had taught a single class or seen the completion of a single building on either of his new sites, Walt was forced to curtail many of his activities due to a sudden, alarming deterioration of his health.

He had begun the new year as grand marshal for Pasadena's Tournament of Roses Parade. To the millions who watched the festivities on television, he appeared robust as ever, if a little thicker in the frame and grayer around the temples. However, in person, without the saving grace of careful makeup and television's discreet long lenses, Walt's face looked more beaten than ever. The pupils of his once-sparkling eyes now seemed foggy and lifeless; his skin knitted into thick, creased patches below his cheeks; his lips turned a cold blue. His entire face seemed to express the distress from what he believed was chronic sinusitis. The pain was often so excruciating he had to apply nightly hot compresses to his face to fall asleep.

The constant pains in his neck and back had worsened in the past months, prompting increasingly less-effective daily sessions with Nurse Hazel George. He upped his daily diet of painkillers, washing them down as always with neat shots of scotch or vodka. The combination no doubt contributed to his increasing bouts of forgetfulness and confusion. Often, he mixed up the names of his children, employees, and celebrities. He began sentences that trailed off without completion. His voice grew softer and windier. On more than one occasion studio workers watched him walk down a hallway and suddenly grab the side of a wall to keep from keeling over, or go down on his knees, holding his stomach as he doubled over in pain. He also developed a chronic kidney condition which required periodic visits to the hospital.

In the early fall, the studio began production on *The Jungle Book*, an animated version of Rudyard Kipling's tales of Mowgli, the Indian boy, and the animals of the jungles of India. Although he had wanted to sit in on some of the early stages of production, he was prevented from doing so when Nurse George's daily treatments failed to relieve his aches and pains. When she suggested the name of a specialist who might be of some help, Disney reluctantly agreed to see him.

Dr. Theodore Lynd, a Beverly Hills orthopedic surgeon, gave Disney a brief office examination, after which he ordered an immediate comprehensive physical workup and a complete set of X rays. The results of both confirmed a severe calcium buildup around Walt's spine and several suspicious shadows on his lungs. A biopsy was performed, and after a brief flight to Virginia to accept yet another in the seemingly endless stream of awards, an exhausted Walt returned to hear the news. The shadows were nodules, probably malignant, and required immediate surgery.

On November 7, 1966, he entered St. Joseph's Hospital, directly across from the Burbank studio, after stopping on his way to spend the morning with Diane and Ron and his grandchildren. Early the next day surgeons removed his left lung, riddled with tumors the size of walnuts. While he was still in recovery, Dr. Lynd informed Lillian the cancer had metastasized to the lymph glands and little time was left for him. Lillian asked the doctor to keep the bad news from Walt. Dr. Lynd agreed.

Lillian met with Roy later that day and told him his brother was dying. He immediately issued a press release in response to the spreading rumors of Walt's terminal condition. It stated, simply, that Walt Disney had undergone surgery to relieve the recurring pain of an old polo injury. Two weeks later, Dr. Lynd, feeling he had done all he could for Walt, released him.

Roy then issued another statement to the press:

During [Walt's] preliminary examination, a lesion was discovered on his left lung. Surgery was decided upon by the doctors in charge and performed the next week. A tumor was found to have caused an abscess which in the opinion of the doctors required a pneumonectomy. The operation was a complete success.

Walt and Lillian spent Thanksgiving Day at Diane's home. He seemed at ease and spent most of his time playing with his grandchildren. After dinner he and Lillian drove to Palm Springs. On November 30, he collapsed at his home there and, after being revived by medics, was driven back to St. Joseph's by private ambulance. Cobalt treatments were begun. Two days later Disney began to slip in and out of consciousness. When awake, he experienced episodes of delirium. He imagined he was ten years old and spoke aloud to Elias and Flora. He pleaded for Miller, his "son," to stay by his side.

On December 5, 1966, his sixty-fifth birthday, Walt opened his eyes to find himself surrounded by his wife and two daughters, who sang happy birthday to him as he stared silently at the ceiling.

On December 14, Lillian spent the afternoon alone at his side. At one point he tried to get out of bed and failed. She hugged him for a long time, until he fell asleep. Later that night he awoke and spent a quiet hour with Roy, who promised that Walt Disney World would open on time. Roy left in tears shortly before ten o'clock. At midnight, Walt requested the head of his bed be elevated so he could look out the window and see his studio. Roy had ordered all its lights be kept on until further notice. Sometime early the next morning, Walt's circulatory system collapsed, and he passed away.

THE WORLD HAD LOST its favorite uncle. In his lifetime he had earned more than seven hundred citations, honorary degrees, and awards, among them: twenty-nine Oscars; four Emmys; the Irving Thalberg Award; the Presidential Freedom Medal; and the French Legion of Honor, all in recognition for his outstanding contribution to the world of film. His cartoons would continue to entertain children of all ages with the antics of a little mouse and the "woman" he adored, a cranky duck, and the dozens of other unforgettable characters. His animated features would return to theater screens every seven years to amaze and delight a new generation, while the international chain of amusement parks that bore his name would continue to showcase a land of eternal youth, as yet unfettered by the responsibilities and restrictions of adult reality. This was the memory of "Uncle" Walt Disney much of the world would embrace.

There would be some who would recall a different legacy, one of shattered careers and ruined lives. Those he had informed on for the FBI would never forget Disney's quarter of a century of radical right-wing antiunionism and his key role in bringing the House Un-American Activities Committee to Hollywood.

Whatever his intentions may have been, one thing remains indisputable. Walt Disney produced a body of work that amplified and, ultimately, transcended his own human frailties by depicting what he believed was, finally, humanity's great moral imperfection.

And the world loved him for it.

EPILOGUE

NEWS OF Walt's death made headlines around the world. Tributes poured in from all over the world. At outgoing governor Edmund G. Brown's directive, flags were hung half-mast throughout the state of California. Governor Brown issued a statement declaring: "I shall miss Walt Disney. Our state, our nation, and the world have lost a beloved and a great artist." Governor-elect Ronald Reagan said, "There just aren't any words to express my personal grief. The world is a poorer place now."

President Johnson sent private condolences to Lillian. J. Edgar Hoover sent the following telegram:

INDEED SORRY TO LEARN OF PASSING OF YOUR HUSBAND AND WANT TO EXTEND MY HEARTFELT SYMPATHY. I KNOW WORDS ARE MOST INADEQUATE TO EASE YOUR GRIEF, BUT IT IS MY HOPE THAT YOU WILL DERIVE CONSOLATION FROM KNOWING THAT HIS OUTSTANDING CONTRIBUTIONS WILL BE A LASTING MEMORIAL TO HIM. HIS DEDICATION TO THE HIGHEST STANDARDS OF MORAL VALUES AND HIS ACHIEVEMENTS WILL ALWAYS STAND AS AN INSPIRATION TO THOSE WHO WERE PRIVILEGED TO KNOW HIM.

J. EDGAR HOOVER

That same day Hoover ordered Disney's name deleted from the FBI's records as an active SAC Contact.

Samuel Goldwyn said, "I have lost a great friend. The world has lost a great man. But in a larger sense Walt Disney has not died because he will live for all time through his work." Richard D. Zanuck, son of Darryl and vice-president of Twentieth Century-Fox said, "No eulogy will be read or monument built to equal the memorial Walt Disney has left in the hearts and minds of the world's people."

The *New York Times* said in its December 16 obituary:

Starting from very little save a talent for drawing, a gift of imagination that was somehow in tune with everyone's imagination, and a dogged determination to succeed, Walt Disney became one of Hollywood's master entrepreneurs and one of the world's greatest entertainers. He had a genius for innovation; his production was enormous; he was able to keep sure and personal control over his increasingly far-flung enterprises; his hand was ever on the public pulse. He was, in short, a legend in his own lifetime—and so honored many times over. Yet none of this sums up Walt Disney. . . .

From England, Julie Andrews told reporters she was "deeply shocked and saddened" by Walt's passing. In Paris, where Disney had been hailed as one of the world's great filmmakers, a newspaper declared that "all the world's children are in mourning." Maurice Chevalier declared on French television, through his tears, that Disney's death was "a disaster for the whole movie world." World leaders from a dozen countries sent their condolences to the studio.

Contrary to rumors that persist to this day, Walt Disney wasn't frozen. Sick jokes about it percolated through the studio for weeks after his death. One animator recalled a running gag at the time that freezing was Walt's attempt to make himself a warmer human being. In fact, his body was cremated.

One day after his death, a private service attended only by the immediate family was held on December 16, 1966, at the Little Church of the Flowers of Forest Lawn Memorial Park, Glendale, six miles west of Burbank. Interment followed at Forest Lawn cemetary, in Hollywood Hills, California. The family requested that in lieu of flowers, donations be made to Cal-Arts.

According to Disney's will, Lillian was named trustee and executor and received all his personal effects. She inherited one-half of Walt's entire estate, at the time of his death estimated to be worth approximately $35 million, most of which he had earned in the last ten years of his life.

At Disney's directive, the other half of the estate was divided into three separate trusts: 45 percent went to Lillian, Diane, and Sharon. Lillian's share was in addition to her full 50 percent. Another 45 percent of the second half went to the Walt Disney Foundation, 5 percent of which was designated to benefit "other charitable organizations at the discretion of the foundation." The remaining 95 percent (of this 45 percent) went to Cal-Arts.*

The final 10 percent of the estate was placed in trust for three nieces, the female offspring of his brothers and sister Ruth, who had married, settled in Portland, and kept in touch with her famous brother mostly by letters at holidays and birthdays. Each, including Ruth, received 2½ percent. Disney left nothing to his two surviving brothers, Raymond and Roy. He believed men were able to control their own destinies. Besides, he never cared much for Raymond and felt he had more than adequately provided for Roy.

Immediately following the services, Roy issued the following statement to the press:

> Walt Disney was irreplaceable. As President and Chairman of the Board of Walt Disney Productions, I want to assure the public, our stockholders and each of our more than four thousand employees that we will continue to operate Walt Disney's company in the way that he has established and guided it. Walt Disney spent his entire life and almost every waking hour in the creative planning of motion pictures, Disneyland, television shows and all the other diversified activities that have carried his name through the years. Around him Walt Disney gathered the

---

*A month after Walt's death, the Cal-Arts board of trustees decided that under his influence the institute he had essentially created had somehow veered off its intended course. With its inheritance from his estate, the board purchased a new site in Valencia, California, about fifteen miles north of Los Angeles, and recruited Robert Corrigan from the East Coast, where he had developed New York University's Graduate School of the Arts, to take over as the new dean. In an effort to restore the school's original commitment to art, Corrigan and his supporters excised all remaining Disney loyalists except family members from the faculty and board.

kind of creative people who understood his way of communicating with the public through entertainment. Walt's ways were always unique and he built a unique organization. A team of creative people that he was justifiably proud of.

Irreplaceable indeed. Walt Disney's passing created an internal crisis of leadership at the studio. For the last dozen years, it had slowly been split into two main camps, one made up of the creative "Walt men," the other the administrative "Roy men." Walt's presence, such as it was, had remained the unifying force. To keep the peace, Roy voluntarily resigned as president and allowed himself to be replaced by two committees, each comprised of both "Walt men" and "Roy men."

Donn B. Tatum, a "Roy man" who had joined Disney in 1955, became the studio's executive vice-president of administration. He was appointed by Roy to head the "executive," or administration, committee. To fill Tatum's previous post, Roy advanced Card Walker, a "Walt man" who first joined the studio in 1938 as a mail-room messenger and had worked his way up to head of the studio's marketing division. The three, including Roy, became known as "the Disney Troika."

The second committee was put in charge of production. It was made up of senior producer Bill Anderson, storyman Winston Hibler, animator Jim Algar, studio executive Harry Tytle, producers Bill Walsh and Ron Miller, and Roy's son, Roy E. For nearly a quarter of a century, Anderson, Hibler, Algar, and Walsh had formed the nucleus of the studio's in-house producers, working under the umbrella of "Walt Disney Presents" television series. Each had been among Walt's most trusted studio allies. Ron Miller completed the "Walt" side of the production team, with Roy E. the requisite "Roy man."

Under this structured duality the studio functioned in relative peace for the next several years, turning out a series of moderately profitable, if mostly forgettable, films, while the Disney television shows and theme parks continued to thrive. During this period Roy concentrated on keeping his promise to his brother that Walt Disney World would open on time.

In 1967, both Ron Miller and Roy E. were elected to the studio's board of directors. Two years later, with his father's financial backing,

Roy E. acquired enough stock to qualify as a principal shareholder and, while remaining part of the production committee, joined his dad, Walker, Tatum, and Miller on the board's executive committee.

In October 1971, Walt Disney World opened its golden gates for business. Two months later, at the age of seventy-eight, Roy dropped dead from a cerebral hemorrhage.

IN 1966, the year Walt died, the studio's gross receipts had reached a then unprecendented $116 million. At the time of Roy's death, under his concept of committee leadership, that figure had swelled to $250 million. The stockholders, the banks, and the board members all were eager to see the studio continue under the two-committee system Roy had instituted.

All, that is, except Roy's son, Roy E. After the death of his father, he first upset the balance of the fragile ruling coalition by expressing his doubts to the rest of the board about the creative direction the studio had taken under the guidance of the production committee. Was the Disney heritage really a mandate to make silly movies like *The Love Bug*, he asked, an alleged comedy about a Volkswagen that could talk? Since when were automobiles lovable? The unnamed but obvious target of Roy's criticism was "Walt man" executive committee member Card Walker. Just as Roy senior had once thought about Walt, Roy E. now felt Walker spent too much time dealing real estate and not enough on the business of making motion pictures.

The situation grew more intense in 1976, when the board named "Walt man" Card Walker president of Walt Disney Productions. Walker then appointed Ron Miller head of studio production.

A year later, on March 4, 1977, citing creative differences, Roy E. handed in his resignation as vice-president of the studio. While no longer active in the day-to-day operation of the studio, he retained his seat on the board of directors and was still the company's largest single stockholder.

With the completion that same year of *The Rescuers*, the last of the still-active "Nine Old Men," Milt Kahl, Frank Thomas, and Ollie Johnston, retired from active studio production. As for the two other surviving members of Walt's "supreme court," John Lounsbery had died before the film was completed, and Wollie Reitherman finished one last coproducing assignment begun before *The Rescuers* and "retired."

A year later, Don Bluth, among the most talented of the "second generation" Disney animators, resigned. His departure prompted sixteen other top-ranking animators to leave Disney. The retirements and resignations all came after Roy E.'s departure, a clear sign of the growing dissatisfaction with the studio's current leadership.

A year later, in 1978, Tatum resigned as chairman of the board, while still retaining *his* seat. He was replaced by Card Walker, who immediately promoted Ron Miller to president and chief executive officer of Walt Disney Productions. Miller, in turn, appointed one of his closest friends, twenty-seven-year-old Thomas Wilhite to head creative development. Wilhite went on to develop a series of expensive flops, among them, *The Devil in Max Devlin* (1980), *The Last Flight of Noah's Ark* (1980), and 1982's high-tech, computer-game-within-a-film *Tron*, which earned Ron the nickname around the studio as "Tron" Miller. The film proved such a box-office dud, Disney's stock fell two-and-a-half points the day after it opened. *Tron's* failure capped the studio's four-year period of financial decline and set the stage for yet another internal struggle for control of the studio, this time between the two most powerful "Walt men," Card Walker and Ron Miller.

As president and CEO, Miller wanted to continue as head of the studio and take it in the direction of what he described as more "sophisticated" *Tron*-like films, on the order of *Jaws* and *E.T.*, two of the most popular and financially successful films of all time, both directed by Steven Spielberg for Universal. Walker maintained it was corporate suicide for the studio to continue under Miller, that films like *Tron* proved audiences would not accept anything from the Disney studio that didn't, in fact, *look* like a "Disney" film.

Another avenue of internal conflict was the ongoing problem of EPCOT. Walt's "City of Tomorrow" had not opened the same time as the Orlando amusement park. For a number of technical, financial, and legal reasons, its debut was delayed more than eleven years, until October of 1982. By then, its cost had escalated to $1.2 billion, three times the original estimate. Every board member attended the opening-week festivities except Roy E., who remained outraged at the amount of money the board had approved for the project.

After EPCOT's debut, Card Walker resigned his chairmanship and was replaced by Raymond L. Watson. Watson, an architect by trade, had first joined the studio in 1964, hired by Walt as a consultant for

EPCOT. After Disney's death, Watson continued in this capacity for Walker. Watson eventually became a key advisor to both Walker and Tatum and, with Miller's support, in 1973 a member of the board.

In 1983, Miller anounced the formation of Touchstone Pictures, a separate division within the company created for the purpose of making more adult-oriented motion pictures. Touchstone's debut feature, *Splash*, developed by Wilhite, was a live-action romantic comedy about a man who falls in love with a mermaid.

In spite of the strong advance word for *Splash*, it proved Wilhite's swan song. His forced resignation by the board before the film's premiere should have been a clear indication to Miller just how soft his support had become. *Splash* opened on March 9, 1984, grossed $25 million its first two weeks, and went on to become one of the year's biggest hits. Miller reveled in the film's box-office success, believing it not only validated his vision but reinforced his power.

March 9, 1984, was also the day Roy E. chose to announce his resignation from the board of directors. For the first time since its inception in 1923, no "blood" Disney held a position of power at the studio that bore the family name.

AT THE TIME of his resignation, Roy E. Disney held 1.1 million shares of Walt Disney Productions. One year later, its net worth had dropped 40 percent, down from $80 million to $50 million. *Splash* proved to be the exception as the studio continued to turn out a series of expensive films that failed to return their investment.

After conferring with his attorney Stanley Gold, Roy E. debated two courses of action to save the family business he now believed would, if its present leadership were not removed, wind up in bankruptcy. He could sell off his shares now, take his $50 million, and end his association with the studio. Or he could attempt one last campaign to regain control of the studio from Ron Miller and the current board. He chose the latter.

Gold got in touch with the man he considered his mentor, former law partner Frank Wells. In 1969, Wells had given up the practice of law to become a vice-president of Warner Bros. Gold inherited several of Wells's clients, including Roy Sr. In 1982, Wells left Warners. Gold asked Wells to join him, and Roy E. Wells agreed, and became the third member of what would later be known as Roy E.'s "guerrilla troika."

Wells's first directive was for Roy to try to convince the board to hire Michael Eisner to replace Miller as the head of the studio. In 1976, at the age of thirty-two, Eisner had been named president of Paramount Pictures by its chairman Barry Diller. The two had first met and become good friends in 1962 after both were hired by Leonard Goldenson as programers for the ABC television network. Diller was one of the conceptual architects of "made-for-TV" movies.

The Diller-Eisner era at Paramount distributed such hit theatrical features as *Saturday Night Fever, Ordinary People, Raiders of the Lost Ark, Urban Cowboy, Star Trek, Reds, An Officer and a Gentleman, 48 HRS., Friday the 13th,* and *Terms of Endearment*. Eisner, along with Jeffrey Katzenberg and executive producer Garry Marshall, was responsible for the development of a string of hit sitcoms for ABC, among them "Happy Days," "Laverne and Shirley," and "Mork and Mindy." During this time, Paramount's annual gross rose from $100 million in 1973, the year before Diller's arrival, to over a $1 billion in 1984.

That same year, the founder and chairman of Gulf and Western, Paramount's parent company, Charles Bluhdorn, passed away and was succeeded by Martin S. Davis. Not long after, a power struggle developed between Diller and Eisner, which many speculated had been instigated by Davis to diminish the team's power. Eisner soon began looking for another studio, and Ron Miller wanted him for Disney. Besides the tremendous profits they generated, of all the product coming out of Hollywood, Miller considered Michael Eisner's output of movies and television shows the closest to "typical" Disney fare.

Miller had first tried and failed to lure Eisner to Disney a year earlier, in 1983. After his relationship with Diller collapsed, Eisner, who knew Roy E. personally—both happened to be board members at Cal-Arts—called him rather than Miller to explore the possibility of joining the studio. However, Roy E., although he had not made his decision known to the public, was already planning his resignation.

Just as Eisner was meeting with Roy E., another gladiator was preparing to enter the arena. A short round man with bullet holes for eyes and black hair that one associate described as not quite as dark as his heart, Saul Steinberg had come to the conclusion that in its present weakened state, Walt Disney Productions was perfectly positioned for a corporate takeover.

WHAT HAD ATTRACTED Steinberg was the continual decline of the value of Disney stock. Early in 1984, Disney was trading at $45 a share, down from the previous year's high of $84. Steinberg wanted to acquire the troubled studio to sell off its individual assets—the film library, the Burbank studio, the amusement parks—for what he figured would bring him the equivalent of $100 a share, an enormous profit of more than twice his investment.

In April, Wells, Gold, and Roy E., working without the board's knowledge, decided to bring in someone to organize a proper defense against Steinberg. The man they chose was the head of the Los Angeles division of Drexel Burnham Lambert. At the age of thirty-nine, Michael Milken had made his name, and a reported annual income of $25 million, by introducing Wall Street to the concept of "junk bonds."

Roy E. was initially against hiring Milken. Disney believed the best way to thwart Steinberg was to buy up enough stock to prevent him or any other raider from acquiring a sufficient amount to effect a takeover. However, based on what they knew of Steinberg's portfolio, Disney's bank advised Roy E. he could not win that battle. Reluctantly, he then agreed to allow Wells and Gold to enlist Milken.

The developments at Disney now caught the attention of Wall Street's new breed of arbitrageurs, investors in large blocks of companies about to be raided whose stocks would therefore suddenly and sharply increase. Overnight, one such arbitrageur, Ivan Boesky, entered the game. His goal was not to take over the studio, but merely to ride the anticipated escalation of the value of stock that would naturally follow from any sudden, large purchases—Steinberg's, Roy E. Disney's, or his own. Boesky thus became the fourth largest stockholder in the Walt Disney studio.

THE BATTLE came to an abrupt end in June 1984 when Saul Steinberg accepted a $325 million payoff from the Disney studio for his Disney stock. Although it was nowhere near what he figured he could make if his takeover had succeeded, he still walked away with a profit of $31 million for *not* buying the company.

The payoff, commonly known as "greenmail," had been negotiated by Roy E.'s team. The strategy had been to convince Disney's board to make several large acquisitions that would increase the company's debt and deplete the percentile value of each share of stock. Eventually, Steinberg, fearing the value of his investment would be seriously eroded by such a strategy, agreed to sell his stock back to Walt Disney Productions.

ROY E. INSISTED it had been Watson and Miller's poor management that had made the studio vulnerable for takeover and vowed to make them pay for it. The third week in June 1984, following Steinberg's withdrawal, Disney's stock began to plummet, due to payments related to the company's planned acquisitions. At that point Roy E. figured the time had come to launch his own proxy fight against the Watson-Miller–dominated board.

The precipitous drop in stock forced a reclusive Lillian Disney to come forward and demand an explanation from the board. Although Lillian strongly opposed Roy E.'s reinstatement, she was even less enamored of Ron Miller. She believed, as Roy E. did, that Miller's and Watson's mismanagement placed in jeopardy the future of the studio her husband had founded. After conferring with Roy E., she agreed to support him in his attempt to oust Miller.

On August 17, 1984, the board of directors asked Ron Miller for his resignation. With the price of stock still seriously depressed and the family no longer behind him, Miller reluctantly agreed to step down. Roy E. was then readmitted to the board and in a show of strength, assigned Miller's vacated seat to Stanley Gold.

Shortly thereafter, Miller retired from the film business. He and Diane moved to northern California to run a vineyard and bought a farm in Colorado to raise sheep. Lillian returned to her Holmby Hills home, where she still lives in preferred seclusion.*

The studio was finally back in the hands of a blood Disney. As far as Roy E. was concerned, he had earned his right to sit on the throne. Emerging from the dark shadows, the nephew Walt had tried to prevent from inheriting the studio had effectively eliminated heir-apparent Ron Miller, an act of vengeance Walt would no doubt have understood and appreciated.

---

*Sharon Disney was never involved in the running of the studio. She was, however, an officer in Retlaw and a trustee for Cal-Arts. For most of her adult life she was involved in numerous charitable activities. Widowed, divorced, and the mother of three children, she died of complications from cancer in February 1993.

ON SEPTEMBER 22, 1984, the board of directors appointed Michael Eisner and Frank Wells, the third member of Roy E.'s guerrilla troika, to head Walt Disney Productions. Shortly thereafter, Eisner brought Jeffrey Katzenberg over from Paramount. "Squirt," as the diminutive, bespectacled, NYU dropout was sometimes called by his associates, had gained his introduction to Hollywood rather circuitously, via New York politics. Katzenberg had worked for New York's mayor John Lindsay in the early seventies. Lindsay then introduced him to David Picker, of Gulf and Western, Paramount's parent company. Picker, in turn, introduced Katzenberg to Barry Diller, who, upon his appointment to head Paramount, hired "Squirt" as his personal assistant.

Together, Eisner and Katzenberg revamped the Disney studio's entire operation. Miller and his team had become accustomed to the lackadaisical lifestyle of two-hour lunches followed by three-hour golf games. Their staff had taken its cues from management, and their film projects reflected the studio's general lackluster. Eisner and Katzenberg immediately shed those employees they considered dead weight. Most of the previous administrative staff were encouraged to resign voluntarily. The rest were either dismissed or demoted. By 1985, more than four hundred pink slips had gone out, with most of those fired replaced by a handpicked team of Eisner's former colleagues at Paramount.

Prominent among them was former William Morris agent-turned-film-producer David Hoberman, who was put in charge of Touchstone Pictures. Under Hoberman, Touchstone produced such Paramount-like hits as 1986's *Ruthless People* and *Down and Out in Beverly Hills* and the phenomenally successful *3 Men and a Baby*. To date, *Baby* has grossed nearly $400 million worldwide.

Richard Frank was recruited from Paramount to help revitalize Disney's television interests. Frank had been responsible for two of that studio's greatest television successes of the 1980s, the syndicated shows "Entertainment Tonight" and a modern variation of the old "Hit Parade" program, "Solid Gold." At Disney, he developed one of the biggest television sitcoms of the eighties, "Golden Girls." With Eisner, Frank supervised the development of the Disney Channel, a premium pay-cable twenty-four-hour service to screen old Disney movies, television shows, and original family programming.

Also in 1985, Eisner agreed to purchase the rights to the MGM/UA library, as well as the famous "Leo the lion" logo. The deal made MGM a strong marketing tool for the company. In addition to acquiring 250 of MGM's and UA's most valuable film titles, Disney was able to add several attractions to the theme parks based on such MGM classics as *The Wizard of Oz* and *Singin' in the Rain*. What made the deal so profitable was the astonishingly low price Eisner paid for it. He was able to acquire everything he wanted from the troubled studio for an annual $100,000 licensing fee, with a built-in cap of $1 million.*

In 1986, Leonard Goldenson, still the head of ABC, repurchased the rights to the Walt Disney prime-time weekly series. "Walt Disney," as the series was last known, had been off the air since 1983. Goldenson, who had given Eisner his first job in television, believed Eisner's easygoing, fatherly demeanor and slightly goofy smile made him naturally telegenic. Eisner seemed the perfect choice as the first host of the Disney television show since Walt's death twenty years earlier.

In 1988, one of Katzenberg's top production assistants at Paramount, Ricardo Mestres, was hired by Eisner to take charge of a second "sub studio" at Disney, Hollywood Pictures. Under Mestres, Hollywood Pictures produced such hits as *Pretty Woman* (1990), directed by Garry Marshall, former television producer under Eisner when both had been at Paramount. *Pretty Woman* became Disney's all-time live-action box-office champ to date, grossing upward of $500 million worldwide. Other Hollywood Pictures hits include *Dick Tracy* (1990) and *The Hand That Rocks the Cradle* (1992).

Eisner also mandated a return to the studio's glory days of animation, beginning with the revival of a project that had languished for years under Ron Miller, *Who Framed Roger Rabbit*. To produce the film, a live action–animation extravaganza featuring virtually every cartoon character who ever graced the screen, Eisner hired Steven Spielberg. To get him, Eisner agreed to give him a share of the film's profits and a piece of the merchandising, two conditions never before

---

*According to Ron Grover in *The Disney Touch*, the deal infuriated Kirk Kerkorian, who owned MGM. At one time during the attempted Steinberg takeover, Kerkorian had been one of Steinberg's partners in the purchase of Disney stock. Kerkorian was not consulted by his board about the sale to Disney. He tried, unsuccessfully, to have the deal nullified.

given to any individual in the history of the studio. The film became the most expensive movie the studio ever made, with a final budget of more than $50 million, plus another $32 million earmarked for promotion and distribution. It eventually grossed $328 million world-wide ($154 million domestic) and spawned more than thirty-four separate licensing agreements for five hundred products of merchandise. In 1993, Eisner opened the "Toontown" exhibit at Anaheim's Disneyland. Visitors to the park could walk through a three-dimensional re-creation of the film's locale where cartoon characters lived when they weren't making movies.

Because of *Who Framed Roger Rabbit* and two other mega-hits, 1987's *Good Morning, Vietnam* and *3 Men and a Baby*, in 1988 the studio, for the first time in its history, grossed more than $1 billion.

The critical success of *Roger Rabbit* signaled to many the studio's return to greatness. In 1989 the studio released the all-animated *The Little Mermaid*, followed in 1991 by *Beauty and the Beast*, the first animated feature nominated by the Motion Picture Academy for Best Picture of the year—*Snow White* had been awarded a special, non-competing Oscar. The studio's big animated feature for 1992 was *Aladdin*, which after only twenty weeks in release took in $200 million at the box office (domestic), making it the studio's highest grossing film of all time.

However, buried among the cheers were the disgruntled voices of many Disney veterans. The old-line animators, especially, were disturbed by the studio's almost totally computerized style of animation. Although Walt himself loved technical innovation, the feeling among many veteran Disney men was that the studio had abandoned its creative heritage, the art of hand-drawn animation in the service of great storytelling.

The new films, they complained, seemed like nothing more than thinly disguised rehashes of much better originals. One longtime Disney animator claimed that *Honey, I shrunk the Kids*, with its larger and smaller motif, was really nothing more than a remake of *Alice in Wonderland*. A veteran storyman suggested the character of Roger Rabbit looked an awful lot like Walt's original Oswald. Even Katzenberg couldn't resist telling interviewers how much *Beauty and the Beast* "owed" to the look, style, and approach of *Pinocchio*.

Still, to most people, Disney's greatness rested on what was and had always been for Hollywood the only line that counted, the one on the bottom. Fiscal 1992 set new records for the Disney studio in every division. Its films took in 29 cents of every dollar spent at the box office in America. "Tokyo Disneyland" opened in 1983 and generates $40 million a year in net profits for the studio. In its five years of existence more people have passed through Tokyo Disneyland's gates than have the entire thirty-three years of the original Disneyland's existence.

Less immediately successful is France's "Euro Disney," opened in April 1992. Located in Marne-la-Valle, about twenty miles east of Paris, Euro Disney was created as a joint ownership venture between local interests (51 percent) and the Walt Disney company (49 percent) at a cost of $4.2 billion. From the beginning there were troubles brought about by construction delays and local protests by those opposed to what they claimed was American encroachment of French property and culture. The hiring of twelve thousand employees nearly caused a complete shutdown when French labor unions objected to Disney's strict dress codes, which the Japanese had accepted without protest.

Disney required employees to abide by a "Le Euro Disney look," which stipulated that men's hair be cut above the collar and ears, no beards or mustaches, no tattoos. Women had to keep their hair one "natural color"—no frosting or streaking—and wear limited makeup. Fingernails were not allowed to pass the ends of fingers. Appropriate undergarments included transparent pantyhose, no black or fancy designs.

The Communist-led Confederation Generale du Travail (General Confederation of Labor) handed out leaflets warning applicants the dress code was "an attack on individual liberty." This led the government labor inspector to issue a formal complaint with Disney, citing French law which prohibits employers from restricting individual and collective liberties.

An uneasy compromise was reached, and the park opened on schedule. From the first day the gates parted and the public was allowed inside, Euro Disney has reportedly been losing $1 million a day. Still, the Disney company's overall profits for the last quarter of 1992 made it the most profitable year in its history.

Late in December 1992, Disney's stock reached an all-time high, doubling in value in a single year from $86 a share to $145, and underwent a four-to-one split. Michael Eisner, wary, perhaps, of

President Bill Clinton's promise of a more stringent capital-gains tax, cashed in most of his stock options and took home a check for $192 million.

IN A BURBANK TAVERN, the son of one of Disney's original team of filmmakers sat in a corner, nursing a scotch and soda. The news of Eisner's stock deal made him chuckle. He shook his head, took a sip, and leaned back. "The irony is, the studio has a reputation for paying the lowest salaries in the business." He wiped the corners of his mouth with two fingers. "What do you suppose old Walt would think about a Jew making so much money from his studio?" He paused, then answered his own question: "He'd either hate it, because the guy was a Jew, or love it, because it meant Eisner had to have enormous talent to produce that kind of revenue. That, of course, was pure Walt. The fearful logic always colliding with the brilliant instincts. His genius, of course, was his ability to survive that kind of internal wreck, and then make great art out of it."

Notes and Sources

General

A good deal of the research for this book was gathered through personal interviews. The list of those interviewed who agreed to be identified may be found in the Acknowledgments.

The primary research facility I used was the Library of the Academy of Motion Picture Arts and Sciences, in Los Angeles. Its clippings files on Walt Disney were extraordinarily well kept and, as always, I found the staff to be courteous, helpful, and altogether professional in every way.

I received Walt Disney's FBI file on March 26, 1991. The Bureau initially released 451 pages out of 570. Approximately six months later, on appeal, I received about 100 additional documents.

The following books were used for secondary research. In places where books have been either reprinted or updated, I have cited the most recent copyright in the edition consulted for research. The chapter notes contain shortened references to the following sources.

Adamson, Joe, *Tex Avery: King of Cartoons*, Da Capo Press, New York, 1975.
Adamson, Joe, *The Walter Lantz Story*, Putnam, New York, 1985.
Almendros, Carlos, *Mojacar, Corner of Enchantment*, Ediciones Savir, S.A., Barcelona, 1990.
Barlett, Donald L. and Steele, James B., *Empire—The Life, Legend and Madness of Howard Hughes*, W. W. Norton and Co., New York, 1979.
Barnouw, Erik, *Tube of Plenty*, Oxford University Press, New York, 1975.
Berg, A. Scott, *Goldwyn*, Knopf, New York, 1989.
Bettelheim, Bruno, *The Uses of Enchantment*, Vintage Books, Random House, New York, 1989.
Blanc, Mel and Bashe, Philip, *That's NOT All Folks!*, Warner Books, New York, 1988.
Bowser, Eileen, *The Transformation of Cinema*, Charles Scribner's Sons, New York, 1990.

Bright, Randy, *Disneyland—Untold Story*, Harry N. Abrams, New York, 1987.

Cabarca, Leslie, *The Fleischer Story*, Da Capo Press, New York, revised edition, 1988.

Canemaker, John, *Felix: The Twisted Tale of the World's Most Famous Cat*, Pantheon Books, New York, 1991.

Ceplair, Larry and Englund, Steven, *The Inquisition in Hollywood*, University of California Press, Los Angeles, 1983, by arrangement with Anchor Press.

Charyn, Jerome, *Movieland, Hollywood and the Great American Dream Culture*, G. P. Putnam's Sons, New York, 1989.

Crafton, Donald, *Before Mickey*, The MIT Press, Cambridge, Massachusetts, 1984.

Culhane, John, *Walt Disney's Fantasia*, Harry N. Abrahms, New York, 1983.

Culhane, Shamus, *Talking Animals and Other People*, St. Martin's Press, New York, 1986.

———, *Animation from Script to Screen*, St. Martin's Press, New York, 1988.

Douglas, Kirk, *The Ragman's Son*, Pocket Books, New York, 1988.

Dunaway, David King, *Huxley in Hollywood*, Harper and Row, New York, 1989.

Eyles, Allen, *Walt Disney's Three Little Pigs*, Collins Publishers, The Walt Disney Company, 1987.

Finch, Christopher, *The Art of Walt Disney*, Harry N. Abrams, New York, 1973; 1983.

Friedrich, Otto, *City of Nets*, Harper and Row, New York, 1986.

Gabler, Neal, *An Empire of Their Own*, Crown, New York, 1988.

Gentry, Curt, *J. Edgar Hoover: The Man and the Secrets*, W. W. Norton and Co., New York, 1991.

Goldenson, Leonard H. (with Marvin J. Wolf), *Beating the Odds*, Charles Scribner's Sons, New York, 1991.

Grant, John, *Encyclopedia of Walt Disney's Animated Characters*, Harper and Row, New York, 1987.

Greenfield, Jeff, *Television: The First 50 Years*, Harry N. Abrams, New York, 1977.

Grover, Ron, *The Disney Touch*, Business One, USA, 1991.

Hamilton, Ian, *Writers in Hollywood*, Harper and Row, New York, 1990.

Hand, David, *Memoirs*, privately printed by Martha Hand. Copyright Martha Hand, California, 1986.

Hollis, Richard and Sibley, Brian, *The Disney Studio Story*, Crown Publishers, New York, 1988.

———, *Walt Disney's Mickey Mouse: His Life and Times*, Harper and Row, New York, 1986.

Johnston, Ollie, and Frank Thomas, *Disney Animation: "The Illusion of Life*, Abbeville, New York, 1981.

———, *Walt Disney's Bambi: The Story and the Film*, Workman Publishing, New York, 1990.

Jones, Chuck, *Chuck Amuck*, Avon Books, New York, 1990.

Kanfer, Stefan, *A Journal of the Plague Years*, Atheneum, New York, 1973.

Kindem, Gorham, ed., *The American Movie Industry: The Business of Motion Pictures*, Southern Illinois University Press, (Chicago) 1982.

Kinney, Jack, *Walt Disney and Assorted Other Characters*, Harmony Books, New York, 1988.

Koszarski, Richard, *An Evening's Entertainment: The Age of the Silent Feature Picture, 1915–1928*, vol. 3 of *The History of American Cinema*, Charles Harpole, ed., Charles Scribner's Sons, New York, 1990.

Leff, Leonard J. and Jerold, L. Simmons, *The Dame in the Kimono: Hollywood, Censorship and the Production Code from 1920's to 1960's*, Grove Wiedenfeld, New York, 1990.

McCabe, John, *Charlie Chaplin*, Doubleday, New York, 1978.

Maltin, Leonard, *The Disney Films*, Popular Library, by arrangement with Crown Publishers, New York, 1973 (additional material 1978).

—————, *Of Mice and Magic: A History of American Animated Cartoons*, NAL Penguin, New York, 1987.

Miller, Diane Disney (As told to Pete Martin), *The Story of Walt Disney*, Dell Publishing, 1957, New York.

Moldea, Dan E., *Dark Victory*, Viking Penguin, New York, 1986.

Mosley, Leonard, *Disney's World*, Stein and Day, New York, 1985.

Musser, Charles, *The Emergence of Cinema*, vol. 1 of The History of American Cinema, Charles Harpole, ed., Charles Scribner's Sons, New York, 1990.

Norman, Barry, *The Story of Hollywood*, NAL Penguin, New York, 1987.

Peet, Bill, *An Autobiography*, Houghton Mifflin Company, Boston, 1989.

Rychlak, Cameron, *Personality Development and Psychopathology*, Houghton Mifflin, Boston, 1985.

Saldinger, Frances, ed., *Walt Disney's Story Land*, Golden Press, New York, 1962.

Schickel, Richard, *The Disney Version*, Touchstone (Simon and Schuster), New York, 1985.

Shows, Charles, *Walt: Backstage Adventures with Walt Disney*, Communication Creativity, La Jolla, California, 1980.

Siegel, Barbara and Siegal, Scott, *The Encyclopedia of Hollywood*, Facts on File, New York, 1990.

Sinyard, Neil, *The Best of Disney*, Portland House, a division of Crown Publishers, New York, 1988.

Solomon, Charles, *The History of Animation*, Knopf, New York, 1989.

Spitzer, Robert L., M.D., Chairperson, Task Force on Nomenclature and Statistics, *Diagnostic and Statistical Manual of Mental Disorders*, Third Edition, APA, Washington, D.C. 1980.

Steinberg, Cobbett, *TV Facts*, Facts on File, New York, 1980.

Taylor, John, *Storming the Magic Kingdom*, Knopf, New York, 1987.

Thomas, Bob, *King Cohn*, Bantam, New York, 1967.

—————, *Walt Disney, An American Original* Pocket Books, New York, 1976.

Walt Disney Company, *Disneyland: The First Thirty-Five Years*, Burbank, 1989.

Walt Disney's Snow White and the Seven Dwarfs, A Studio Book, Viking Press, New York, 1978, 1979.

Wiley, Mason and Bona, Damien, *Inside Oscar*, Ballantine Books, New York, 1986.

Notes by Chapter

1. Fathers and Sons

Information regarding the Disney family genealogy is taken from the following: The Register of Births, city of Chicago, 1890 and 1893; Cook County Clerk Stanley T. Kusper, Jr.; Bureau of Vital Statistics, 118 N. Clark, Chicago, Illinois; twelfth Census of the United States: 1900 Population; thirteenth Census of the

United States: 1910 Population; Index to Birth Records, Cook County, Illinois Bureau of Vital Statistics, 1871–1916. Additional information on Disney's ancestry was researched by Larry L. Piatt, Larry L. Piatt Genealogical Services, Salt Lake City, Utah, Reference Consultant in the U.S.–Canada unit of the Family History Library of the Church of Jesus Christ of Latter-Day Saints.

The story of the brothers sharing the same bed and body fluids is from Taylor, *Storming the Magic Kingdom*, p. 11.

Details of the newspaper home-delivery job are taken from Miller, *Story of Walt Disney*, pp. 18–19. Although presented in book form as a "biography" of Walt by his daughter, Diane Disney, according to Ward Kimball (quoted in Leonard Mosley's biography of Walt Disney): "Around this time [1954–1955] Walt was being interviewed on tape by Pete Martin for a series of articles dealing with Walt's life . . . which appeared subsequently as a book, *My Dad, Walt Disney* [Ed. note: actual title: *The Story of Walt Disney*]. By using this ploy, Walt avoided sounding too egotistical. . . . "

The detail of Walt's sleeping in alleys comes from an interview conducted by Charles Champlin, recollected in Champlin's piece entitled "The Wonder Years," *Los Angeles Times*, April 14, 1991, Calendar section, p. 8.

The information regarding Walt's favorite childhood book series, "Jimmy Dale," is from an interview conducted by Eliot with Disney's brother-in-law, Bill Cottrell, at his home in North Hollywood, spring, 1991, and a telephone conversation by Eliot with Ron Miller, spring, 1991. Years later, Disney purchased the rights to all the Packard "Jimmy Dale" novels, hoping to develop them into a series for the studio. The series never materialized.

Information regarding the forged signatures is from Miller, *Story of Walt Disney*, pp. 39–40.

2. Kansas City Ad Infinitum

Background information on Ub Iwerks is from a series of interviews by Eliot with Iwerks's son, David Iwerks, 1989–1991.

Otto Messmer, in his foreword to Crafton's *Before Mickey*, p. xv, wrote of his creation of Felix: "In 1916 I joined Pat Sullivan [at] Universal. . . . In 1919 I created a character which Paramount named 'Felix the Cat.' I used the style of Charlie Chaplin and kept him alone in his antics, unhampered by supporting characters. . . . I gave Felix a personality. . . ." Although Disney claimed to have based his early concept of Mickey Mouse on Charlie Chaplin, Messmer's Chaplinesque Felix preceded Mickey by ten years.

Background information on Margaret J. Winkler from ibid., pp. 206–208.

Excerpts from Disney's May 24, 1923, letter to Winkler are from Thomas, *Walt Disney, An American Original*, p. 53.

The story of Walt's meeting the elderly gentleman on the train was recalled in an interview with William Cottrell, April 1991.

3. Of Men and Mice

Disney's letter to Margaret J. Winkler is taken from Hollis and Sibley, *Disney Studio Story*, pp. 12–13.

The Winkler telegram is from ibid.

Ub Iwerks's hesitation about rejoining Disney and their "lifelong" partnership is from Iwerks interview. The trash-can anecdote is from an interview by Eliot with journalist Shirley Thomas.

The figure of $2,250 per "Oswald" short is from Miller, *Story of Walt Disney*, p. 85.

" . . . I'm telling you . . . on one condition": Ibid.

"Out of date crap": Mosley, *Disney's World*, p. 92

Background information regarding "Oscar the Rabbit" is from Crafton, *Before Mickey*, p. 209.

"Harsh taskmaster": Freleng in ibid., p. 208.

"Mice gathered in my wastebasket": Miller, *Story of Walt Disney*, p. 92.

"It's pretty clear now": Iwerks interview.

4. The Sound of Fame

"I started in as an artist": from a 1948 RKO press release.

"We had a showing with sound": Maltin, *Of Mice and Magic*, pp. 34–35.

Background material on competing sound cartoons is from Crafton, *Before Mickey*, pp. 210–215.

"A youngster named Jackson": Miller, *Story of Walt Disney*, pp. 95–96.

"Why should we let a few dollars": Thomas, *Walt Disney*, pp. 86–87.

5. Heroes and Villains

Background information on Edison and the Trust is from Musser, *Emergence of Cinema*, p. 145.

Background on the history of early Hollywood censorship is from information that appears in Koszarski, *An Evening's Entertainment*, pp. 194–208.

Background on Will Hays is from Leff and Simmons, *Dame in the Kimono*, p. 84.

"Presbyterian censorship" quoted in ibid., and from FBI report, "Communist Activities," August 15, 1922.

"Bunches of Jews": Leff and Simmons, *Dame in the Kimono*, p. 8.

"It was around eleven o'clock that night": Cottrell interview.

According to Anthony Slide's article, "Hollywood's Fascist Follies," *Film Comment*, vol. 27, no. 4, July–August 1991, both Giannini, the founder of the Bank of America, and Disney shared Cohn's admiration for Mussolini. In 1936 Giannini welcomed Carolo Roncoroni, president of Italy's Fascist National Confederation of Builders and member of the Joint Executive of the Fascist Confederation of Industrials, to Hollywood to discuss filmmaking co-ventures with Rome. The following year, during the course of the filming of *Snow White*, Disney visited Italy and was entertained by the Italian dictator at his private villa. One further aspect of the "Italian" connection—Gunther Lessing arranged an introduction for Vittorio Mussolini, the dictator's son, to Hal Roach. Mussolini wanted to study film production in Hollywood, and after their meeting Roach put together a deal for a joint venture—RAM Productions (Roach And Mussolini), funded by MGM. Roach believed the partnership, which failed, would have actually reached production had it not been for the World War II, and because, according to Roach, "The Jewish people in the picture business didn't like it."

"Ub and Walt": Iwerks interview.

"I guess I was working too hard": Miller, *Story of Walt Disney*, p. 113.

6. Fairy Tales and Fatherhood

Background information on the special Academy Award presented to Walt Disney is from Wiley and Bona, *Inside Oscar*, pp. 40–48.

The financial information on the cost of the black-and-white "Mickeys" is from Eyles's afterword to *Walt Disney's* Three Little Pigs.

The financial figures regarding merchandise are from Schickel, *Disney Version*, p. 163.

"I made a deal": Disney quoted in Miller, *Story of Walt Disney*, p. 120.

"We were told": Kinney, *Walt Disney and Assorted Other Characters*, p. 26.

"The life and adventures": The quote appears in "Storyboard: The Art of Laughter," *Journal of Animation Art*, vol. 3, no. 5, Oct./Nov. 1992. The original date and source of the quote are not identified; however, Walt's reference regarding how he still spoke for Mickey and vice versa suggests it was probably said in the first eight years of Mickey's existence, when Walt did the on-screen voice for his character.

"Well, that might not be such a bad imitation": Disney quoted by Louella Parsons in her column which appeared in the *Los Angeles Examiner*, August 11, 1935.

"For American animation": Jones quoted in Eyles, *Disney's* Three Little Pigs, p. 3 of afterword.

Description of Walt's acting out *The Three Little Pigs* is from Cottrell interview with Eliot.

"Mad about you": J. P. McEvoy, from his King Features syndicated column, December 12, 1933.

"It was good": Hand, *Memoirs*, p. 139–141.

7. Disney's Folly—The Making of Snow White

Regarding the first feature-length cartoon: In fact, in 1917, Argentinean film-maker Quirino Cristiani had made a full-length animated feature, *The Apostle*, and while the film received little attention in the United States, it did enjoy considerable success in Europe. It's doubtful Walt was aware of its existence when he was thinking of making *Snow White*.

"Early in 1935": Marc Davis interview with Eliot, January 1990.

"When the cartoon": Ward Kimball interview with Eliot, January 1990.

"I actually got a call": Joe Grant interview with Eliot, January 1990.

"I'd just graduated from high school": Marcielle Ferguson interview with Eliot, June 1990.

"There was a guard": Michael Murphy interview with Eliot, July 1990.

The information regarding Disney's signature is from Smith, "Storyboard: The Art of Laughter," p. 9.

The story transcript is from a meeting regarding *Tiger Hunt*, held on September 30, 1943. It is taken from Kinney, *Walt Disney and Assorted Other Characters*, pp. 91–92.

"Actually, he had no knowledge": Arthur Babbitt interview with Eliot, June 1990.

The letter explaining Disney's role at the studio is from the *Hollywood Citizen-News*, March 19, 1934.

"A drop of mercury": Jack Cutting, quoted in Hollis and Sibley, *Disney Story*, p. 27.

"Walt confided to me": Hand, *Memoirs*, p. 70.

"[One time he]": Ibid, p. 76.

"That preview was unsettling": Wilfred Jackson quoted in Solomon, *History of Animation*, p. 224.

8. A New Language of Art

Hollywood liberalism had been in decline since the FBI's World War I draft-dodger "Palmer" raids and the campaign to destroy the IWW—"Wobblies." During the Merriam campaign, Louis B. Mayer described the Democratic candidate as "a most dangerous Bolshevik beast," a comment which became one of the battle cries of the anti-Merriam right and served to reawaken the dormant American Socialist party. By 1938, there were over 100,000 registered members of the party in America, with an estimated additional quarter-million active sympathizers.

The anecdote about the Lorna Doones comes from Babbitt interview with Eliot. He added the following postcript: "I swiped the notice and showed it to Bill Cottrell. He just howled with laughter. I thought it was a classic."

"You took it," Kimball interview.

"This one Saturday": Grant interview.

9. A Means of Absolute Identity

"We worked every night": June Paterson interview with Eliot, June 1990.

The anecdote regarding the midgets hired for the opening of *Pinocchio* is from Boller, Paul F., Jr., and Ronald L. Davis, *Hollywood Anecdotes*, William Morrow and Company, New York, 1987, p. 381.

"I remember Roy": Miller, *Story of Walt Disney*, p. 149.

Background information regarding the Fleischer strike is from a 1980 interview with Arthur Babbitt conducted by Harvey Deneroff.

"In the immediate years before": Babbitt interview with Eliot, 1990 (with portions from 1980 Deneroff interviews). All Babbitt quotes in this chapter are from these two sources.

"A company union": Bill Littlejohn interview with Eliot, December 1989. All Littlejohn quotes in this chapter are from this interview.

"The studios made payoffs": Moldea, *Dark Victory*, pp. 4, 26–27.

At one point Walt told the *Los Angeles Times* that he didn't "want to come out of this business old and broke. . . . I could buy a big place in Florida. . . . I belong to this studio, this 'thing' that has grown up. . . . This is where my money goes." *Los Angeles Times Sunday Magazine*, December 4, 1938, p. 20.

"I knew the Federation" David Hilberman interview with Eliot, May, 1990. All Hilberman quotes in this chapter are from this interview.

Although certain Guild members at the time challenged the legality of the Federation, insisting it had never been approved by the NLRB, according to the Disney company's Prospectus of April 2, 1940: "Under date of July 22, 1939, the National Labor Relations Board issued its Decision and Certification of Representatives, finding that the employees in certain specified classifications, i.e., animators, artists, directors and their assistants, etc., constituted a unit for the purposes of collective bargaining, and certifying that the Federation of Screen Cartoonists had been designated and selected by a majority of the employees of Walt Disney Productions, Ltd., in such classifications as their representative for the purposes of collective bargaining, and that the Federation of Screen Cartoonists was the exclusive representative of all such employees for the purpose of collective bargaining in respect to rates of pay, wages, hours of employment and other conditions of employment."

Homer S. Cummings's 1937 book, *Federal Justice*, examines the start of the General Intelligence Division of the FBI in 1919. In Gentry, *J. Edgar Hoover*, p. 73, the early, previously unknown history of Hoover's association with the FBI is discussed. Gentry states that if Cummings's sources were correct, then "the Intelligence Division in 1919 . . . was organized under the direct administrative supervision of J. Edgar Hoover, since 1917 in charge of counter-radical activities as special assistant to the attorney general."

Hoover's letter to Disney regarding his "absolute identity" is from an FBI memo dated July 17, 1936, index number 62-41936-41, obtained from the Bureau by the author under the Freedom of Information Act. All subsequent FBI memoranda are henceforth referred to as FBI, with an identifying index number.

"Walt Disney Strolls" and "Simply came to see the sights": From FBI, 94-4-4667A, and ibid.

The information regarding the salaries of Disney's workers is from an article by Paul Hollister: "Walt Disney: Genius at Work," *Atlantic Monthly*, December 1940, pp. 689–701.

10. Strike!

"While dining alone": Solomon, *History of Animation*, p. 67.

T. S. Eliot's comment on D. H. Lawrence, another neo-Freudian Modernist, from his review of *Son of Woman: The Story of D. H. Lawrence:* "The whole history of Lawrence's life and of Lawrence's writings . . . is the history of his craving for greater intimacy than is possible between human beings, a craving irritated to the point of frenzy by his unusual incapacity for being intimate at all. His struggle against overintellectualized life is the history of his own overintellectualized nature."

"Grandiose venture into culture": Friedrich, *City of Nets*," p. 34. The anecdote involving the "colors" of passages is also from Friedrich.

Stravinsky eventually relocated to the United States and in December 1939 paid a visit to the Disney studio where he was afforded the courtesy of a private screening of *Fantasia*. Disney's version of the visit to the studio was that Stravinsky had been "visibly moved." Furthermore, according to Disney, Stravinsky had been paid $10,000, not $5,000, and that his perfectionist standards had led him to ask for modifications, but that he admitted the concept of creation and prehistoric life were "really" what *Le Sacre* was all about. Stravinsky later replied that he was, indeed, moved by the screening because the Stokowski interpretation of his music had been "execrable" and Disney's visuals were "an unresisting imbecility." Stravinsky's opinion of the Disney studio and Hollywood in general was that it was a place where "they killed you to keep you from starving to death." Disney: *Saturday Review*, January 30, 1960; and Stravinsky: Stravinsky and Craft, *Expositions and Developments*, p. 159; and Stravinsky, *Themes and Conclusions*, p. 49.

The anecdote involving Frank Lloyd Wright is from Finch, *Art of Walt Disney*, p. 254.

Lillian's impressions of *Fantasia* are from remarks made by Roy E. Disney to the invited audience at the first official screening of *Beauty and the Beast*, at the El Capitan Theater, Hollywood, March 1992.

The reference to Alexander Woollcott is from Cottrell and Grant interviews.

"I'll never understand": Mosley, *Disney's World*, p. 176.

The weather report for the week of *Fantasia*'s opening is from the studio "Bulletin," dated November 15, 1940.

"Roy called me into his office": Babbitt interview. All Babbitt quotes in this chapter are from this interview.

"There was just": Bodle interview with Eliot, January 1990.

The anonymous memo which begins "After the two and a half years" is from Culhane, *Walt Disney's* Fantasia, p.31

"Damn, I didn't think": This quote and the anecdote about opening the bottles of Harvey's Bristol Cream are from Finney, *Walt Disney and Assorted Other Characters*, pp 137–39.

"No overtures toward": *Hollywood Citizen-News*, May 28, 1941, p. 1.

"The union offered": ibid., June 4, 1941, p. 3.

"One of the . . .": Bodle interview with Eliot.

"I got a call": Anonymous. interview with Eliot.

"I didn't particularly": Hilberman interview with Eliot.

"We are compelled": Lessing quoted in the *Hollywood Citizen-News*, July 18, 1992.

The Mickey Mouse cartoon strip and support documents are from FBI 61-7560-7276

Details of the settlement comes from *Daily Variety*, July 31, 1941, front page.

11. The Mojacar Connection

Source material for this chapter comes from a research investigation personally conducted by the author in the village of Mojacar, Spain, in February, 1990. Interviews included Paco Flores, and Senor Jacinto Alarcon, the former mayor of Mojacar. Additional information is from Almendros, *Mojacar, Corner of Enchantment*, p. 83; Julian Ruiz, "Walt Disney Was from Almeria," *Interview* magazine, no. 242. Genealogical research was conducted by Larry Piatt (see chapter 1 Notes).

12. Disney Goes to War

"I was fired": Babbitt interview with Eliot.

"We knew that Walt": Hilberman interview.

"He called me in": Swift, quoted in Mosley, *Disney's World*, p. 207.

The story concerning Sharon's schoolmate is from an interview conducted with her. The source wishes to remain anonymous.

"The motion picture business": Miller, *Story of Walt Disney*, p. 188.

The National Conference of Christians and Jews, Inc., film proposal is from a letter dated May 15, from the organization to Sol Lesser.

Information regarding the Council for Pan-American Democracy is from FBI 100-45254 and FBI 62- 60527-25.

"Unprecedented demonstration": *Sunday Worker*, Section Two, p. 13.

"Find ourselves": *New York Sun* (A.P.), February 2, 1944.

The anecdote concerning James Cagney is from a *New York Times* review by John O'Connor of a TNT documentary on the life of James Cagney, July 3, 1992, Section B, p. 12.

Cagney's membership in an organization called "The Free World Association" came to the attention of the FBI when it held a meeting the same night as the announcement of the formation of the MPA. It was a meeting Walt Disney attended and reported on. As noted in Disney FBI file LA100-22299 ("Internal Security"): "The Free World Association has a dazzling roster of film names— DUDLEY NICHOLS, THOMAS MANN, JIMMY CAGNEY, ORSON WELLES, JOHN GARFIELD, WALTER WANGER, WALTER PIDGEON and many other box-office stars on the male side; RITA HAYWORTH, OLIVIA DE HAVILLAND, JOAN FONTAINE, BETTE DAVIS, INGRID BERGMAN, ROSALIND RUSSELL and others in the ladies lineup."

Details of the letter to Senator Reynolds is from Ceplair and Englund, *Inquisition in Hollywood*, p. 212.

Ironically, the success of *Dumbo* had nearly resulted in Goldwyn's becoming Walt's boss anyway, as Disney's product was considered one of the relatively few reliables in RKO's chaotic organization. Having gone through a series of take-overs, challenges, and flops, Goldwyn considered acquiring the studio before settling for a distribution deal. As a result, Goldwyn and Disney had become partners of a sort; both were independent filmmakers distributing with the same studio RKO.

Background and details for the Sam Goldwyn/Disney Reno affair are from the following: *Up in Arms*: Berg, *Goldwyn*, pp. 382–91; Disney's involvement: FBI 60-86, 60-3020-13, 60-30-17, 60-3020, 60-3509-15, 60-308.

13. Disney, HUAC, and the Blacklist

Fiscal information for 1944 is from Walt Disney Productions 1944 Financial Report to stockholders, and from *Daily Variety*, January 16, 1945. The actual net profit total for 1944 was $486,287, as compared with $431,536 for 1943.

"Disney discovered the power": Jules Engel interview with Eliot, March 1991.

Apparently, Walt was able to free up a sufficient amount of Technicolor film by enlisting the help of the FBI. In file 60-8509 "Antitrust," much of which has been marked "confidential" by the Bureau, enough information remains to suggest that by 1948, Special Attorney James M. McGrath considered instituting an antitrust lawsuit against the company, after which Disney experienced no further difficulties obtaining as much film and processing as he required.

Walt maintained absolute control over the editorial content of the *Look* piece, a policy he insisted on for all articles that sought his cooperation. This practice is still very much in force today for writers seeking cooperation from the studio.

In the *Look* article, "Walt Disney—Teacher of Tomorrow," vol. 9, no. 8, April 17, 1945, the opening paragraph describes a very different Donald Duck than the one that starred in *The Three Caballeros*. It reads: "His Donald Duck and Mickey Mouse have made millions laugh; now they will teach other millions to read. Symbolically speaking, a celluloid duck is emerging from World War II as the greatest potential education force this world has ever known. His name is Donald Duck, and he stands for the international picture language developed and perfected over 25 years by his 43-year-old creator, Walt Disney."

The Interracial Guild description of its personnel was given by Harry Levette, its publicity director, to the *People's Voice*, January 25, 1945.

The details of Walt's resignation are from the *New York Times*, September 12, 1945, and the *Motion Picture Herald*, September 15, 1945. Additional background is from the *Los Angeles Times*, September 11, 1945.

"Totally disinterested": Crowther quoted in Schickel, *Disney Version*, p. 282.

"He did everything": Babbit interview.

Information concerning the 1945 CSU strike is from Ceplair and Englund, *Inquisition in Hollywood*, pp. 216–25.

The story is told of no less a thirties Hollywood liberal (and future political ally of Walt Disney) than Ronald Reagan, taken with how the American Communist party was actively involved in "helping the dispossessed, the Okies, the unemployed and the homeless," sought membership. Many of the then Roosevelt-liberal Reagan's Hollywood friends had already joined, and he let it be known he was considering it himself. However, the leaders of the Hollywood branch of the party, believing Reagan something of a flake, rejected his membership, preferring to keep him working as a so-called friend of the party, and supporter of party-related projects.

Background information on the Waldorf Statement is from Ceplair and Englund, *Inquisition* in *Hollywood*, pp. 328–31.

Disney's testimony before HUAC is taken from FBI 26239, which contained the full testimony as recorded by the *Congressional Record*.

Background on *Red Channels* in Ceplair and Englund, p. 386:

"The people and organization which assembled in HUAC's shadow threw their nets far wider than the committee and obeyed far fewer rules. The important 'smear and clear' organizations were:

1. American Business Consultants, formed by three ex-FBI agents in 1947. They published *Counterattack* on a regular basis and in June 1950 printed the 'bible' of the graylist, *Red Channels*, a list of 151 people in show business and statement of Communist-front activities of each.

2. Wage Earner Committee, formed in October, 1951. Published the *National Wage Earner*, which listed 92 "subversive" films, picketed selected movies, and issued defamatory circulars on many others.

3. 'Aware Inc.,' established in December 1953 by a group of New York actors and Vincent Hartnett, who formerly worked for ABC. They published *Confidential Notebook* regularly and supplements similiar to *Red Channels* periodically.

"These groups followed the lead of [Disney's] Motion Picture Alliance for the Preservation of American Ideals. . . ."

14. New Directions

According to Ceplair and Englund, Hughes was such an avowed anticommunist he devised a plan to ensure he never knowingly hired one at RKO. He liked to offer prospective directors a chance at making *I Married a Communist*. If a director turned it down, Hughes took that as a sign of fear and concluded that director was a Communist. Thirteen directors lost potential jobs turning the film down. It was finally directed by Robert Stevenson (1950). A box-office bomb, it was retitled *Woman on Pier 13* and later sold to television.

All Stanley Myers quotes in this chapter are from an interview with Eliot, March 1991.

One year after Walt declined to take over RKO, Hughes sold 750 feature films to a television distributor (C and C Corporation) for $15.2 million, then sold the studio's remaining inventory and real estate to the General Tire Corporation, which restructured RKO as a studio involved exclusively with the production of original television programming.

15. King of the New Frontier

As a way of protecting their personal assets, Lillian was specifically omitted from any participation in WED. At the same time Walt signed over his interest in the Holmby Hills home to her, to insure it wouldn't be exposed to any financial risk.

Retlaw's present estimated worth is said to be in excess of $150 million. It owns six television stations (all CBS affiliates), 1,150 acres of prime California real estate, and a private jet-leasing firm. It continues to collect approximately $600,000 a year for its share of twenty-six Disney live-action films made in the 1960s. In 1982, Retlaw sold the rights to the Walt Disney name and Disneyland's monorail and steam railroad back to the Walt Disney Company.

The breakfast and 10-cent tip story is from Michael Murphy interview with Eliot.

The information regarding Wallerstein is from Goldenson, *Beating the Odds*, p. 26.

Information regarding the Melancon lawsuit is from *Hollywood Reporter*, June 18, 1953; the *Hollywood Citizen-News*, August 28, 1953; and the *Los Angeles Herald Examiner*, August 28, 1953.

"Benevolent monarch": Thomas, *Walt Disney*, p 238.

The city councilmen's quotes are from Bright, *Disneyland—Untold Story*, p. 31.

The Sarnoff turndown is from Goldenson, *Beating the Odds*, p. 122.

Details of the ABC deal are from ibid., pp. 122–26.

Lillian's article is quoted in *McCall's*, February 1955.

Arthur Godfrey responded to Disney's ratings success in the April 18 issue of *Newsweek*: "I love Disney," he declared. "I wish I didn't have to work Wednesday night and could stay home to watch his show." The magazine also reported that both CBS and NBC were hunting "desperately" for new "family oriented" programs to put opposite ABC's Disney shows.

Some incarnation of the Disney one-hour television series was on the air from 1954 through 1990, including "Disney's Wonderful World" "Disneyland," "Walt Disney Presents," "Walt Disney's Wonderful World of Color," "The Wonderful World of Disney." In the mid-eighties the Disney Corporation began the Disney Channel, a highly successful premium cable service still in operation.

The FBI memo regarding Disney's promotion is from FBI 66-new and is dated December 16, 1954, in response to an SAC letter (54-54) dated October 7, 1954, which recommended Walt for promotion within the ranks of the Bureau.

"He'd call all hours": Kimball interview.

About the financially pinched Disneyland: Because of the contractual separation of WED and Walt Disney Productions, WED was unable to directly benefit from the studio's profits from television to help defray the enormous cost overruns connected with the construction of Disneyland.

"We had no idea": Disney quoted in Maltin, *Of Mice and Magic* p. 122.

16. Disneyland: Forward to the Past

Extensive news footage exists of the opening day. In addition, the Disney studio has aired several television specials which includes footage.

The welcome plaque at the entrance to Disneyland reads: "To all who come to this happy place . . . WELCOME. Disneyland is your land. Here age relives fond memories of the past . . . and here you may savor the challenge and promise of the future. Disneyland is dedicated to the ideals, the dreams, and the hard facts that have created America . . . with the hope that it will be a source of joy and inspiration to all the world."

"The worst thing": C. V. Wood in Bright, *Disneyland—Untold Story*, p. 96.

C. V. Wood, Disneyland's first official employee, left in 1956 to form a consulting firm specializing in amusement parks. In 1964 he supervised the building of Freedomland in the Bronx, New York, which he envisioned as an East Coast Disneyland-type theme park. Freedomland closed within a year.

"My group of studio employees": Kinney, *Walt Disney and Assorted Other Characters*, p. 176.

"We have to charge": Disney in Bright, *Disneyland—Untold Story*, p. 108.

About Disney standing at the window of his Main Street apartment: Sheri Alveroney interview with Eliot, March 1990.

"Walt used to talk": Cubby O'Brien interview with Eliot, January 1990.

"Walt was warm": Sheri Alveroney interview.

By the end of its first full year, more than three million people had paid admission to pass through Disneyland's front gates, which, along with the profits from the prime-time television series, netted more than $30 million dollars for WED.

As a result of its participation, the Walt Disney studio's net profits rose to an unprecedented $1,352,852, which escalated the price of a common share of stock to an all-time high of $2.07. In Feburary of 1956, the board of directors of Walt Disney Productions voted a two-for-one stock split (*Wall Street Journal*, January 10, 1956).

Apropos of the Douglas lawsuit: The most famous incident of this type, popularly known as the "Begelman Affair," involved Cliff Robertson's accusations against Columbia Pictures executive David Begelman that he forged and cashed a $10,000 check in the actor's name. Although completely innocent, Robertson suffered a two-year blacklisting for taking his accusations public.

" 'Uncle Walt' . . . invited": from Douglas, *Ragman's Son*, pp. 229–30.

Both Disney's and Douglas's statements regarding their lawsuit are from the *Hollywood Citizen-News*, August 3, 1956.

"I thought, what am I doing?": Douglas, *Ragman's Son*, p. 230.

The Nichols/Kemper memo is from FBI 94-4-4667-2x.

The March 7 memo to Tolson is from FBI 94-4-4667-3.

The March 15 memo to Malone is an addendum to FBI 94-4-4667-3.

The March 21 internal memo is from FBI 94-4-4667-4.

The memo regarding *Moon Pilot* is from FBI report 94-4-4667-37.

A copy of President Eisenhower's letter to Hoover regarding Disney's being considered for appointment to the Advisory Committee on the Arts is in Disney's FBI file.

The details of the Milestone award ceremony are from the *Hollywood Citizen-News*, February 18, 1957; the *Los Angeles Times*, February 17–18, 1957; and the *Los Angeles Examiner*, February 18, 1957.

17. Final Destinations

"Well, she's your problem": Disney in Thomas, *Walt Disney*, p. 324.

"What now?": Disney interview with Philip K. Scheurer: "Realist Disney Kept His Dreams," *Los Angeles Times*, June 26, 1960.

"I thought it was time": Goldenson, *Beating the Odds*, p. 124.

"No man can go on forever": Disney in *Los Angeles Times* interview with Bob Barnes (AP staff writer), December 24, 1961.

"The idiot nephew": Taylor, *Storming the Magic Kingdom*, p. 14.

The Bob Hope and Herman Wouk anecdotes are from Bright, *Disneyland—Untold Story*, pp. 149–150.

Unlike most of Disney's other animated features, *Fantasia* had only been rereleased once before, in 1956, and did poorly at the box office. In his review Crowther omitted the effect of the strike on Disney's studio one reason for the film's initial "failure." In its 1969 rerelease, the so-called psychedelic factor accounted for the film remaining in general release for nearly a year, as it became a favorite cult film for the campus marijuana and LSD crowd.

The Bosley Crowther review of *Fantasia* appeared in the *New York Times*, November 18, 1963.

The specifics of Disney's estate are from *Variety*, December 12, 1966.

Epilogue

Much of the information regarding the evolution of the studio has been gathered from articles that appeared in the *Wall Street Journal*, the *Los Angeles Times*, the *New York Times*, *Variety*, and *Hollywood Reporter*.

In addition, John Taylor's *Storming the Magic Kingdom* and Ron Grover's *The Disney Touch* offer detailed accounts of the events that took place at the studio in the years following the death of Walt Disney. Taylor's book deals primarily with the Steinberg greenmail episode. Grover's book outlines the Eisner era.

Katzenberg told an interviewer from the American Movie Classics channel that *Beauty and the Beast* "would not have been made the way it was" if it were not for *Pinocchio*. The interview has been broadcast several times over the cable channel.

The source for the anecdote regarding Disney's logic and instinct wishes to remain anonymous.

Index